In the Claws of the Eagle

Praise for *Wings Over Delft*, Book 1 in the *Louise* trilogy:

'A remarkably engaging story, in which themes of love, art and history are power-fully combined. The unfolding narrative is dramatic, passionate and brilliantly set. The quality of the writing throughout is superb and the ending unforgettably moving.'

Robert Dunbar, critic and broadcaster

'The gentle love story takes the reader through dark intrigue, religious unrest and the palpable, cultural atmosphere of life in a Dutch city, to an unexpected conclusion. A well-tailored and absorbing read for adults as well as for age 12-plus.'
The Sunday Tribune

'Flegg gives us an exquisitely crafted novel which will stay in the reader's memory long after the closing pages are read. The ending is unexpected and dramatic and leaves the reader eagerly awaiting the subsequent books in the Louise trilogy.'

Valerie Coghlan, *Inis*

Praise for *The Rainbow Bridge*, Book 2 in the *Louise* trilogy:

'An original, interestingly-imagined and challenging book. Its finely-textured writing with historical flavour and a strong plot make this a rare achievement.'
The Irish Times

'Flegg is one of the finest writers of children's literature in Ireland today. Many passages in this novel are a pure pleasure to read.'
Inis

AUBREY FLEGG was born in Dublin and spent his early childhood on a farm in County Sligo. His later schooldays were spent in England, but he returned to Dublin to study geology. After a period of research in Kenya he joined the Geological Survey of Ireland; he is now retired. Aubrey lives in Dublin with his wife, Jennifer; they have two children and three grandchildren.

As well as the *Louise* trilogy, he has published two other books for young people: the first, *Katie's War*, is about the Civil War period in Ireland and won the IBBY Sweden Peter Pan Award 2000. His second book, *The Cinnamon Tree*, is a story of a young African girl who steps on a landmine.

Wings Over Delft is the first book in the acclaimed *Louise* trilogy, followed by *The Rainbow Bridge* and *In the Claws of the Eagle*. *Wings Over Delft* won the Bisto Book of the Year Award 2004, Ireland's most prestigious children's literature prize, and the Reading Association of Ireland Award 2005. It was also chosen for inclusion in the White Ravens 2004 collection – a selection of outstanding international books for children and young adults made by the International Youth Library in Munich.

Aubrey's books have been translated into German, Swedish, Danish, Serbian and Slovene.

In the Claws of the Eagle

*Book 3: the **Louise** trilogy*

Aubrey Flegg

THE O'BRIEN PRESS
DUBLIN

First published 2006 by The O'Brien Press Ltd,
12 Terenure Road East, Rathgar, Dublin 6, Ireland.
Tel: +353 1 4923333; Fax: +353 1 4922777
E-mail: books@obrien.ie
Website: www.obrien.ie

ISBN-10: 0-86278-827-7
ISBN-13: 978-0-86278-827-8

British Library Cataloguing-in-Publication Data
Flegg, Aubrey M.
In the claws of the eagle. - (The Louise Trilogy; bk.3)
1.Portraits - Fiction 2.Holocaust, Jewish (1939-1945) -
Fiction 3.Art thefts - Fiction 4.Young adult fiction
I. Title
823.9'14[J]

1 2 3 4 5 6
06 07 08 09

The O'Brien Press receives
assistance from

Editing, typesetting and design: The O'Brien Press Ltd
Cover artwork by Henriette Sauvant
Printing: Creative Print and Design, Wales
Author photograph: Jennifer Flegg

The *Louise* trilogy is dedicated
to Bill Darlison

I see something of God each hour of the twenty-four,
and each moment then,
In the faces of men and women I see God,
and in my own face in the glass,
I find letters from God dropt in the street,
and every one is sign'd by God's name,
And I leave them where they are,
for I know that whereso'er I go,
Others will punctually come for ever and ever.

Walt Whitman. 'Song of Myself' Canto 48.

In the Claws of the Eagle is dedicated to
The children of Terezín

ACKNOWLEDGEMENTS

I am once again deeply indebted to my family and friends for their help, criticisms and observations, this time with the writing of *In the Claw of the Eagle*. I particularly thank my wife Jennifer for reading and commenting on my manuscript, for her patience and support, and for her skill with *The Rough Guide* during our travels.

I would like to thank Maeve Broderick of the *Royal Irish Academy of Music* for allowing me to attend a series of master classes for violin students of the Academy. And so too Mary O'Brien, whose master classes were an inspiration not only to her students but to the writer in the audience. Violinist Clodagh Vedres gave me her time and help, particularly with the question of musical memory. Rosemary O'Connell helped me with some of the German words used in the text, and Ewa Rudolf gave Helena Stronski her name, and also provided me with the Polish for *Frère Jacques*. I, however, claim sole responsibility for any errors that may have crept in.

My thanks to Mandy Gelbmann for suggesting Mödling as an appropriate retreat for Izaac, and to her and her family for their hospitality when we visited that lovely little town.

I acknowledge with gratitude the *Arts Council of Ireland* for travel and mobility bursaries that enabled me to research the Paris side of this story and also, while on another mission, to visit the Terezín Concentration Camp near Prague. A week's residency at the *Tyrone Guthrie Centre* at Annaghmakerrig provided the starting blocks for me at the commencement of this project.

Finally, grateful thanks to Michael and Ivan O'Brien, and all at The O'Brien Press for their skills, patience, encouragement and good humour. To Íde ní Laoghaire who has been a guiding light throughout the writing of the *Louise* trilogy, and especially to my editor, Mary Webb, for her inspired suggestions, and meticulous editing of this book, my heartfelt thanks.

CONTENTS

Louise: The Story so Far

Wings Over Delft

Nearly two hundred and sixty years before Izaac Abrahams was born in 1910, a master painter, Jacob Haitink, who lived in the tiny town of Delft in Holland, undertook to paint the portrait of a sixteen-year-old Dutch girl, Louise Eeden. He did so against his own best judgement because he knew that if he failed to capture this girl's illusive beauty it would destroy him. But he did succeed, just as she succeeded in capturing the heart of his young apprentice Pieter. When the portrait, probably his finest work, was nearing completion, the Master prophesied that one day, long after they were all dead, Louise Eeden would live again in the hearts and minds of people who saw her portrait.

The Rainbow Bridge

And so it happened. Certain people, who had the eyes to see, were indeed so captivated by the girl in the portrait that she became real for them, and shared in their lives. Gaston Morteau, a young French hussar, who rescued her painting from a Dutch canal, had Louise as his riding companion as he crossed the frozen Rhine and journeyed south through France. Young Pierre, his cadet – too gentle for a soldier's life – turned to her portrait to tell her of his fears, and of his heart's

9

yearnings. Then there was Colette, the girl who was destined to become Gaston's wife. There was also the Count du Bois, in whom dark forces stirred, so that not only her portrait, but Louise herself were put in jeopardy.

When her portrait was sold to a Jewish pedlar in exchange for a few trinkets, Louise was ready to move on.

After *The Rainbow Bridge* ...

In the Jewish pedlar's family, Louise found herself valued: first as an investment, then as a work of art, and then as a companion to Mitsu, the teenage son of the family. When the family were forced to flee France, following a local pogrom against the Jews, they crossed the border into Switzerland. It was with Mitsu that Louise saw mountains for the first time, and stood on a bridge, watching the pearl-green glacier-water creaming over the rocks of the riverbed. For several years they shared each other's interests and activities.

Mitsu had hoped to get an apprenticeship as a clockmaker, but soon found that the clockmakers of Switzerland kept a closed shop and did not take kindly to strangers. Then one day, desperate for work, he undertook to mend his landlady's piano and discovered that he had perfect pitch. His ear could tell him to the tiniest turn of the tuning key if a string was in tune or not. With Mitsu's new-found skill, the fortunes of the Abrahams family changed. Mitsu's descendents all had good or perfect pitch and followed his trade as piano tuners. They graduated from pubs to parlours, to drawing rooms, to concert halls. But they also migrated, inching eastwards towards Austria and ultimately to Vienna, the music capital of the world. Here, David Abrahams and his brother Rudi divided the great concert halls and salons between them. Though they were too busy to pay more than passing attention to the portrait that had hung on their walls since they could remember, Louise never felt neglected; she had a place in their lives, even if it was now a passive one. Then, in 1910, baby Izaac was born to David and Judit, and Louise was to find herself called back to action by an imperious demand from a most unexpected quarter ...

CHAPTER 1

The Performer

It was a spring morning; a light breeze stirred the muslin curtains in front of the open windows of the Abrahams' apartment in Vienna. Motors passed, horses clopped, and carriages occasionally clattered on the cobbled street below. Trams hissed and clanged over the nearby crossing. Izaac Abrahams, aged three months, stirred restlessly in his pram; his nurse Lotte had placed it facing the wall with instructions for him to 'go to sleep!' But Izaac had no intention of going to sleep; he had just learned to put both of his big toes into his mouth at the same time, and was in urgent need of an audience.

For some time now he'd been examining an object on the wall above him. The image was a bit fuzzy because his eyes didn't focus well on distant things yet. His view of the world was, therefore, mostly made up of shapes and colours. There were shapes that didn't move and on which no amount of charm had any effect, then there were shapes that did move, and therefore had to be entertained. For these he reserved a repertoire of gurgles, squirms and smiles, or if these failed, a variety of cries, roars and wails.

Nothing was moving now so he turned his attention back to that thing on the wall above him. For some reason he felt it had potential; there was a shape inside it that intrigued him; he gathered himself to work on it.

Louise felt Izaac's attention on her as a flow of energy, a small dynamic focus in the already sunlit room. At first glance there didn't seem to be anyone else present, but energy was clearly coming to her from somewhere. She was out of practice and was bothered that she could see no source for this attention. Izaac, however, sensed her growing interest and tried an exploratory:

'Ba?'

She looked down in surprise. Two large eyes, inky pupils bright with curiosity, were staring up at her picture. She had to smile. To her amazement he smiled back, tentatively it is true, but a smile nonetheless.

'Well, who are you?' she asked herself. He wriggled – she smiled; he tried a gurgle – she smiled again; they could go on like this. Now he tried her with his word again, repeating it in case she hadn't heard.

'Ba ... ba?' Now Louise laughed outright. That was all the encouragement he needed. He lifted both legs in the air and whumped them down on the bed.

What followed was a gala performance of all the tricks that Izaac knew, the climax of which was, of course, putting both big toes in his mouth. He concluded the show with his own tumultuous applause. Louise joined in, it didn't seem to bother him that her applause was silent; he was a very engaging creature. The effect of all this attention was, of course, for him to start again. It was when he started on his third performance that Louise began to get a little desperate. She had no experience of babies; she was afraid of encouraging him and equally afraid of stopping him. Fortunately at this moment Lotte appeared.

'*Ach Liebchen, du bist so* fröhlich*!* Little one, you are happy!

She picked him up and turned her back, leaving Louise with a glimpse of a triumphant small face looking at her over Lotte's shoulder.

As the days, weeks and months passed, Louise became genuinely fascinated with Izaac, and she could see him growing, not just in body but in mind. It was like watching frost patterns growing on a windowpane; tiny branches thrusting out, dividing, spreading until they met and became part of a network that was a small human being. Because the music room, where her picture hung, was where he was put to rest in the afternoons, Louise had him to herself. Sometimes he would be content to watch the shifting light on the ceiling. On other occasions his urge to show her what he was seeing was so strong that she would find herself seeing the world through his eyes. When a bumblebee landed on his pram and then spread its wings, unfolding them like transparent fans, and flew off with a buzz like a hornet, she experienced anew his surprise and amazement at the phenomenon of flight. Then the vision would fade, and it might be weeks before he felt compelled to share some other experience with her. How was it that this little fragment of humanity had such complete command over her?

But, now that Izaac had co-opted her as an audience for his dress rehearsals for life, Louise joined in with enthusiasm. It was she who first saw him rise up from his stomach like a caterpillar until he formed a hoop and then, miraculously stand. She also saw him take his first steps, and later heard the cries of joy from the next room when he gave his first public display of this new skill. Months stretched to years. For long periods Izaac would appear to forget about Louise. Then something would arise and he would urgently require an audience. On other occasions he would go out of his way to avoid attracting her attention.

It was young Mitsu (Izaac's great grandfather) who had reinstated music in Louise's life, when he had reassembled his landlady's piano in Switzerland, and in doing so had discovered his perfect pitch. As the three generations of piano tuners had worked, struggling to establish themselves, there had always been a piano, harpsichord or other instrument in bits in the parlour. Later, as the family flourished, and there were workshops to which these poor wrecks could be banished, there would be new or borrowed instruments for the family to play on. None of them played the piano professionally but they were enthusiastic amateurs making music for the love of it. Also it went down well with clients to hear short pieces played when the tuning was done. Inspired perhaps by the music in Vienna, or even to get away from pianos for an hour or two, the family turned to strings. Soon there were violinists, viola players, or cellists in the family ready to play the duets, trios and quartets that they loved. As they always played in the parlour, Louise was in on their performances and on their practising too. It was as if they enjoyed having someone to play for, often positioning themselves so that they could play to her portrait.

She had become used to their Jewishness as well. Sometimes observant, more often not, they struck her as being very comfortable with their God. Their main observance seemed to concentrate on the ancient traditions that welded the community together. On Friday nights, in particular, music and tradition were melded together on the eve of the Jewish Sabbath. She would look forward to these evenings with relish. One evening, however, things did not go quite to plan.

CHAPTER 2

Of Cats and Viols

It was the turn of the Abrahams family to host the other members of the *Tuning Fork Quartet*, first to music, and then when the sun had gone down, to join their Sabbath dinner. Every week they would gather in one or other of their homes to play, mostly quartets and trios, with lots of enthusiasm and equal toleration of each other's mistakes. As the afternoon wore on the music would get less demanding, steins of foaming beer would appear beside their chairs, and any piece that ended with all of them still playing, and still together, would be greeted with a cheer.

'At least we look like a real quartet,' laughed Uncle Rudi, who was their first violin. He was completely bald, with a head like the pointy end of an egg, and a beard that flowed out generously over his violin. He had to tuck his beard in, in case it got tangled up with his bow. Uncle Rudi's son, Nathan, who played second fiddle, was a medical student, while Uncle Albert, their viola player, was neither an uncle nor a Jew, but became honorary ones on Fridays. Father played the cello, and the piano if needed. Today, however, they had a very special guest, an old friend of the family, none other than the great Madame Helena Stronski, still one of the most sought-after solo violinists out of her native Poland.

She had arrived towards the end of their session, sweeping in like a ship under full sail in a billow of diaphanous scarves.

She was a large woman, once strikingly beautiful, now inclined to weight and to ruff and gruff to hide a heart alloyed equally of steel and gold.

'Don't stop, don't stop!' she called as the music faltered, 'I love it. This is what I've come for, real music on the hoof.'

The quartet, however, rose to a man, not the least offended. She offered both cheeks to her host David Abrahams, and the same honour to Uncle Rudi. She gave young Nathan a hearty shake of the hand, and let Uncle Albert kiss the back of it. Having dealt with them all in accordance with her code of intimacy, she declared: 'Well gentlemen, what will we play?' From Uncle Rudi's music stand she picked up a sheet of the music they had been playing. 'Good heavens, dears, this is far too difficult for me.' She searched deeper among his sheets of music. 'Here … this is much more my standard these days.' They all burrowed through their music, eager as squirrels, while she surveyed the room with a smile of content. This was what she loved; people making music together. But they would all enjoy it more if they could play something within their ability.

Judit, Izaac's mother, came in, holding her guest's violin case and leading a boy of about three and a half by the hand. He was wearing a sailor suit; his eyes round in awe at the sight of their visitor.

'This is Izaac.' They shook hands solemnly. 'You will play for us, won't you? Izaac would love to hear you,' said Judit.

'Humph,' said the great lady, looking down at Izaac. 'I bet you'd prefer to be pulling the cat's tail? Makes the same sort of sound if you think about it.' She gave him the nearest thing to a wink that a great lady can make and turned to Uncle Rudi. 'Rudi, all right if I double up with you on the first violin?' Uncle Rudi made to rise. 'No no no, don't get up, I'll read over your shoulder.' She put her violin case on a chair, opened the lid and folded back the silk scarf that was wrapped around the instrument. It lay for a moment in its case like a freshly opened horse chestnut in its husk. Izaac leaned forward for a better look. 'It's very, very old,' she explained. 'It was made by Stra...di...var...ius, I call it Strad for short.' She took up her bow. 'And this is the cat's tail. It looks all floppy now, so we'll tighten it up like this.' She turned the tiny mother of pearl nut on the end of the bow until the hairs were tight and straight. 'Now, all I need is my rosin and we are ready.' She showed him how she rubbed the rosin on to the hairs of the bow. 'So, where will I put it? I could put it on top of Uncle Rudi's head?' Izaac was still a little awed.

'Wrong shape, my dear,' said Uncle Rudi.

'Uncle Rudi's a little-ender, isn't he Izaac?' she laughed, and dropped the rosin back into her case. 'Lead off when you're ready, Rudi,' she commanded.

The home team launched into the first movement of their quartet tentatively, as if shy in the presence of the maestro. To begin with, she appeared just to be playing very softly, a mere shadow of Uncle Rudi's lead, but as they got used to her presence she began to play with them, leading them, nudging them, and a subtle transformation took place. They seemed to relax, their bow strokes became longer and they were moving better in time. They found themselves glancing at each other with secret smiles as they passed the notes and phrases back and forth between them. *Her* magic seemed to be flowing through their fingers and into their bows. When it came to Father's entry on the cello, the deep notes of the instrument rang out rich and sweet. His eyebrows shot up with pleasure. When they paused between movements they didn't chat, as they often did, but sat held in a trance. They approached the dramatic finale like ships entering harbour in a line, swinging up into the wind and dropping anchor as one. Only when they turned to applaud their leader, did they realise that Madame

Stronski had stopped playing, and that their triumphal finale had been all their own; she had her fiddle under her arm and was applauding them.

While the musicians were recovering, happily congratulating each other on this or that entry, Madame Stronski adjusted her scarves, which always seemed to be about to fall off, but never did, and took up a position near the piano. She raised her bow and launched into the first notes of a piece of music that none of them had heard before.

At her first notes Izaac Abrahams whipped about like someone stung. He had been accustomed to music since babyhood. Father would practise his cello in the evenings, and Mother played the piano in the afternoons, when she thought no one else would hear her. He would go about his business, arranging animals from his ark, putting them in fields outlined in dominoes, building castles from bricks, or stalking the cat. From time to time the music would inspire him to perform acrobatics and other things. Unfortunately people engrossed in making music tend not to notice other people's performances, so Izaac would have to contrive his own audience. The animals of his ark would be arranged in appreciative rows and performed for, but their attention span was short. After they had been knocked over a couple of times he would dismiss them. Then he would turn his attention to the picture on the wall and would perform for the girl in the green dress. She could be relied on for the correct level of applause; she understood him. On this occasion, when the quartet had finished and everyone else was preoccupied, he had treated her to headstands, and he was doing this when Madame Stronski started to play her solo.

Izaac had never heard music played by a maestro. He had never heard a bow bite into the strings as if the note to be played had existed in the air, expectant and impatient ever since the composer had first conceived it. His small body became rigid; two powerful forces were running through him like competing electric currents. The first, a sustained vibration, came from the music, the outward flow of something both beautiful and terrifying. The second came from his own sense of affront. He, Izaac, was the performer in this house! This was his territory. That Cloud Woman, the one with all the billowing scarves who talked about cats, was his competitior. He stamped his foot in temper.

As if sensing his challenge, the Cloud Woman half turned towards him; the violin gave the smallest dip of acknowledgement, her eyes glinted, but she played on. How dare she! He stood his ground, small, dark and sturdy. But Izaac had no defence against music like this, not in the hands of a master. In minutes he was overcome. The music penetrated every fibre of his small body, running like liquid silver into his bones where it hardened into something both brittle and sensitive. When the Cloud Woman finished playing, Izaac was the only one in the room who did not clap; neither did he turn somersaults.

Madame Stronski observed Izaac's reaction and had a pang of conscience. She had noticed his sudden rigid attention when she had begun to play. It was a compliment, and what musician can resist the compliment of complete attention? So, she had played for him, a personal message of power and beauty, an example of musicianship that she was delighted she still had in her. But had she laid a trap for him? Oh, Helena, she said to herself, what have you done? Perhaps there was still time to get the genie back into the bottle. She pulled herself together and called out to Izaac's father:

'Come David, soon Judit will be lighting your Sabbath candles for our dinner, let's play a round for Izaac before he goes to bed. How about '*Pani Janie*', as we call it in Poland, '*Frère Jacques*' in French, what is it in German?' They laughed and told her, '*Bruder Jacob!* But with variations!' They smiled as they bent for their instruments. 'Rudi, you begin. Then Nathan, then Uncle Albert, you, David, and then me. One, two, three.' Uncle Rudi started playing the simple tune. Then, while he played on, Nathan started, beginning again so the tune was overlapping on itself. Uncle Albert came in on the viola, followed by Father on the cello, and last of all came Madame Stronski. Now they were all playing and the tune became a little symphony. Faster and faster they played until they all had to give up in laughter. The double doors opened and Mother stood there smiling. Dinner was ready. With a sweep of scarves Madame Helena laid her violin in its case.

'Judit, I'm starving,' she said, and led the way into the dining room, while Izaac was picked up by Lotte, and carried off to bed.

Voices rose and fell behind the double doors that separated the dining room from the music room. Dinner was progressing at a leisurely pace. Next door in the music room, Izaac, in pyjamas, was edging silently along, hugging the wall under the picture where he thought the girl inside it wouldn't see him. This wasn't a performance, it was more like a commando raid, and she had a habit of making him uneasy about his plans.

He was also apprehensive about the Cloud Lady. Her reference to cats had disturbed him; he still had scars from the time he had given their cat a loving hug. His interest was in her violin; he wasn't sure whether it was alive or not, so he must be careful. Uncle Rudi and Nathan both played violins, but clearly these were just toys when compared to the Cloud Lady's instrument. It, he had decided, was the key to her performance. If *he* could tame it, then *he* would turn everyone's head and make their legs go wobbly as his had just done.

He could see the chair with her violin case on it, a tongue of the scarf she had wrapped around the instrument peeped from under the lid. Even the case had a special magic; it was old and scarred, the only bright thing about it was a scarlet hotel sticker on the lid with a picture of a dancing clown. He was afraid of it now, but the more he looked the more strongly it drew him, filling his vision until his feet had no alternative but to move. The case lay on a chair at chest-height to him. He reached out. The lid was unclasped; he lifted it cautiously, alert in case the violin might spring out at him. The silk was soft on his hands, but so had been the cat's fur. He parted the folds, and there it was – the violin. The grain of its wood seemed to pulse with life. He reached out cautiously and touched the polished surface. It wasn't cold like the marble floor in the hall; it was warm. He decided that it was probably alive. When he ran his fingers across the strings, they murmured back at him the familiar notes he heard whenever his uncles tuned up. Perhaps it liked him. He got it firmly by the neck and lifted; it was lighter than he expected, but when he tried to put it under his chin he found that his arms were too short. He looked around for the bow. The silly woman had called it a cat's tail – nonsense – it was a sword. Uncle Rudi called *his* a sword and used it to duel with Izaac and the toy sword he'd been given for his birthday. There were two bows in the lid of the case; he put the violin on the floor behind him so he could pull properly. But the clip holding the bow was old and the bow came away in his hand. Izaac reeled backwards, waving it above his head for balance. For a moment his backside wavered dangerously above the violin before thumping down on the floor only inches away from it.

Louise, observing from the confines of her picture, was in an agony of apprehension as this saga developed, but all she could do was watch. Izaac did a swash and buckle or two to save face and then examined his prize. The hairs were floppy. He remembered that the Cloud Woman had had the same problem. He was good on technical details and he found the small mother-of-pearl nut on the end of the bow and turned it. That made it worse. He made a couple of rather angry swipes in the air and then got the direction right and the hairs tightened. Now he turned his attention to the violin. The music he was about to play was already loud in his mind. As he couldn't manage to put the violin under his chin, he laid it on his knees with the thin end away from him and prepared to play.

Izaac knew that the place where the music came from was where the strings were held up on a wooden little bridge. So, gripping the bow by the middle, and still thinking more of a sword than of a bow, he thrust it lustily into the gap between the strings and the fiddle. To his surprise and amazement the creature let out a most terrible screech, not at all the music that Izaac had expected. He looked at the impaled instrument in horror; he hadn't meant to hurt it. An unnatural silence had fallen over the house; it gave him a sense of urgency. There was only one thing he could do, and that was to pull out the offending bow A second appalling shriek rang out. He heard the clatter of knives and forks, the cries of 'Izaac'. They were coming for him. However he still had the violin, and even to a three year old, possession is nine tenths of the law. All he needed was a little time to tame the creature.

━✦━

An appalling, jarring screech cut through the quiet conversation about the dining room table. In the shocked silence that followed, only the flames of the Sabbath candles dared to move, shifting in the summer air from the half open door into the music room. Forks were arrested on the way to mouths; knives were held poised.

'What on earth was that?' breathed Father.

'The cat?' wondered Mother.

'A violin?' said Uncle Rudi. A second screech rent the air.

'Izaac!' burst out as one voice from around the table. There was a clatter as the entire company dropped their cutlery onto their plates and headed for the door.

At any other time the sight of all four members of the Tuning Fork Quartet trying to get through the dining room door at the same moment would have had him in stitches, but today Izaac meant business. When eventually they uncorked and burst into the room towards him he waved his bow menacingly. Their expressions changed to horror as they all realised that what Izaac had on his knees was not one of their own violins but the priceless Stradivarius. They faltered to a man, held back by the thought that at a wrong move from them Izaac might do literally anything. They were hopping around him like vultures when a cry rang out from the door.

'Stop. Leave the boy!'

The four men fell back, walking on the tips of their toes in an agony of apprehension. Izaac had a momentary glimpse of the Cloud Lady standing like a fairy godmother in the doorway. This was his moment. He lifted the violin as if to fit it under his chin as Uncle Rudi did, but that's where things had gone wrong last time; his arms were too short. He was aware of the expectations of the audience gathered about him; it was clearly up to him to entertain them, but whether with a solo performance or a full-scale tantrum he wasn't sure. The Cloud Lady was standing above him, but for some reason she seemed to be encouraging him. At that moment he remembered how Father held his cello. So, still sitting, he spread his legs wide and put the bottom of the violin on the carpet. He exercised his right arm, remembered how his father played and took a cello-like swipe at the strings. It was not a success; the bow slipped and skittered across the strings, but fortunately the noise was deadened by his grip on the neck of the instrument. The Cloud Lady bent down and gently guided his left hand so that he was holding the violin by its shoulder; now the strings were free. As he drew back his arm, he could feel her fingers over his on the bow, light but firm. Now at last the magic he had been looking for was flowing through him. His bow found the lowest of the four strings, the G string. As if of itself it began to move and the full rich tone of the open string sang out.

The next three seconds would prove to be Izaac's most enduring musical memory, the moment when he realised that it was *he* who was making this magical sound. And what a sound! Not just a single note but the countless other notes and harmonics that make the sound of the violin unique. His mind, like a well-prepared plot of land, was ready for this and he would remember the moment as minutes not as seconds. Half a bow was all that his reach would allow but he used every inch of it and sustained that note to the very end.

Now came the applause, but Izaac was too shocked and dumfounded even to acknowledge it. He dropped the bow as Madame Stronski swooped forward and lifted the violin from his hands. Without saying a word he rushed out of the room, past his mother, and buried his head in the neutral starchiness of Lotte's apron.

Some hours later, when the visiting members of the *Tuning Fork Quartet* had departed, still laughing at the incident, Madame Stronski came back into music room to collect her violin. For a moment she shed her merriment and turned to Izaac's parents.

'About your little Izaac ...'

'Oh, we're so sorry. We hope he didn't ...' they exclaimed in unison.

'No, my dears, it's for me to apologise. I'm very much afraid I have woken a monster in your little fellow. Hopefully he will get over it and become a banker or keep bees, but if he takes an interest in the violin, keep him away from it till he is six or more. Then send for me, and I will help him if I can.'

She gathered up her things and turned to leave, looking around the room with affection. Her eye was caught by the portrait of the *Girl in the Green Dress* hanging on the wall. 'You know, this really is a little gem, have you told me where she came from?' she asked, sailing up to look at it closely.

'Oh, Louise? She's been in the family, passed down from father to son, ever since we had to flee from France at the beginning of the last century.'

Madame Stronski shook her head. 'I would say she had broken a few hearts before that,' she said and she sighed: 'You won't believe this, but I was once as slender as her. Look how she challenges us! I'd like to think that I looked like her when I told the Academy selection board in Kraków what I thought of them. Lot of old fuddy-duddies, misogynists to a man. "*The concert platform is no place for a woman.*" Pah! I told them. So I came to Vienna instead. I still miss Kraków though,' she sighed.

She smiled at the portrait and said: 'Look after my little protégé for me, won't you.' Then, gathering her scarves about her, she left.

CHAPTER 3

Partners in Crime

Autumn changed to winter. Izaac was restless and irritable and inclined to interrupt people when they were playing or practising. Mostly he ignored Louise; if he wanted her attention he would either act out his frustration in front of her picture or try to explain it in long speeches that would end in frustrated gobbledegook. Then, quite suddenly, the situation changed; he found he could lift the lid on top of the piano keyboard. Louise couldn't see him from where her picture hung but could hear him playing notes, as if searching for a tune. Then there would be clashing chords, some of which worked, some of which didn't. He was self absorbed, not looking for an audience, so Louise withdrew into her own distant thoughts. Then, all at once she was in demand again.

'Lees, I want you! Come here!' Izaac had never addressed her directly like this before. Invariably their exchanges had been his one-way commentary on life, with her just making encouraging thoughts. Clearly something had happened over by the piano, the one part of the room which she couldn't see, and where he couldn't see her. She could feel his frustration and anger mounting; he wanted her and he wanted her now! There was only one thing she could do to avoid a scene, and that was to go to him. She didn't want to frighten him by suddenly appearing, but she needn't have worried. As soon as he began to see her outline forming, he waved her forward.

There, he commanded, waving her into the curve of the grand piano where she could see him. Now that she was looking down at him, he could start. Using one finger on his right hand he began to pick out a tune. Louise recognised it at once – *Frère Jacques* – the round game that Madame Stronski had got the quartet to play the last time she had been here. She was impressed; he even managed the quick notes *Sonnez les matines* at the end. She raised her hands to clap.

'Bravo Izaac …' she began, but he hadn't finished; he shook his head impatiently, his mouth set in a hard line. Louise stood, hands still raised, hardly able to believe what she was heard next. At exactly the right moment, he had started to play the tune again with left hand, eight notes lower on the keyboard, just like Nathan following Uncle Rudi that day when they had all played. Louise had never been good at the childhood game, 'Rub tummy, pat head' – her hands would never obey her, but here was Izaac, standing at the piano, both hands working away independently. All went well until his left hand came to the quick bit at the end, and he lost the tune. It was too much for him; he crashed his hands on the keys in frustration and rushed for the door. There he seemed to recover his dignity. He turned to Louise and bowed to her, a perfect replica of Madame Stronski bowing at that first concert, and left the room. Louise hadn't even recovered enough to clap.

⌒⫻⫻⫻⊱⌯

Gone now was the frustration, gone were the tantrums. It was as if Izaac had found a new and better language to speak. He and the piano became inseparable. While he was at the piano his whole character changed. This wasn't play; it was work. His roguishness disappeared. The only expression he would allow himself was a small smile of satisfaction when some phrase or chord pleased him. The family noticed too. The men thought of him as a budding piano tuner, while Mother dreamed of seeing him on a concert platform. But Louise was finding another side to Izaac altogether; the flip side of the coin.

His and Lotte's daily routine, winter and summer, piano or no piano, included a walk down the street, over the busy Ring Road to the Volksgarten, the People's Garden, where Lotte would talk with other nannies, and Izaac would potter and sometimes play with the other children. Recently he had demanded that Louise come too. It didn't seem to bother him that nobody else could see Louise, in fact it he seemed to enjoy it.

'He's got this imaginary friend,' Lotte explained to her fellow nannies. '"Lees" he calls her. Insists that she comes down here with us. I hear him chatting away to her as if she was really there. I wonder if he's alright in the head?'

'Is Lees a rabbit?' Frauline Kreutz, one of the more experienced nannies, asked. 'I had a little girl once who had a pretend rabbit. Nearly drove me mad, Kani was his name. Kani had to have breakfast at every damned dandelion between here and home, one of hundreds I can tell you, and then we had to stop while Kani ...' The nanny snorted with laughter, and then went on. 'She married a Councillor ... the girl did, not the rabbit ... and had triplets. Perhaps that was Kani's influence in the end.' They all laughed and Lotte was reassured. At least Izaac's friend didn't stop at every dandelion. She suspected that Lees was his idea of the girl in the picture back home; he'd talked to that since he was tiny. She wasn't jealous, if anything Izaac was easier to handle when he had his 'friend' with him.

These walks to the park were a delight to Louise. All she had seen of Vienna so far was the small square of stucco on the building opposite their third floor apartment. Izaac wanted to watch everything, so their progress down to the Ring Strasse, the wide tree-lined street that embraces the old city, was slow. The stately fronts of the houses towered above her, gleaming white in the morning light. As they reached the Ring, the view opened out and Louise gazed in wonder; there seemed to be palaces in every direction. The trams – just passing sounds to her before – clanged their bells and swayed and hissed as they passed. There was so much that was new to her, so much she wanted to know. How did these move without horses? What was the purpose of the wire that occasionally sparked above them? Beyond the trams and the trees was the main road, loud with traffic: carts, drays and smart carriages and, more startling to Louise, motor cars that growled, purred, and occasionally back-fired. Everywhere she could see the work of science, just as her father had predicted all those years ago. But, as they waited while ranks of drab-uniformed soldiers passed, she wondered what had happened to the brave new world that he had predicted. Lorries and guns drove past too, the men sitting up with rifles between their knees. The talk was of war. Had they learned nothing of the folly of war in all these years?

Lotte would be edgy until they had crossed the terrifying stream of traffic and had plunged into the sudden tranquillity of the Volksgarten. Here gravelled paths formed a labyrinth to be followed between beds of scented roses and lawns lined with low box hedges; there were fountains, statues, even a Greek Temple and a small area where children were allowed to play. In the early morning, hoses made rainbowed arches in the low sun, and the grass would glisten with fresh drops. There were ducks in the park that enjoyed the watering and were a particular attraction to Izaac.

Louise noticed his interest in the ducks but didn't think more of it, apart from hoping that he wouldn't start chasing them, because there was so much for her to look at and to see. There were the distant buildings of the Hofburg palace and a stirring statue of some great man rearing his horse. She thought with nostalgia of how Gaston would rear his horse just for the fun of it. She was lost in her dreams when Izaac passed in front of her. He looked perfectly innocent, but there was something about his walk that caught her attention, a certain busyness that said, as loud as words, 'look at me'.

Sure enough, as soon as he saw that he had her attention, his walk changed to a waddle. Louise blinked, for a second she could have sworn that she was looking at one of the park ducks. The transformation was extraordinary; the hand behind with the two curled fingers for a tail was obvious, but it was his walk that had Louise choking with laughter. His small body was tilted forward at an improbable angle, his toes were turned in, so his feet appeared to be flat, giving his body just the right swaying motion, while the bright-eyed movements of the head and eyes gave him a knowing very duck-like look. Louise laughed out loud, and then, forgetting that the men mowing the grass nearby could not hear her, put her hand over her mouth. One of the men, who had seen Izaac's performance, quacked.

For the next few days Izaac entertained the park regulars with his duck impersonation. The only person who did not approve was 'the General,' the park warden, and the ogre of the Volksgarten. He was a bearded replica of the old Emperor Franc Joseph himself. Unlike the Emperor, who was a kindly man, the General was a sworn enemy of all small boys whether they were pretending to be ducks or not. He carried a long polished wooden stick and a whistle on a silver chain, given to him, he claimed, by the Emperor himself. He was a Hapsburg man to the core and had a row of campaign medals to prove it. He terrorised everyone in the park, from doddering pensioners to small children, his one aim being to keep all and sundry, particularly Izaac, off the grass.

32

As Louise was new to the park, she knew nothing about the General or the taboo about the grass; she was as tempted by the smooth perfection of the lawns as any small boy. She therefore accepted Izaac's kind invitation to sit beside him in the middle of the greenest and most perfect sward in the park where he propped himself comfortably against a small metal notice that seemed made for his back. An expression of content settled on his face and he closed his eyes. Louise was happy just to sit and gaze at the pinnacled excesses of the Rathaus – the Town Hall – that she could see through the trees. She was just wondering where all this wealth had come from, when she was woken from her reverie by a whistle followed by a roar like a lion from the nearest path.

Izaac had leapt to his feet and was busily gazing about him, pretending not to know where the roar had come from. To Louise, a law-abiding Dutch girl, the source of the rage was obvious: a bearded figure with an upraised stick, who was making enough noise to command a parade ground. She hadn't met the General but she recognised authority when she saw it. Izaac was going to get into terrible trouble and it was *all her fault*.

The man was gesticulating, pointing at the notice that Izaac had been leaning against; surely he couldn't expect the boy to be able read? Louise glanced down, and for the first time had reason to doubt Izaac's innocence. The notice needed no words; it was a picture of an elephant leaving huge footprints on the grass, the message was clear even without any words. Izaac was now walking towards the enraged keeper, his shoulders hanging, a picture of injured innocence. Louise bit her knuckles; surely the man wouldn't beat someone so small? She need not have worried. Before Izaac got within range of the long stick he turned parallel to the path and began walking along just out of reach, taking huge elephant strides and glancing at the keeper as if inviting him to put his polished boots on the grass and come after him. What Izaac knew, and Louise didn't, was that nothing would induce the General to walk on the Imperial grass, grass that he had protected for a quarter of a century.

She could see Izaac's plan now, but so could the General. In a moment Izaac would be opposite to where Lotte and the gaggle of nannies sat behind a wall of prams, watching the standoff like spectators at the races. The General felt he had him now, he was cut off from his only retreat; the prams. He and Izaac stood facing each other. Behind the General's back Louise could see a ripple of movement. The nannies, seeing Izaac's predicament, were quietly turning their prams to face out, leaving just one small-boy-width between them. Izaac saw his chance, made a start to the right, then dodged left, and in a flash was across the gravel and inside the corral before the General could turn. When he did the boy had disappeared. There was nothing he could do, and his wrath bounced harmlessly off the starched uniforms of nannies.

Izaac got a very light clip over the ear and a scorching from Lotte but the other nannies seemed delighted with him. The General stamped and fumed; it all seemed harmless enough, but Louise, standing close when he turned, heard him mutter: *Juden!* under his breath, Jews. Where had she heard 'Jews!' uttered in just that way? Then she remembered; a hundred years before, when the Abrahams family had been turned out of their home in France, 'Juif!' was the word in French, but the hate had been the same. She looked at the gaggle of nannies, fair homely Austrian faces, and then she looked at their charges, mostly dark, mostly Jewish in looks. Did these nannies have to stick together because their small charges were Jews? The incident passed, but for a moment it had been like a cloud on a sunlit day.

One day Louise noticed that Izaac was preoccupied. It was as if he wanted her to be there, but equally didn't want her to see what he was up to. She was beginning to understand his moods and guessed that he was preparing some surprise for her. Sure enough, in the park a day or two later, he drew her out of sight of the others and treated her to a preview of his latest transformation, not a duck this time, but into a miniature version of the General himself. He had the parade-ground walk, imperious glance, and wielded an imaginary version of the General's stick with that special swagger which the General used to show that he was no ordinary park warden. Soon there wasn't a nanny or an old hand in the park who hadn't enjoyed Izaac's impersonation of the common enemy. Louise thought uneasily of the old man's muttered comment about Jews and warned Izaac never to do his impersonation in front of the man himself. He shrugged and didn't argue, but he couldn't resist just a step or two to tease her whenever he saw the General coming.

Louise was beginning to feel uncomfortable. Perhaps she should have been less responsive to Izaac's performances; now they were likely to get him into trouble, and she felt partly responsible.

Her new-found sense of responsibility was soon put to the test and all because of the Countess von Tischelstein. The 'Countess' was a fey creature who wandered about the park greeting invisible friends on empty seats. She was a harmless entertainment to them all. Louise watched Izaac's careful observation of the Countess with apprehension. Could she trust him not to poke fun at the old lady with one of his impersonations?

'Izaac,' she cautioned, 'you understand; you must be nice about the Countess.' Even as she said it, Louise realised her mistake. Izaac was indeed going to imitate the Countess, but he would have given her a dress rehearsal first. All the time he had been thinking about the old lady he had been imagining Louise's delight in his imitation. Now she had shown that she didn't trust him and was tut tutting at him like a nanny. The devil got into him and he put on an imitation of the poor Countess that had all the nasty mocking elements that Louise had wanted him to avoid. What could she do now? She knew that this was not the performance he had intended to give, but yet he mustn't be allowed to get away with it!

'Izaac! You will not mock her like that, it's cruel and nasty!"

'You can't stop me!'

'I won't come out with you any more!'

'I don't care.' And that was that.

Izaac stopped looking for Louise to come out, and she made no effort to join him. It had all ended in a silly little childish spat. The loss for Louise was profound. She had lost the trust of someone who she felt sure wanted and needed her, and, on top of that, in what she thought must be the most beautiful city in the world, all she had to look at now was the wall of the house opposite.

～～◆〰

The music room was where family matters, and matters of wider importance in the world outside, were discussed by the Abrahams. Without Izaac as a constant distraction, Louise began to pay more attention to what the family was talking about. Lately their anxieties had been focused on a war, which, Louise remembered from a year ago, everyone had thought would be over in a few weeks, but now seemed to be dragging on, and worse, spreading wider. David Abrahams, Izaac's father, had been called up and appeared from time to time in uniform, looking distinctly uncomfortable. He was lucky; he had been given a musical post in Vienna so that the

Opera would not be deprived of their favourite piano tuner!
Uncle Rudi was too old to be called up, but Nathan might get
his papers any day. Louise had always liked Nathan and was
fearful for his safety; from what she was hearing, the losses to
the Austrian army seemed terrible.

CHAPTER 4

The Brahms Lullaby

While Louise listened with anxiety to talk of the war, and grieved over her tiff with Izaac, a new life was beginning in the little town of Mödling, a few miles south of Vienna at the point where the Vienna woods swept down and met the plain that stretched east to the borders of Hungary. A woman's voice, thin but pleasing, was singing the Brahms Lullaby.

'*Guten Abend, gute Nacht, Mit Rosen bedacht,*
Mit Näglein besteckt, schlupf unter ...'

'Lullaby ... lullaby. It's not nighttime, it's morning. Can't you rock the brat to sleep without all that noise?' The singing faltered and then faded; Sabine always faded in the presence her father-in-law. There must be bad news from the war, she thought. 'Well, can't you answer?' his voice demanded from inside the kitchen.

'I don't want to wake little Erich,' she called softly.

'Little Erich!' The voice was scornful. For a second the girl's mouth hardened into a firm line. You're jealous of him, she whispered to herself. The voice went on, 'As if the Emperor didn't have enough to cope with without another mouth to feed.' Veit Hoffman appeared in the doorway, a crumpled newspaper in one hand. His grey hair still had a military spikiness to it, his moustache drooped and blue eyes glinted fiercely from under deep brows. He was wearing a hunting jacket with green lapels as a substitute for the army uniform he had worn all his life. As a former soldier of the Austrian Imperial Army, he had risen from private to corporal, to sergeant major. Now, with the greatest fight in the history of the world underway, he had been swept aside like so much flotsam. One minute he was a vital cog in an army of armies that included Hungarians, Czechs, Slovaks, Poles, Ruthenians, Croats, Serbs and Slovenes, Romanians and Italians, and now, due to age, he had been retired without ceremony. God rot them all! Now he was left with nothing better to do than to listen to lullabies while the Empire that had been his pride and glory crumbled about him.

It had never occurred to Veit that the amazing conglomeration of countries making up the Austro-Hungarian Empire had been acquired, not by his army, but almost entirely through the judicious marriages of the ruling Hapsburg dynasty. The entire empire had been built like a house of cards: aces were played, kings and queens produced daughters who married kings, and occasionally knaves, with alliances balanced precariously one against the other, until, in 1914, a disgruntled Serbian student had shot dead the heir to their throne, Archduke Franz Ferdinand, in Sarajevo. Austria then invaded Serbia, and the entire structure that had kept Europe at peace came tumbling about their ears.

Sabine braced herself; she would have to listen to the latest round of disasters. She looked longingly towards her easel, which stood at the far end of the room. Painting was her refuge, the one place where she dared to be herself, but she knew that the sight of her 'doing nothing' would provoke Veit even more than singing a lullaby. She gave Erich's cradle a gentle push to leave it rocking, and braved herself to face the outraged ex-sergeant major at the door.

Over a lifetime Veit had devised a hundred tricks with

which to terrorise his young recruits. It seemed perfectly natural to him to use these devices on his daughter-in-law. Sabine never seemed to be able to anticipate what he would do. He was obviously enraged by what he had seen in the newspaper; he lifted it up in front of her. Naturally, she leaned forward to see what it was he wanted to show her. In the next second the paper seemed to explode in her face as he banged the back of it. She gave a small shriek.

'What is the matter with them?' he sneered, glaring at her with satisfaction. 'We invade Serbia and are defeated, not just once but twice! We can't even hold our lines in Poland!' The paper was swishing back and forth now like a lion's tail; she couldn't stop her eyes following it. He raised his hand as if to bang the paper again and noticed her wince. He had the ascendancy now. 'Lost 4,000 men, pushed back to Krakow, and then we have to be rescued by the Germans.' At each expostulation he forced her back half a step into the room where Erich was sleeping. 'Defeated in Ivangorod and now Italy attacks us from the south. We can't expect the Germans to help us down there, can we?' Sabine had stopped listening; the pure animal instinct to protect her young was stiffening her. When he thrust his face up into hers she didn't step back. It worked; his voice changed. He shrugged his shoulders; his next question was almost solicitous. 'So when will Franz get his papers then?' Franz was her husband and of an age to be called up.

'Papa, you know very well! Franz has been turned down by the army because of his heart.'

'Heart be damned! He's as fit as I am. Don't you dare try to make excuses for him, woman!'

Sabine looked at him in confusion. How did it always end up like this, with him blaming her for something that he had done? Years ago, when Franz, was a boy, Veit had decreed that the lad needed to be toughened up. *Make a man of him.* His solution was to take the boy camping in winter. Franz, already heavy with a cold, had been put to sleep in damp bedding and had got chilled to the bone; rheumatic fever followed. By a miracle the boy survived, but was left with a heart murmur that even an army doctor could not ignore. Sabine knew this story because Franz's mother had told her about it before she died. Sabine was grateful to her now. Perhaps Veit didn't know that Sabine knew. For once she had a small hold over him but she had the wisdom to keep it to herself.

'He should be at the front. My own son, clerk in a timber yard, making money for a Jew!'

⸮⸮⸮⸮

Having vented his spleen, Viet was civil over breakfast. When he left the house to walk to the shop for tobacco, Sabine checked that he really had gone before crossing to her easel. There she squeezed several inches of carmine and then black on to her palette and painted Veit. As she worked, she could feel the brushstrokes starting deep in her body, rising up, tearing at her insides until they broke on to the canvas with little cries of pain, or could it be rage? After an hour it was done and she stepped back, shaking, her face wet with tears. She looked at the canvas with a mixture of terror and joy: terror that Veit might see it, joy at having expressed her feelings for once.

By the time that Veit returned, carrying a cabbage as a peace offering, the canvas was safe. A gnarled old tree wrapped deeply around with ivy now replaced the enraged Viet. Sabine watched him pass the canvas, pause, snort, and walk on. She breathed again. Then, just short of the door, he turned and came back to look again. Surely he could see nothing of himself in that tangled mass? He caught sight of her watching. His eyes glinted, but it was some time before he bullied her again.

CHAPTER 5

The First Violin

Nobody could blame Nathan Abrahams for his generosity; he had not been there when Madame Stronski had warned Izaac's parents to keep him away from the violin until he was six. Izaac's success on the piano had eased his petulance with regard to music, and he would sidle up to Nathan when the quartet met in their house and persuade him to let him hold his violin, or better, to let him use the bow while Nathan picked out the notes on the fingerboard for him. In the days coming up to Izaac's fifth birthday, Nathan might have been seen scouring the many musical instrument shops in Vienna looking for a suitable small-size violin for his little cousin. He loved the idea of using money from his first job on such a present. He arrived on the day of Izaac's birthday, calling out his congratulations and carrying a parcel that declared its contents by every curve. If Izaac's parents remembered Madame Stronski's warning they just had to forget it now.

The sight of that parcel eclipsed all else. Cakes and presents were graciously accepted, but everyone could see that Izaac's mind was elsewhere. If the half-size violin looked tiny to the adults, to Izaac it looked like a key to heaven. This was no mere toy: the feel, the strings, the pegs, the bow that tightened with a little twirly nut, all the intricate details assured him that this was the real thing. He demanded a lesson from Nathan immediately and for the rest of the day he carried the violin –

safe in its case – with him everywhere. When he went to bed, the violin went too, so that he could reach out and touch it as soon as he woke.

Perhaps the family had felt shy about taking up on Madame Stronski's offer to teach him, since she was, after all, much sought after. So an elderly neighbour, Herr Müller, who had once played on the very lowest desk in the Volksoper agreed to come in and give 'the little boy' some lessons.

Louise watched with amused apprehension while the 'little boy' absorbed in seconds what the old man had to offer, and then had to wait patiently through many repetitions and explanations until he was alone and could practise and perfect what he had been told. Within weeks the old man was floundering. It was little wonder; Izaac could already read music far better than he could read words. He would sit looking at a sheet of music and hear the notes in his head; he simply devoured the elementary primers that his teacher produced.

As the euphoria of his first lessons began to wear off, Louise sensed that Izaac was unhappy. She longed for him play for her, as he used to play on the piano. Nearly a year had passed since their tiff over the poor Countess; if he didn't want her company, there was nothing she could do about it. But now he was like a hobbled pony. Every time he tried to trot he tripped. She had seen his hands flitting over the piano keys as light as butterfly's wings, now she saw them on the violin looking like arthritic sausages. The coordination that had had him playing *Frère Jacques* was gone too. She watched in dismay as, week by week, his shoulders began to droop like an old man's, as if the violin was pulling them down.

He started practising in front of her portrait. She longed to be able to make suggestions, but they had lost their common language. All she could do was look on in horror as Izaac gradually transformed himself – not to a duck, nor yet to the

General – but to a second Herr Müller! It had taken the old violinist years of sawing away in his dusky corner of the pit at the opera to acquire his hunched shoulders and the aches and the cramps that Izaac, a natural mimic, now copied from him in weeks. She would watch Izaac putting away his violin like an old man after his lessons, and would feel his despair. Then one day, after Herr Müller had gone, Izaac looked up at Louise's portrait.

'Lees, I'm sorry. I wouldn't have done it really.'

'What do you mean, Izaac?' she asked.

'The Countess von Tischelstein, I never would have poked fun at her to any one else. I just pretended to you that I would. I liked her, it was just ...' Tears were balancing precariously on his lower lids. Louise realised how much she had missed sharing things with him.

'Just that I didn't trust you, that you didn't want another nanny?' she suggested.

Izaac nodded but his shrug suggested that there was something more here that he couldn't express. She noticed his arm tightening on the violin tucked under his elbow.

'I love your new violin,' she said.

'But not how I play it!'

'How do you know that, Izaac?'

'Because when I play for you, Lees, I just *know*. You don't have to say anything but I feel it. Oh help me, Lees ... why can't I do it? I hear the music in my head, but my fingers ...' he trailed off. He was crying properly now, the tears running off his chin. He closed the lid of his violin case to keep it dry, and managed an apologetic grin.

'Izaac, listen to me. Do you remember a woman with lots of scarves who played for you years ago?'

Izaac looked puzzled; then he nodded. 'Oh yes. I called her the Cloud Lady; I did something terrible to her violin!'

'You did indeed,' Louise smiled to herself. 'She played her violin for you, and then you played a lovely long note on her violin for us, remember?' He was nodding; he would never forget that moment.

'Well, would you like her to give you a lesson?'

'Me?'

'Yes, you! Why don't you ask Papa?'

'But I don't even know her name.'

'Tell him that she was the one who let you play her violin; he'll remember.'

'You'll stay, won't you, if she comes?'

'Only if you want me.'

The front door at the bottom of the apartment stairs opened and closed and Madame Stronski's distinctive Polish accent rose over Mother's voice in the hallway.

'I know... I know. Nathan has a heart of gold, but not the sense he was born with. Izaac, the poor mite, is he still playing it like a cello?' Her laugh rang out richly while Mother murmured apologies. The door swung open and the maestro made her entry. 'I left Strad at home. Lost his nerve after last time, the coward.' Now she spotted Izaac, who had been practising. 'Izaac Abrahams, is it really you? Good heavens, they've been watering you.' She swept a pale blue scarf over her shoulder as she bore down on him. 'So this is the new violin. Bless me, Cousin Nathan *has* done you proud! Now we must have a chat, you and I.' Turning to Izaac's mother, she said, 'Judit, Izaac and I have important matters to discuss.'

Then she turned to Izaac with a conspiratorial smile. 'I hate to have people about when I'm practising, don't you?' Louise, from the security of her picture, wondered if she should go too, but Izaac had specifically asked her to stay. Now the maestro stood back and assessed the boy with narrowed eyes. 'Let me see you hold the violin for a moment. Just tuck it under your chin. Now raise your bow as if you were about to play.' She swept around him like a comet, trailing scarves. Louise watched Izaac's eyes swivel anxiously as she passed. 'Harrumph! Aged about seventy ...' she muttered. 'Vintage? Vienna café-orchestra perhaps.' Then to Izaac: 'Now, let me hold this little beauty,' and she held out her hand for his violin. She ran her fingers over the strings. 'In tune too.' She put it down into its case.

'Now, let's look at the other half of the equation, that's you, Izaac. You don't mind if I push you around a bit do you ... you don't bite?' Izaac managed a nervous smile. 'Just stand in front of me, will you, feet comfortably apart, left foot a little forward, as that's where the weight of the violin comes.'

Louise watched, fascinated, as the great lady got to work on Izaac. She was like a sculptor working with soft clay, pushing his body around and moulding it while murmuring the reasons for each adjustment as she did so.

'If we get this right now, Izaac, you will never have trouble with your body. We are athletes, you see, we go out on to the platform and we do things with our bodies that would leave the average person from the audience tied in knots.' She stood back, head on one side, to admire her work. Then she reached out and put her hand on Izaac's head.

Louise thought that she was going to give him a blessing; in a way she was.

'Now, Izaac, push up against my hand. This is the most important thing I can teach you. Every thing about the violin strives upwards. The only thing that presses down is the bow, and that you hold in your fingers. Reach up with your body, and so will your violin, so will your music, and your audience will feel themselves rising too. This is why they sometimes even rise to their feet … they can't help it, you see. But before that, my love, there is work, a lot of hard work.

Madame Stronski came every week when she could, and Louise watched and listened with silent admiration as she quietly undid the damage inflicted on Izaac by the well-meaning Herr Müller. Izaac would play her the piece she had given him to work on. Louise noticed that she would always begin by pointing out something that he had done well.

'Your open strings are really buzzing now …' Then having softened the blow, she would begin to tackle the problems. 'Your thumb, Izaac, your thumb! Get your left thumb perched on the neck as I show you and it will be right for life!' One time she got cross. 'Izaac, don't you think it would be polite if you were to play to *me* and not to the wall.'

Even though she could only manage one lesson a week, Izaac was now streaking ahead. He only had to be corrected once, would remember what he had been told, and would build on it. He was able to look at a page of music and hear it in his mind; his problem was to get his fingers, his arm, and his whole body to translate this into sound. Here *Madame Helena*, as he now called her, was his guru. She would pounce on him, holding his violin by the scroll and getting him relaxed until the violin came to be like a feather in his hands. When his notes became thin and wispy she would make him use his bow so slowly that the sound came out grating like gravel. 'There, Izaac,' she would shout, 'horrible isn't it, but that is what sound is, those pebbles and the stones rattling around in your violin are what you turn into your castles and palaces. We have to shape them and cast them into sound.'

One day, when his lesson was over and Izaac had been taken out to buy a new pair of shoes, Madame Stronski lingered on in the music room with the excuse that she wanted to practise, but she soon put her violin down and began to prowl, moving about the room as if trying to find the exact position where Izaac had been standing during practice.

'This is the spot,' she said to herself. Then crouching down to Izaac's height, she looked up and gazed directly into Louise's portrait. 'Well, well, well, I guessed as much. So he's not just playing to the wall. Well, young lady. What have you got to say for yourself? If I remember rightly, I asked you to look after my little wonder for me. Fat lot of good you've been.' She heaved herself to her feet. 'So, he plays for you, does he? Well, we all need somewhere, or something, don't we, some rock or tree or marble saint to which we can speak our minds and hear ourselves think. But you're no saint, are you, dear? That's why I like you. You're like my Copernicus.' She smiled at the memory. 'There is a statue of him as a young man outside the University in Kraków holding his astrolabe, and I thought he was wonderful. He was the first man, you know, to work out that the earth moves around the sun and not vice versa. A sad story: he didn't dare publish his discovery in case he was excommunicated, or worse. I would tell him, his statue, all about my love life and woes. One day I was giving out to him about the fuddy-duddies in the conservatory, when I heard his voice – remember, I was only eighteen – "Wake up Helena! Where is the musical sun? In Vienna, of course. So off you go, my little planet, stop expecting the musical world to spin about you, and go and spin about it." I'd like to think he said, "I'll miss you,"' she added wistfully, 'but I don't suppose he did.'

While Madame Stronski was talking, Louise kept seeing little glimpses of – Kraków surely – through her eyes. A great square lined with cafés and restaurants, carriages passing; a trumpet that called from a high spire and then stopped, tantalisingly, in mid-phrase. Then they were walking under trees where a statue rose in a small clearing, and there he was! Copernicus, looking down at them, holding his astrolabe. Louise wasn't surprised that the young Helena had brought her troubles to him; his was a face to confide in. She looked at her companion, and saw Helena as the eighteen-year-who had stood under Copernicus's statue that day: rebellious, troubled, but at that moment glowing with her new idea. Had Louise known it, she was seeing the same radiant beauty that she herself had shown one day in Delft, the day when the Master had captured her likeness. The vision faded ... her new friend was now at the window gazing down on the Viennese traffic.

About this time Izaac first walked into the music room wearing a school uniform. It came as a surprise to Louise, who was inclined to forget that Izaac had a whole life of his own that was beyond her ken. Perhaps he was as good at his homework as he was at his violin, because it was always a very short time between hearing the bang of the apartment door and his eager appearance in the music room, particularly when Madame Stronski was waiting for him. As his confidence returned, so too did his good opinion of himself.

'Izaac! Stop, stop, stop! You are swelling like a toad. If you swell any more you will burst and I will have to mop you up,' Madame Stronski shouted. Louise was amused. Izaac was standing with his violin, the picture of offended dignity, but Madame Stronski gave no quarter. 'I want to hear *Izaac* playing, not *Master stuck up little Abrahams*. You're not in the Musicverein, nor yet at the Carnegie Hall in New York. You are plain ordinary Izaac, a little squirt of a schoolboy who happens to be good at the violin. Just be kind enough to play for *me*. I like Izaac's playing, but, frankly, *Master Abrahams* gives me a pain.'

'But Madame Helena, how do I know when *Izaac* is playing and when it is *Master Abrahams?*'

'*Um Gottes willen*! Because I begin shouting at you for a start! Don't you *feel* it when you are swelling like a toad, eyes boggling, buttons about to burst, imagining that you are the great Mr Kreisler himself?'

Izaac opened his eyes wide. 'But when you're not here to shout at me?'

'Well, play for your friend, Louise!' Izaac looked at the ceiling, then at the floor, studiously avoiding any glance towards Louise's picture. 'And don't go all innocent on me; you know perfectly well who I mean. You've been playing to that picture since I first came here.'

'Oh, Lees!' he said. 'But she doesn't know anything about music.' Louise gave a mental sniff.

'She doesn't have to,' Madame Stronski snapped. 'Izaac, get this into your head: *ninety percent* of our audiences know nothing about music, but we still play for them, and if we play like self-conceited little brats they will tell us. Just as I tell you – sure as rosin-your-bow – if you play for Louise here as you played for me just now, either she will reach out and bop you on the head with her telescope, or you will know in your conceited little heart that Master Abrahams, the toad, has just pushed you off the platform! Now go away and play, I need to negotiate pay and conditions with Miss Louise!'

For a while she paced the room, then she paused near Louise's picture and said, half to herself, half to Louise. 'I want him to mature into a man, Louise, not just a prodigy. We have a huge responsibility.'

Izaac was still miffed the following day. He had rather fancied himself as 'Master Abrahams,' who felt far more important than the Izaac he was familiar with. He rubbed his tummy, wondering if he really had swelled, then he turned away hastily in case Louise was watching; she was in on this conspiracy against him. Hiding his violin behind his back, he tiptoed across the room and sidled along the wall till he was as near to her picture as he could get. He then plucked his violin from behind his back and played the most rasping discord he could devise. No reaction, she was pretending not to hear. He came out from the wall to face her, put on a look of angelic innocence, and started practising his scales, carefully hiding a series of small mistakes in them.

This was more difficult than he'd imagined. Still no reaction; so he put his tongue out and played: 'La da di da da', just to tell her what he thought of conspirators. She knew nothing about music, and Madame talking of Louise bopping him on the head with her telescope was just silly. A thought crossed his mind; what was that he'd just played? 'La da di da da'… he played it again. Then he moved it up a key and modulated back down. Variations on a theme of La da di da da! He'd *have* to play this for her. So he turned to Louise's picture and played it again, this time in a longer variation in which his violin chased the original tune around the room like a bird in flight. When he heard Louise's laugh, the sound came from behind him.

'Bravo, Izaac!' He span about.

'But how did you know, Lees?' he asked.

'Know what?'

'When I was playing well?'

'Because you told me, you mutt!' she was laughing at him.

'No, I did not!'

'Oh, but you did. You said, "This is Izaac here, not beastly little Master Abrahams."'

'But how do you *know*? Madame Helena said you would.'

'Once you said that playing for me was like playing in a mirror,' she reminded him. 'Because you really, really want me

51

to hear and love your music, you share your thoughts with me. Not thoughts about what's for lunch, or how beautifully you are playing, but your thoughts as a musician. Just like when Madame Stronski said that you had stopped being Izaac and had turned into Master Abrahams.' Izaac frowned, that hadn't been his favourite moment.

Louise wondered if she could turn it into a game. 'Try me,' she teased. 'I bet I can tell you when you make a genuine mistake, and when you are just fooling.' Rather suspiciously, Izaac raised his violin to his shoulder. Louise crossed her fingers. He played a few sombre notes for her. 'Good,' she encouraged him. Then he played a simple scale on G. 'Good again.' Then, without changing his expression, he played the same scale with a rogue sharp in the middle of it. 'You did that on purpose, you rascal. You can't fool me.' She taunted.

'Oh yes I can!'

'Oh no you can't!'

By now Izaac had a glint in his eye that was new to Louise; she laughed nervously as he rose to his toes and began to play. She found herself mentally ducking as he pelted her with every note and musical trick he had in his armoury. Louise had meant this to be a game, but now she realised she had started something far more serious. Izaac was testing her, and in doing so, was testing himself. Slow-moving semibreves were used to disguise a sharp attack of crotchets and semiquavers. He practised up-bows and down-bows and then tickled her with pizzicatos.

Years ago, as a little girl in Delft, Louise had played catch with the boys. They would go to great lengths to disguise where they were about to throw the ball, but Louise soon learned to watch their eyes and could quickly move in the right direction. Though Izaac tried to distract her in every way possible, he could do nothing to disguise the minute frown or flicker of his eyelids or even the mental 'oops' when a genuine mistake slipped through.

'Mistake!' Louise would respond. 'I don't know what you did, but that was wrong!' Izaac would stare at her furiously in disbelief.

The continued with their 'game' over the next few weeks, and Louise discovered an Izaac who would argue over every note. They would have shouting matches just because Izaac, eager as always to get on with a new piece or exercise, would pretend to himself that the old one was perfect. As Louise had predicted, the more he played for her, the stronger became the voice of the musician. She was no longer relying on a wince or a frown. Soon it was Izaac the musician who knew he had made a mistake, and who felt bad when he cut short his practice.

Louise didn't always get it right either, but as time went on Izaac trusted her more and more, sharing his musical thoughts and feelings willingly with her as he played. Louise was reminded of the moment when the Master had begun to paint her portrait and her image had appeared as if it had always existed in the canvas, emerging as if from behind a frosted glass. Now Izaac was looking past her image in her portrait and finding the musician that lay deep inside him.

⌒≫

As Louise learned more about music, she was able to appreciate what Izaac called his 'musical chuckles'. His variations on La da di da da were just the first of a whole series of 'chuckles' that would later become famous in his encores. He was nearly seven now, and playing better than many a graduate of the Academy. When working on some particularly beautiful piece he could reduce them both to tears, and Louise would wonder what would happen if he felt like this in a performance. After a while, however, she realised that these emotional moments belonged in rehearsal. At his performances it would be for other people to weep. She found it more and more difficult to draw a line between herself and him. They were partners in his music now, merging into a single resonance.

CHAPTER 6

Mutual Understanding

Erich was hungry. He was always hungry, and he had been drawing food. That amoeboid blob in his drawing book was a huge Wiener schnitzel, and those things like marbles were potatoes, drawn small so he could have lots of them. His tummy gurgled; perhaps drawing food had not been a good idea. He listened. For some time he had been hearing an interesting scraping and scratching sound which seemed to be coming down through the high dormer window that was set into the sloping ceiling of his attic room. Mother had lifted him up once or twice so that he could see out, and he had felt like a bird looking down on the little patch of lawn at the back of the house. At present all he could see was sky.

He looked around for something to climb up on so that he could see out. The only thing to hand was an old nursing chair with a high ladder back. Abandoning his schnitzel and potatoes, he set-to to drag the chair to a place under the window, and climbed up on the seat. Now he could get his hands on the sill; it was tantalising, another few centimetres and he would be able to see out. He felt the chair-back against his knee. If he could just … Groping with his foot, he found the first rung on the back of the chair. He rose cautiously and looked out.

The lumpy green of the Vienna Woods rose beyond the end of the garden. He could see the vine trellis on the far wall of the garden, but the lawn, from where the scraping sound was coming, was obscured by the slope of the roof. He felt for the next rung on the chair and pulled himself up. Now he could see! There was Grandpa Veit's head.

'Granp–' he began, raising a hand to wave, but at that moment the chair shot from under him and Erich found himself suspended with his arms over the windowsill, his legs thrashing in the vacant air below. Instinct told him that dropping back into the room onto the top of the fallen chair was not a good idea. Another instinct, more obscure, prevented him calling out to his grandfather for help. If he could just make it onto the windowsill he'd be all right.

He tried to push himself up on to his hands but his arms were not strong enough. If only he could use his legs. He lifted a knee but it got caught under the sill. His strength was running out now, but grim determination was making him hold on. He used his head to work out a move, and in one last effort he managed to swing one leg up and hook his heel over the top of the sill. Now, like a rider mounting a horse, he rolled tummy-wise onto the windowsill. In fact his effort was so successful that he only just stopping himself from continuing his roll on out of the window, down the roof, and into the garden where Grandpa Veit was looking up at him with interest.

What Veit was doing was digging up Sabine's lawn in the hope of planting some late potatoes in time for an autumn crop. He was stripped to the waist. He had lost so much weight that his lederhosen swung loose about him from their leather braces. The war was over, and since November the year before, soldiers had been returning home hungry and weary from trenches and billets and barracks on a dozen different fronts. Real starvation threatened all but the wealthy in the capital.

He only had a small patch of lawn still to dig. All morning as he turned the grass, sod by sod, Veit had designated these as the countries lost to Austria as a result of the war. He had dug up Poland first … let them have their Republic, if the Russians didn't get them first. Then Czechoslovakia went under his heel, followed by Serbia – now part of Yugoslavia, of all improbable alliances. Hungary was still with Austria, but it was sure to go, so he spat on his hands and dug it to oblivion too. He looked at the pathetic patch that represented all that remained of Austria, and then he remembered that they had also lost the Sudetenland – the German-speaking Alps – now part of Italy.

All of the things that he'd looked to as a source of pride were dead or gone. The Emperor was dead. Sergeant Major Veit Hoffman was gone … retired. Even his uniform was gone. Viet gazed down at his lederhosen with distaste. The government had once been a source of pride, but now the country was being run by the Jews. His son should have been a source of pride too, but his mind winced away from that topic. A daughter-in-law, who looked like a Rhine maiden from the myths, but who had as much spine as an earthworm. And finally there was her brat. He drove his spade into the last of 'Austria'. As he did so he heard a shout.

'Granp–' Veit looked up, saw the startled face of Erich in the attic window, and then saw it disappear. What was the brat doing now? He had re-emerged but he seemed to be struggling. Perhaps Sabine was holding him from below? But that was Sabine's voice singing in the kitchen. Veit's interest quickened. The boy's face was scarlet with the effort that he was making. He'll shout for help in a moment, Veit speculated, but the boy didn't. He watched as Erich got his heel, then his calf, then his knee over the window sill and prepared for the final heave. Veit didn't move, even when he realised that the boy might overdo it and tip himself down the roof and into the garden at his feet. He was interested, but quite detached, like a general watching his men streaming into battle; what would be would be.

Erich straddled the windowsill, having corrected his roll by bracing his foot against the warm tiles of the roof. He knew Grandpa Veit was looking up at him. At least Grandpa wouldn't fuss, though if Mother saw him now there would be panic. He needed time to work out what to do. Going back had no attractions; the dark space behind him seemed threatening and dangerous. In front of him the roof sloped down to a gutter that stood out a few centimetres from the tiles, and while it was only a small protection from the drop into the garden below, it was reassuring. Below and to his right a high wall met the house at right angles and then ran down the side of the garden to where it supported a lean-to shed. If he could move diagonally across the roof from where he sat, then down onto the top of the wall, he could make his way along this and slide down the roof of the shed. It wouldn't be that big a drop from there into the garden.

He rolled onto his tummy and started lowering himself down; suddenly this seemed all wrong His knees had no grip and he was sure that once he let go of the windowsill he would just slide inexorably over the edge. He hauled himself up to the window again. His heart was racing. Grandpa Veit was pretending to dig, but Erich guessed that he was watching. Sitting on his bottom he felt more stable, his bare feet gripped well on the tiles. He hitched himself forward gingerly, his fingers finding little overlapping places between the tiles. Now he was moving sideways towards the top of the wall. He looked up. Above him the sky arched in a cloud-flecked dome, beneath him the tiles seemed warm and friendly; he had a wonderful feeling of freedom and of being suspended in space with air both above him and below.

Perhaps he'd wave to Grandpa. He looked down, and quite suddenly it all changed; his legs, his arms, and his spine turned to jelly. The tiles were no longer friendly. While he had been moving, the overlaps had been forcing him ever closer to the edge of the roof. As he froze, his toes knotted and began to slip, his hands began scrabbling for a grip. Veit was looking up at him; he didn't even look anxious. Erich took control of himself, but only just in time; as he relaxed, his feet began to grip again, and his hands became as tactile as limpets. By working methodically against the grain he hitched himself up and away from the edge.

The passage from the roof onto the top of the wall was tricky, and when he reached it, it was quite narrow so he straddled it and hitched himself along until he reached the lean-to shed. Once there it was a simple matter to slide down the corrugated iron roof to the edge. It seemed a long way down. Perhaps Veit would be cross, but the old man's silent observation suggested approval. He would take a risk.

'Grandpa,' he called. 'Can you help me?' Veit, sighing audibly at the interruption, dug in his spade, came over, and reached up to lift Erich to the ground.

'Listen to me, young man,' he said. 'You must never climb up something you can't get down. Do you hear?'

'Yes Grandpa, thank you Grandpa,' Erich said, backing away.

Veit watched him as he turned to run. 'I'll make a man out of him yet,' he said.

CHAPTER 7

A Prodigy Steps Out

Louise was sick with nerves. Izaac, now aged seven, had grown considerably in the year and a half since Madame Stronski had ousted Herr Müller as his teacher. Today he would perform for the first time to a group of family and friends. The concert double bill featured *The Tuning Fork Quartet* and the as yet unheard boy violinist Izaac Abrahams. Preparations were well under way.

Uncle Rudi passed in front of Louise's picture, walking backwards, dragging a heavy armchair over the carpet towards the wall where he angled it towards the performing end of the music room. Beads of sweat glistened all over his head. He rubbed himself down with a large handkerchief, then he joined Nathan, who was assembling a line of chairs robbed from the dining room. They both went off to see what chairs they could find in the bedrooms. Izaac struggled in with a stool from the kitchen and put it at the back, where it would do for any latecomer.

It was the calm before the storm. Members of the family had gone off to bedrooms to change; there were distant shouts of laughter. Izaac, scrubbed to within an inch of his life, appeared. He had been dressed up in a frilly white shirt with a large, floppy blue bow tie, a grey jacket and shorts.

'Will I be all right?' he asked, glancing in the direction of Louise's portrait. 'I think this jacket will be too tight.'

Louise reassured him.

'What if I forget my notes?' he went on.

'You won't forget!' He began to relax. A mischievous smile crossed his face.

'I think I'll do my duck act!'

'No, you won't do your duck act! Don't tease me.'

⌐–⟋⟍⟋⟍–⌐

The applause was polite as the four members of *The Tuning Fork Quartet* rose to their feet, pleased, perspiring, and bowing. The chairs were all filled now. The ladies were comfortably ensconced in armchairs around the edges of the room, while the men eased themselves on the upright ones in the middle. While the quartet put their instruments away and moved their chairs back to form a semi-circle, Izaac, looking small and scared, took his violin from its case. Madame Stronski leant forward and whispered some words of encouragement. All eyes were on the boy. They had heard about him, but that not that he was a pupil of the great Madame Stronski, and they were impressed. They all leant forward now, putting their will behind him as he tightened his bow. No one noticed when the door behind them opened to let a tall distinguished looking man slip silently into the room. He looked about him; spotted the high kitchen stool that Izaac had brought in, and tiptoed over to it.

Louise noticed him straight away. Who could this be? His suit was well cut with a discreet stripe, his hair was dark with wings of grey over the ears, and a fine moustache was just flecked with grey. The only other person who could see this stranger was young Izaac, and he was struck dumb.

Izaac gaped, his hands freezing on his violin. He had heard the great Fritz Kreisler, who was certainly Vienna's, and possibly the world's, greatest violinist, play only a month before, when Nathan had taken him to the Great Hall of the Musikverein. What could he be doing here? He could feel the audience becoming uneasy, but didn't they know who was sitting behind them? Suddenly he heard Louise calling him.

'Izaac, Izaac … listen to me!' She was pleading. 'Don't worry about him; he's just a man come in off the street. Remember Madame Helena's instructions: your feet, relax your shoulders, breath deeply.' But his violin felt like lead, how could he ever lift it? Then he realised that the great man was looking at him sympathetically, with an amused smile hovering over his face. As if reading Izaac's mind, he raised an imaginary violin to his shoulder and rested an invisible bow on the strings, as if about to play. It was all so relaxed, so confident, so full of music that a great weight seemed to fall from Izaac's shoulders. His violin responded and rose like a feather to his chin.

⌐╼╫╫╫╌◞

Over the next two years the list of composers and pieces Izaac mastered grew and grew: Bloch's 'Abodah', Wieniawski's 'Scherzo-Tarantelle', and Schubert's gorgeous 'Ave Maria'. To begin with, these were just names to Louise, but now it was dawning on her that when people talked of Izaac as a prodigy, they really meant it. Though Izaac would fret that Madame Helena was holding him back, he seemed gloriously unaware of his genius. Finally he was ready for his proper debut concert.

When Izaac had played in the music room to his family and their friends, the applause had sounded like a sudden shower of rain. As if it had caught them all by surprise. How could this seven year old, in short pants and a floppy bow tie, produce sounds that wrenched forgotten emotions from their hearts? Today, however, the applause was of a different magnitude; it swept over Izaac like a wave, crashing about his ears as he stared, bewildered, at the audience from which this amazing sound was coming. The uniform black of the men's suits was enlivened by a speckle of colour from the ladies' dresses. Their faces merged, hands blurring, clapping as if their lives depended on it. A rumble began that seemed to rise through the boards at Izaac's feet, like rocks churning in the backwash of a wave. The audience were stamping their feet in an ecstasy of delight.

The nine-year-old glanced towards the safety of the door at the side of the platform. There was Madame Helena, signalling urgently, bending almost double to get her message across. Of course … he should bow! His paralysis passed and he bowed and then bowed again. He let his eyes sweep the audience, as Madame Helena had told him to do. 'You won't see a thing, Izaac, but they will love it,' she had said, but he was looking for someone special. There, beyond the blur, a spot of colour stood out sharp and clear. There was only one green like that in the world: Louise was there, just as she had promised. He could see her standing at the back, clapping like everyone else. A broad smile lit his face, and the crowd loved it. Those generous Viennese hearts that love music and musicians above all else opened to him as one. A final bow, and he turned to leave the stage.

Once through the door he was engulfed by his dear Madame Helena, simultaneously cuffing him for having forgotten to bow, hugging him, and trying not to cry. Having held him as long as she dared, she turned him around and sent him out to play his one short encore.

Once again he scanned the audience, looking for Louise, and there wasn't a mother in the crowd who wasn't convinced that his look was for her alone. He found Louise on a second pass, at the back in a seat just vacated by an early leaver. He could feel her laughter and delight running through him. As he played his encore, the laughter got into his fingers and they danced on the fingerboard.

Three times he was called back. He pleaded with Madame Helena to be allowed to play again, but she was adamant. In the end she just took his violin from him and pushed him out for his final bow. She heard the wave of clapping break, saw Izaac's last bow, and without waiting for him, gathered her scarves and proceeded towards the Green Room. She had a thing or two to tell him about his vibrato. At that moment there came a roar of laughter from the auditorium. Madame Helena turned, but all she saw was Izaac lunging through the door from the stage, a broad grin on his face.

The following morning, Madame Helena's maid, Hanna, had been sent out to buy the morning papers and had stacked them neatly on the side of her mistress's breakfast tray. Helena ran her eye over the front page of the *Neue Zeitung* while she buttered her roll, postponing the reviews until she had both hands free to open the papers. '*Food Shortages Ease,*' was the banner heading. Beside it was a short column about a young comedian. Sliding that paper to one side, she looked at the *Tages Bladt*; its headline reported on a meeting of a new political party in Munich that seemed to be upsetting the Communists, but she didn't mind upsetting the Communists. She was about to read further when she noticed that the comedian had made it onto the first page again. She read the first line and her heart nearly stopped. '*Prodigy violinist Izaac ...*'

Hanna heard her mistress's shriek from the kitchen and came running. She found her enveloped in as many newspapers as she normally wore scarves.

'Listen to this, Hanna,' she commanded as she read from the paper. 'Infant prodigy entertains audience with duck dance ...' She raised her eyes, saucer wide, to the mystified Hanna. 'Oh, Izaac, how could you do this to me?' Papers flew and Hanna rescued sheets on demand as Helena plunged after the serious reviews that were always hidden on the inner pages. Little by little she relaxed. *'Superb technique for one so ... pure musicianship ... a credit to his teacher.'* Then a gratifying mention of the great Madame Stronski. Hanna, who had been worrying about where she had put the smelling salts, relaxed too. *'A bit too heavy on the vibrato ...'* Yes, she had been going to tackle him on that when he had careered off the stage, but there was more to come. She read on in trepidation: excellent reviews, but one and all critical about Izaac's behaviour after his encore. *'Vienna expects her young performers to behave with decorum in the halloed precincts of the concert hall, where the ghosts of the great composers linger yet.'* Even while she cringed for Izaac, Madame Stronski couldn't entirely suppress a little snort of laughter. 'Stuffy old fuddy-duddies,' she muttered to herself. 'Mozart would have loved it.' She rather wished she had seen exactly what the little monkey had done.

Izaac was hanging his head as Madame Helena whirled around him like a Dervish, berating him about his fooling on stage.

'Izaac Abrahams, what ... did ... you ... do?' Louise, who knew only too well what he had done, was quite glad of the protection of her picture frame. She was already feeling guilty for having been so ready to laugh at Izaac's antics.

'I did my duck act,' he whispered.

'Your duck act!' He made to show her. 'No! I don't want to see it. I don't want to know about it. I particularly never want to hear about it again. You are never, ever, to put on one of your little performances on stage again. You have disgraced me, and apparently the whole musical profession in the process. I don't know, in the circumstances, if you even

deserve to hear what the reviews actually say. However ...'
Now, walking up and down, Madame told him about the reviews, as if reading him his school report. Musicianship: excellent. Technical ability: good. Vibrato: too much. Intonation: good except in pizzicato. 'No time to slide about looking for the note, is there?'

As she went on, adding glowing comment to glowing comment, her voice softened. Her prowling slowed. 'I don't know if I should tell you this, but you know that the Konzerthaus is part of the University?' Izaac nodded. 'Well, the Professor of music heard you and suggested to me, after your performance, that you should enrol at the University and study with me there.'

'But I'm only nine!' Izaac said, his jaw dropping.

Helena reached forward and raised his chin. 'You'll still have to go to school, but well done, my little wonder. Now give the old dragon a kiss. I deserve it. We can talk vibrato later.'

CHAPTER 8

The Face in the Ivy

Erich was doing his homework while his mother painted. He liked the smell of turpentine as it mixed with the piny smell of his pencil parings. She was relaxed, singing quietly to herself, *Röslein, Röslein, Röslein rot ...* They were like two overlapping circles, each with their own centre but each aware of the other. Erich didn't understand her paintings, splashes of colour and criss-cross lines, but he liked cutting out pictures of 'real things' from her monthly magazine and pasting them on to the walls of his room. He would imagine walking into the pictures and having adventures.

He looked up. Grandpa Veit was resting, and Father was still at his work. Erich could see his mother over the top of her easel. The light falling over her right shoulder was catching the curtain of fair hair across her face. Grandpa called her a *Rhine maiden,* so Erich thought Rhine maidens must be the most beautiful people in the world. Yet there was something in the way that Grandpa said it that made Izaac feel protective and possessive about her. People said that he looked like her. Once, when Grandpa had him on his own, he had pushed Erich's shoulders back and lifted his chin, and had told him he was 'good Aryan stock'. Erich had no idea what this meant but, like most things Grandpa told him, he kept it to himself.

That evening after work, Mr Solomons, the owner of the timber yard, knocked on their door. They were all there,

Father, Mother, Grandpa and Erich, about to have dinner. Though there was little enough food, Mother, impulsive as always, invited Mr Solomons to join them. He refused politely but stood there awkwardly, a book under one arm, twisting his hat. Then he explained that he had been in Munich on business. While there he had gone to an exhibition of modern art. Knowing Mrs Hoffman's interest, he had taken the liberty of bringing her the catalogue of the exhibition, if she would be so kind as to accept it.

Mother's face lit up. 'Oh, how kind, how wonderful.' In a moment, forgetting all about dinner, beckoning them to her, she said, 'Come and look, everyone!' She began turning the pages of the catalogue, exclaiming over the pictures with cries of delight. 'Oh look: Picasso, and Matisse, that's Miró surely ...'

As his mother was excitedly turning the pages, Erich felt Grandpa's hand on his shoulder, biting in and drawing him back from the others. When he had been pulled to a safe distance Grandpa Veit bent and whispered in his ear.

'Mustn't let you get contaminated, boy.' He made a dusting gesture at Erich's front as if Erich had rubbed up against something dirty. Confused and embarrassed, Erich tried to move away but Grandpa Veit held on to him. 'Notice that he wouldn't eat with us?' Erich supposed he meant Mr Solomons. 'Because we're not kosher ... we're unclean, might give him pig.' The old man's stale breath blasted in his ear. 'He's poisoning her now with all that rubbish – modern art – it's a conspiracy, son! All cut-up people, and nudes that nature wouldn't recognise; it looks like kid's art, but it's corrupting; all part of their plan.'

'Whose plan, Grandpa?' Erich whispered.

The old man bent even closer. 'The Jews', he whispered in his ear.

Erich stopped on the stairs to listen, his pyjamas cold on his shoulders. No one had heard his scream. He had woken in a sweat. Mr Solomons had been cutting up people with scissors and mixing the pieces in a drink for mother. Could Mr Solomons really be trying to poison her? He could hear Grandpa snoring and was glad; this was something Erich wanted to investigate on his own. He had never understood his mother's paintings, but if she was happy, he was happy. He took a deep breath and turned into the sitting room where there was a row of them propped up against the wall. He approached them suspiciously and began to move methodically down the line.

Some were very simple, just lines and blocks of colour; he felt safe with these, and began to wonder what the fuss was about. All these were the elite, the few that had survived Sabine's frequent over-painting and scraping-out of old canvasses. They were in many styles, mostly abstract, shapes and colours that were meaningless to Erich. It was just as he thought – her playthings – nothing even as meaningful as his Wiener schnitzel. He had reached the end of the line and was about to go, when out of the corner of his eye, one of the pictures appeared to move.

He whipped around. Nothing. He was sure though. He *had* seen a person move! He turned away slowly and there it was! Out of the corner of his eye there *was* a person that had not been there before. He turned back, careful not to lose the image. It was a girl dancing, head thrown back. How had he missed her? Now, as he looked down the line of painting, he realised that there were more. Not moving, that had been an illusion, but people and faces, and possibly places, emerging and fading as his eyes moved from picture to picture. Some of the pictures gave him feelings of sadness.

'Poor Mother,' he murmured, as his eight-year-old mind unwittingly revealed the pain his mother had so successfully concealed from the world. He moved slowly, falteringly, back down the line. Here was one he could hardly look at now: a seascape or a troubled sky? Then suddenly out of the tormented blues his father's face emerged, cyanose, as Erich had seen it one time when his heart was bad. The image went and he could not see it again. Feeling shaken, he arrived at the end of the line. The last canvas had been turned to face the wall. Erich turned it and looked at it curiously; it was easier, much more realistic than the others, a gnarled tree covered in ivy. He knelt to prop it up, and then nearly reeled back as the ivy seemed to burst apart in his face, and there was Grandpa Veit, his face staring out at him. Erich dropped the picture back against the wall and covered his eyes.

What evil magic was this? What spell was Mother under that made her paint these terrifying things? Still half covering his eyes, he ran for the door and nearly straight into Grandpa Veit who stood blocking his way, spindle-shanked in his nightshirt. Erich staggered to a stop and stood, waiting for a blow to the head or a blast of the old man's anger, but none came. To his amazement, his grandfather began speaking to him seriously, as if talking to a young soldier just back from patrol.

'So you have seen it, have you? You have been looking into the heart of darkness, boy. The pure apple infected by the worm. The Rhine Maiden sings, but the worm has the ring. Who will be our Siegfried, Erich, where are our heroes?'

Grandpa had told him the Siegfried saga at great length, even so, Erich had only the vaguest idea of what the Rhine Maidens were, except that they must be beautiful, and that Siegfried was a hero of heroes. But Veit had seized Erich by the shoulders. 'We have work to do, lad. Not only have we an empire to recover, but a race to save.'

The words and the passion behind them stirred Erich like the rousing music that would boom out from Grandpa Veit's hissing gramophone. Nobody but Grandpa spoke to him like this: man-to-man. His words made Erich proud, so that when his grandfather reached forward, lifted his chin, and looked him in the eye, Erich felt his own shoulders broadening and his chest expanding, as if some great purpose was being revealed to him.

But then something happened. The old man's eyes were boring into him ... piercing but changing ... the face was transforming, wrinkles deepening into rugged bark. Now ivy leaves were crowding round his face, framing it. Erich pulled back in terror, but the evil mask remained, it was a warning and he knew where it came from. He turned and fled for the stairs.

CHAPTER 9

On the Crest of a Wave

'Follow me, Mr Abrahams.' Maestro Herzfeld, Izaac's conductor, a formidable man with fierce bushy eyebrows and a shock of grey hair, swept past him and out onto the stage. Izaac followed, holding his violin high above the seated players. He had given dozens of recitals, had played several times with student orchestras and had loved it, but this was his first full professional engagement. Helena had intentionally held him back until he was sixteen, saying that he was too volatile.

'This is your chance, Izaac. Play well for Maestro Herzfeld and you can call yourself a professional. I want no histrionics ... Understand?'

Izaac had never felt less volatile, or more in control. He sidled past the violins, and exchanged grins with the woodwind players on his left.

'And remember to shake hands with the leader;' Helena had reminded him. 'He's a better violinist than you are! No bobbing up and down; turn to the audience and give one polite bow. The years when you were applauded just because you looked cute in short trousers are over.'

Izaac had wished she'd shut up. He was well able to look after himself.

Louise found herself an empty seat tucked away to the right

of the platform where Izaac could see her without turning if he really wished. She relaxed, relishing the anonymity of the crowd. She was exhausted, but elated too. They had worked so hard on the Dvorak that she was sure that nothing could go wrong. As they had worked, bar by bar, line by line, she had felt the music drawing them closer and closer. Most of the time her role was to help Izaac to stand back and listen and 'feel' the music while tackling its technical difficulties. As they approached performance standard, however, the concerto began to grow, developing into a living thing, no longer a succession of lovely notes, but at one moment a monster that raged and terrified, leading them into the dark places of the soul; and next a friend that walked them through fields and gardens. Locked in the world of music, they shared the drama and pain, laughter and tenderness, as if they were one person. But when their practice together was over, they shed their intimacy and walked away as if their close encounters had never happened.

Izaac was lucky, he had the release of his performance to look forward to, but Louise had no such release. Without her noticing it, the cumulative effect of these collaborations began to grow. She thought back to her own short life, and her cruelly interrupted love for Pieter, the Master's apprentice back in Delft. Then there had been Gaston, her French Hussar; if she hadn't loved Colette like a sister she could never have stepped aside for her.

Why did she have this so human need for love and affection, if it was never to be fulfilled? Her love for Izaac might be that of an older sister, but bitter experience had taught her that such love can spill over. She had no right to his heart outside of their music. And time, her enemy, would inevitably take him beyond her. The sadness of her immortality, of being constantly left behind, was a bitter pill. Now, as she watched him on the platform, relaxed and confident, she let go her hold on her feelings. The audience enclosed her, sending out their own warmth to him; a little more affection from her could do no harm.

Izaac looked towards the conductor, his smile confident. Madame Stronski could have told Louise that the one thing Izaac needed at this moment was a sharp slap on the backside and a reminder to place his feet correctly. But just now Louise was not on duty. He raised his bow, the conductor's baton fell, and the music from the orchestra swept over him.

There is probably no greater moment for a violin player than to experience for the first time the full strength and power of a seventy-piece orchestra surging in behind. Izaac felt himself being lifted up and thrust forward, like the bowsprit of a ship under full sail, reaching far out over the waves. The playing of the orchestra had the power of the wind behind it. No matter which way the ship turned, he would be there.

This was the moment at which Izaac must abandon all flights of fancy. Now he must enter his own private tunnel of sound where there was nothing to distract him but the remembered pages of music sliding before his eyes, and the strange designs and shapes that represented harmony and rhythm to him. But suddenly something infinitely sweet and alluring was pouring into him, lifting him headily higher. He had no idea where it was coming from but it manifested itself as a bright line of sound which danced about his playing, illusive, disarming, passionate but yet infinitely sad. It flooded him, drove him, intoxicated him. His ship was riding on the crest of a wave. Had he been a sailor he'd have known to fear for his life.

Louise realised, far too late, that something was seriously wrong. It was only when Izaac's body started to weave to the music that she realised that he needed her help.

'Come down Izaac, come down,' she pleaded, but he was

gone beyond her call. She had no access to him now. He was playing with a brilliance that he surely could never sustain. The opening passages of the first movement were passing, but at this pitch there was no room for error, nothing to stand between him and musical disaster. Louise closed her eyes and prayed.

Izaac never heard Louise's call to 'come down' but he noticed when the intoxicating harmony began to fade. His mind groped desperately for other indulgences to buoy him up. He became conscious of himself, of his good looks, of his technical skills, of his musicianship. He reminded himself how brilliantly he was playing. In Madame Stronski's language, he was beginning to swell, and Louise saw it all.

'Oh, where are you, Izaac?' she whimpered in anxiety. That wasn't him on the platform; it was the dreadful *Master Abrahams*. 'Stop. Stop,' she pleaded, echoing Madame Stronski's cry, but Izaac couldn't stop even if he wanted to. Seventy musicians, eyes lifting from their music to the conductor and back, were dependent on him, and he loved it.

At last the movement came to an end. Louise sank back in her seat, exhausted. He'd made it! Let him come down to earth now while the conductor was mopping his brow and while people coughed. He would be mentally turning the page in preparation for the next movement. But what in fact Izaac was doing was writing a rave review of his own performance.

The conductor glanced down, a courtesy glance to see if his young performer was comfortable, a smile of reassurance perhaps? He felt a slight prickle of apprehension. Those glazed eyes could just mean that the boy was preparing himself. On the other hand …

Izaac was called back from faraway by that glance. Ah yes, the third movement. But no, it couldn't be, there'd been no pause yet. Doubt flickered across his mind like a black-winged bat. This must be the second movement, surely. But the page he was seeing in his mind belonged to the third! Panic spread through him like a fever; he began to sweat. He would have to ask the conductor for a look at his score. He had heard of this happening, but he'd also heard that performers who did this were seldom seen again. 'Louise, help me!' He didn't deserve it, but he needed her now as never before.

Louise felt his call with a mixture of guilt and alarm. While they worked together she would watch the musical score through his eyes, one sheet sliding down over the other as the first was played. Most of the time the notes would appear as a comfortable blur, a sufficient reminder of the shape of the passage. When he was approaching a difficult section, however, she would know because here the notes would be crisp and clear. Now she realised that she hadn't been paying attention. She closed her eyes to concentrate, and her heart sank; what she was seeing through his eyes now was chaos. A page would appear, and then be snatched away. She could feel his panic mounting. She gripped her seat and tried to concentrate.

The conductor, realising that time was up, tapped his leg with his baton. What could have gone wrong? What *should* he be showing her? Surely the beginning of the second movem... She sat up. Of course! In the Dvorak violin concerto the first and second movements are always played as one continuous piece without a break. The mutt had forgotten; they had always practised the first two movements separately. He had let the orchestra carry him clean through into the second movement without thinking, and was now looking for the beginning of the wrong movement.

'Izaac, listen! You have played the second movement; it's the THIRD: Laa laa la la lee laa la la la lee la ... '

A look of enlightenment crossed Izaac's face. He turned to the conductor with an apologetic smile; he was ready.

After that Louise never left him for a second, thinking ahead for reminders and associations should he need them, but Izaac was safe now; she had saved him. The applause poured over her, but she was too drained even to clap. Izaac looked down and saw her hunched in the vacant seat, invisible to all but him.

The following morning Madame Stronski called to congratulate Izaac on his performance. He was exhausted and deflated, a condition that she knew from her own career, so she postponed her enquiries about what had happened at the end of the second movement until she was about to leave.

'Well, what happened at number three? I thought Maestro Herzfeld was going to run you through with his baton. I would have done!' Izaac hung his head and explained to the carpet that he had forgotten where he was in the score. 'What? With that lovely tune to remember? Oh Izaac!'

'I was playing so well in the first two movements, too.'

'No *you* weren't. It was bloody *Mr Abrahams* who was playing, wasn't it?'

'How can I explain, Madame Helena? I heard another line, a harmony like nothing I have ever heard before, it was so beautiful, but so sad. It just lifted me up and up.'

'Pah! I'd put that down to a bad case of inflated ego!' Madame Stronski snorted.

Louise sighed with relief. Ever since the concert she had been wondering if what had happened had anything to do with the feelings she had directed at Izaac.

Madame Helena wasn't interested in his excuses. There were new challenges ahead, she warned him. She wanted him to study some more modern composers, saying darkly that these would be brutes to learn.

CHAPTER 10

Night in Vienna Woods

Erich woke from a dream of family picnics, but the campfire smell persisted. He sniffed, and turned on his bedside light. A thin haze circled the shade. He let his eyes follow his nose upwards towards the skylight. Smoke was gently cascading into the room. He threw back his sheet, jumped for the ledge of the skylight and pulled himself up. He was twelve and lithe and active. Resting his chin on his hands, he peered down into the garden.

The smell wasn't from Grandpa Veit's bonfire. He looked left and saw a sudden flicker of red light illuminate the underside of a rising column of smoke. His arms went rigid; he hung for a second longer to be sure of his bearings, and then dropped back into the room, pulled on his shorts, grabbed a shirt and ran barefoot down the stairs.

'Fire! Papa ... fire; the sawmill is on fire!' The doors to the two bedrooms opened together. Grandpa Veit in his nightshirt, bleared and confused, started shouting loudly for water. Father, more practically, was pulling on his trousers. He reached into his pocket, took out some groschen and pressed the small coins into Erich's hand. Against the rising volume of Grandpa Veit's military-style commands, he shouted to Erich.

'To the telephone, Erich. First the Fire Brigade, that's free, then Herr Solomons. The operator will know his number. Run! I'll follow.'

At that moment Erich felt a surge of pride in his father so strong that he wanted to give him a hug. Instead he pelted down the road to the public telephone, and wound the handle until it nearly came off in his hand. At first the operator was reluctant to take orders from a boy, but when he said, 'Well, you tell Herr Solomons then!' she realized it wasn't a hoax.

Erich arrived at the fire almost as soon as his father.

'Papa!' he said. 'They're coming.' Already they could hear the clang of the bell in the distance. The fire glowed ominously, outlining the buildings facing on to the road. Father had keys to the iron gates of the yard and was opening them in anticipation.

'Erich,' he said. 'Run to Herr Bookmann, the yard supervisor. He knows where all the men live. Do as he says.'

For the next half hour Erich ran and ran … and ran again, knocking on doors, throwing stones at windows, and shouting through letterboxes.

'The sawmill's on fire, come and help!'

He didn't wait to explain; the glow against the sky told the startled men all they needed to know. When he arrived back at the sawmill it was like a scene out of hell. The fire engine was pumping curved jets of water in through the windows of Father's office and dousing the sawing-sheds behind. Erich noticed that someone had painted a yellow star on the door. As he looked, and wondered what it meant, flames burst through the cracks and flickered around the new paint. A line of men had formed a chain, passing buckets of water to douse the fire as it tried to encroach on the piles of new-sawn timber. Erich could see his father, his face ruddy in the fire's glow, directing operations, picking up fallen buckets, filling gaps in the chain at need.

'You take it easy, sir ... leave it to us,' one of the workers cautioned him, but Father appeared not to hear. A motorcar had arrived; Herr Solomons was there. Erich ran towards him; 'Father's over there!' Erich wanted everyone to see – Father was saving the yard!

At that moment everything seemed to stop. The chain of buckets faltered and the fire gave a great gasp as part of the roof fell in. Erich turned to see the men dropping their buckets and running towards Father, hands reaching out too late to catch his fall. They closed around him. Erich ran and beat his way through the encircling men. One of them had a torch, and as Erich watched, he turned its pale beam on Father's face, robbing it of the fire's glow. Father's face was blue, just as he had seen it for a moment in Mother's painting. The crowd was parting to let Herr Solomons through.

'Franz!' He said anxiously, using Mr Hoffman's first name for the first time. 'We will get you a doctor!'

Father shook his head. 'The fire sir, the fire!', he murmured.

'Don't you worry, my friend. You have done a hero's work, and what is insurance for?' He promptly organised for Father to be carried home. Later, when the fire was under control, he came and stayed until the doctor had declared Father to be out of danger.

Erich watched the movements of the adults through the open door of sitting room. He felt detached, in a misery that was all his own. They were like actors entering a set, saying their lines, and then leaving it again. Mother, tousled but beautiful, still in her dressing gown, emerged with the doctor. Herr Solomons, holding his hat, waited anxiously for the prognosis. Grandpa Veit, now partly dressed, appeared, saw Herr Solomons, and retreated into his room again, aiming a stage grimace towards Erich. Eventually the doctor left, with reassurances to them that Father would be all right with a little rest.

Herr Solomons was the last to leave. At the door he turned and said, 'Anything, Frau Hoffman, anything, you just have to ask.' The door closed behind him. As if on cue, Grandpa Veit appeared from his room, shaking with apparent rage, and confronted Mother.

'Why did you let him go?' he snapped.

'Who? The doctor?'

'No, you stupid woman. Franz. You know he's not fit. You could have killed him.'

'Well, who should I have sent? Erich?'

'No, me. I'd have sorted out that bloody Jew.'

'You! If I remember rightly, you were standing here in your nightshirt shouting for water! Go back to bed, old man, and stop blaming me. I have Franz to tend to.' At that Sabine went into their bedroom and all but slammed the door.

Erich closed his eyes and held his breath, willing his grandfather to turn about and go back into his room, but Veit had been stood up to, he had not had the last word, and he didn't like it. Erich heard the shuffle of his coming.

'It was your mother's fault. She's responsible, you know.'

Erich kept his eyes closed. This wasn't the first time Grandpa had blamed Mother when Father had one of his attacks. What did he mean about Mother being responsible? Responsible for what?

Veit, pleased with his ambiguity, now turned his attention to the consequences of the fire. 'So the timber yard is gone? That will be the end of your father's job. She'll have to go out to work now; no more messing about with paints.'

Oh, go back to bed, old man, Erich thought. But Veit wasn't finished.

'Solomons did it on purpose, you know – the fire. It's all part of their conspiracy to bring the country, and our civilisation, to its knees.'

'But why would he burn his own sawmills?' Erich queried.

Viet bent down and his voice sounded hot in Erich's ear. '*Insurance,* boy. Destroy the industry, make twenty honest men jobless, collect the insurance, and laugh all the way to the bank.'

Erich liked Herr Solomons, and he just didn't want to know about this. Herr Solomons's words to Father had been said out of kindness, he was sure. He remembered the yellow paint on the door: the Star of David, that's what it was. He had heard how it had been painted on other buildings when they were wrecked by the right-wing mobs that were becoming commonplace.

'But Grandpa,' he said. 'Somebody had painted a yellow star on the door like they do when they attack Jewish premises. I saw it myself.'

'Oh no! Don't you be fooled by that, lad. They do it themselves; just to make it look like it was sabotage. They don't want to be charged with firing their own premises, do they?'

⁂

Erich was in bed, but he wasn't dreaming this time. His nightmare was live: a rollercoaster that had no sooner completed one terrifying cycle than it would start all over again. Father would be out of a job; Mother would have to go out to work instead; he would deliver papers like Hans in school. Herr Solomons was kind – Mother liked him; Herr Solomons was evil – Grandpa said so. What had Mother done to make Father sick? He hated Grandpa with all his heart, but … there were Mother's pictures – surely art was supposed to be beautiful, not terrifying. Herr Solomons liked her pictures; he had started the fire. If he hadn't, who had? And he would be back for another stomach-churning round.

Erich sat up in bed. He had to do something to quiet the

turmoil in his mind. Action, that's what he needed. Something, anything to stop worrying about uncertainties, to hone himself for some great endeavour. His vision stopped short of shining armour, but only just. He kicked the sheet off and swung his legs over the side of the bed. He dressed quickly, choosing a dark top. He pulled his lederhosen up by their braces, and tied a pair of black rubber-soled shoes about his neck. He turned the key in the door of his bedroom so that they'd think he was asleep if they came up, walked to where he could stand directly under the skylight and jumped.

He stood for a moment beside the garden shed, listening. Nothing moved, no lights in the house, the neighbour's dog hadn't barked. He knew the path through the garden well enough, the only obstacle turned out to be his grandfather's wheelbarrow. He rubbed his thigh and cursed the old man quietly. A well-used path led up beside the vineyard. If he looked at it directly, it wasn't there, but if he looked a little to one side he found he could see it, a lighter density in the black about him. His night vision was improving and as it did so the darkness began to reveal other dimensions. It was as if objects in the dark carried an almost tactile aura about them. He flinched away from a branch that overhung the path; he hadn't seen it, but yet had known it was there. He reached a stile and crossed it, stepping onto a wider path, one of the numerous *Wander Wege* or wanderer's paths that lace the Vienna Woods.

This was familiar territory. He had walked all these paths a hundred times: as an explorer (intrepid), as an Indian (swift and silent), as a cowboy (easy in his saddle, finger on trigger). Tonight however was for real. He put his feet down as silently as possible; if he met someone he wanted to be the first to know. When a leaf rustled, he froze, pulse racing. It was so silent that he could hear the hiss of his own blood in his ears. Snakes, they said, would lie on the paths enjoying the lingering warmth of day. It was amazing how easily the mind turned even the most modest stick into a silent menace. He decided to put on his shoes.

He could see the path clearly now. As he leaned into the slope, climbing above the reek of the still smouldering timber yard, he noticed the air freshening. Erich was aiming for the old ruins from where he could get a view over the town below. The trees were thinning about him now and the high cloud was breaking up, allowing scatters of stars to shine through. The path widened here, this was a popular place and there was a circle of stones where someone had lit a fire. It had been carefully banked over. He laid a hand on the top stone; it was still warm. He looked about. Whoever had been here had gone. He walked over to the edge of the clearing and looked out over the lights of the town, pallid in contrast to the ruby glow from the embers of the timber yard. Far to his left the sky was lit from underneath by the lights of Vienna itself. A string of bright beads extending towards him picked out the towns and villages at the foot of the wooded hills.

'*Guten Morgen,*' the voice came from only inches behind him. Erich stiffened but did not turn. Whoever it was had come up to him without a sound.

'It's still night,' he corrected.

'You missed the best of it.'

'What?'

'The fire down there, it looked spectacular from up here.' Erich tried to size up the voice behind him. It was a boy's voice but older than his; it had already broken. The voice came from above him, so the boy was taller.

'It looked spectacular from down there too.'

'You were watching?'

'No, trying to put it out.'

'Why?'

'My dad works … worked there.'

'But you're not a Jew!' It was a statement.

'How do you know?'

'What! With that thatch of fair hair?' The boy behind him laughed. For some reason Erich felt jealous of that laugh. It was relaxed … assured. Perhaps one day he would be able to laugh like that. He realised also that perhaps the boy was right about it being morning. The palest of light was beginning to fill in panels of darkness about him. Erich stepped to one side before he turned to face his companion. He had been right about his height, what he hadn't expected was to find himself looking into a face that could have been his own, given a year or two in the difference. The same thought must have struck them both. The older boy recovered first saying with a laugh, 'You need a haircut.' He held out a hand. 'Klaus,' he said introducing himself.

Erich took his hand. 'Erich,' he said, and the older boy silently clicked his bare heels.

'Come on over. We are camped in the ruins. We won't wake the others, they are just lads, but like you, they have been busy tonight. There will be life in the fire if we uncover it, and we can talk.' Erich watched as the boy uncovered the coals and swiftly fed it twigs until a bright flame danced. Immediately the remaining darkness closed in around them, leaving them to examine each other across the flames. Erich noticed that Klaus was wearing a type of uniform that he hadn't seen before.

'Are you Vandervögel?' – Scouts,' he asked. He'd always rather liked the idea of 'Wander-birds'.

'Sort of,' the boy replied, eyeing Erich, still sizing him up. 'The lads are scouts,' he said, waving towards the ruins.

'Not you?'

'I'm not from here. Not now. I live in Germany with my father but I come home here to stay with my mother in the summer. It's boring so I join up with your *Vandervögel* and teach them things.'

'Like?'

'How to bank up fires,' he shot Erich a grin. 'Then I tell them stories of our great Germanic past.'

'Rhine maidens?' asked Erich absent-mindedly.

Klaus laughed. 'You're too young to be thinking of Rhine maidens. But you have the right idea.' Klaus went on, 'You see, Austria has lost its way, hasn't it? We've lost an empire and have nowhere to go. It's time for us to join up with Germany.'

'*Ein Volk, ein Reich,*' Erich quoted.

'Exactly! We are one people so we should come together – *Anschluss* – to form one state: Germany and Austria together. We could conquer the world!'

'How do you know about these things?' Erich asked. Klaus reached into the top pocket of his shirt and pulled out an armband with a swastika on it.

'Hitler Youth,' he said. 'I'm a group leader back home in Germany. Not everyone likes us here in Austria, so I don't wear it in public.'

'Am I public?' Erich said.

'Perhaps. Why don't you tell me a little about yourself?'

Erich told Klaus about himself and some of his frustrations. Klaus said very little; he was a good listener. When the boys, who had been sleeping in the ruin, began to stir, he didn't introduce Erich to them, but suggested that he would walk a little way with him. Though still early, it was broad daylight when they said goodbye and promised to meet in a week's time.

Only one person saw Erich's return, a quick fluid run this time along the top of the wall from the roof of the garden shed, then like a shadow across the tiles and in through the skylight. Grandpa Veit scratched at his stubble. He needed to feel young again after his performance last night. He wouldn't tell Sabine that the boy was going wild. Let the woman rot.

Up in his bedroom Erich undressed quickly, preparing to slip back into bed for as long as he could get. He noticed a smear of yellow paint on his right hand. He must have picked it up at the timber-yard. Never mind, he'd wash when he got up. He dropped off to sleep dreaming of the Star of David dancing in the flames of the burning yard.

CHAPTER 11

Holiday in Mödling

This looks like one of those posters of families setting off for the seaside, Izaac thought, as he watched his extended family embark on their summer holiday in Mödling. Uncle Rudi had borrowed a large motorcar for the journey; its leather hood was folded back into a neat concertina so that they could travel open. In the front sat Madame Helena, once again an honorary member of the family, because it was she who had been responsible for finding them a suitable house for their holiday. She was wearing a wide straw hat, held down by a gauze scarf tied firmly under her chin. She also had with her a longer scarf, which Izaac guessed she would 'fly' once they were underway.

Mother and Nathan's pretty wife, Krystal, sat in the back with their precious cargo, Krystal's new baby, in a basket between them. Father and Nathan sat opposite to them, facing to the rear on two rather uncomfortable fold-down seats. Lotte, like a life belt in case of emergencies, had been inserted into what Uncle Rudi called the Dickey seat at the back, her head almost invisible between the folded hood and the mountain of trunks and cases on the rack behind.

Izaac watched with a mixture of alarm and amusement as the car gathered speed, everyone waved, and, yes he had been right, there was Madame Helena's scarf floating like an admiral's pennant in the slipstream. Izaac turned back into the house; he was to travel on the 'Bim,' the special tram named after the bell that it clanged at every stop, crossing, dog, and wandering pedestrian as it ran south from Vienna along the edge of the Wienerwald.

The whole idea of a summer holiday had started with a rebellion. For weeks Vienna had sweltered under a blanket of air so dense that it felt as thick as soup. While officially a graduate, and with a diary full of concert engagements lined up – the Konzerthaus Vienna, Prokiev, Schuman and Kreisler, then off to Graz – Izaac still regarded Helena as his professor and relied on her advice and guidance. For her part, she was beginning to worry that his repertoire was too old-fashioned. Her plans for his summer included a whole new raft of composers: Stravinsky, Schoenberg, Berg.

Izaac was not impressed. 'Why must we study these wretched twelve-tone-wonders? They don't even use the normal scales.'

'The point is, Izaac, they are all composing. And somebody will have to be able to play them.' As the University was closed for the summer, Helena came to their apartment. Despite the open windows, Izaac's violin, slippery with sweat from his hands, developed the properties of an eel. It slithered under his chin, his fingers skated on the fingerboard, and his bow, which he couldn't grip properly, writhed like a live thing in his hand. Suddenly it was all too much.

'Plink plank plonk... how does anyone learn this stuff, let alone play it, it's not even music? Take five hundred assorted notes, throw them in the air and scribble them down where they fall!' He turned on Madame Helena. 'You are a slave driver! Other people have *lives*. They have holidays, they have friends, and they don't have to spend the summer rotting in

Vienna. Look, I could wring water from my violin.' He gave the neck a graphic twist, then he fell, pleading, to his knees. 'Please, Madame Helena, most gracious, most wise, just tell our agent that Izaac Abrahams has melted away, and is now no more than a stain on the carpet.'

Helena attempted a snort, failed, and sank instead into a cane chair; it creaked fatalistically. 'Two stains on the carpet, Izaac, mine will be pink,' she sighed. 'I feel like a marshmallow about to melt.'

Rescue was at hand; the door opened and Lotte came in carrying a tray with two tall frosted glasses of lime-juice. The ice tinkled as she placed the tray on a small table beside the collapsed Helena. Louise looked longingly at the tall glasses of green juice. She felt exhausted after their practice. It had been heavy stuff, like their old game of musical tennis, with Izaac scattering Mr Stravinsky's notes about the room as he grappled with this most modern of modern composers. She imagined reaching out and feeling the cold glass in her hand and then lifting it! What would Helena say if her drink suddenly rose up and emptied itself into clean air? She chuckled; she was never quite sure whether Helena might not see her one of these days.

'Bless you, Lotte,' Madame gasped. 'Delicious!' Then to the world at large, 'We need a holiday.'

'The mistress was saying that too, only this morning, but all the hotels is booked, so she says.'

Izaac looked disappointed, Madame Stronski, however, swirled the ice around in her glass as if thinking.

'I wonder?' she said. Then she put her glass down and pulled herself upright. Izaac looked up questioningly. 'Mödling ...' she said. 'Friends of mine have gone to Prague for the summer months; they won't be back till September. It's a barn of a house. I'm sure they'd let me have it, but we'd have to do for ourselves. It might not be so much of a holiday for you, Lotte. Would you mind?'

'Anything to get out of the heat here, Mam.'

'Just think, Izaac, you could be walking in the steps of Beethoven, Schubert, Wagner, Mozart; they all went to Mödling to work.'

'Work! Am I going to have to work?'

'Izaac, my love, an artist never ceases to work,' she looked dreamy. 'You lie under a tree watching the sky and you say you are working; you meet with friends, and you are working; you sleep, and you work in your sleep; you walk in the woods, and your friend Igor Stravinsky will walk beside you.'

'Heaven forbid,' Izaac laughed, but Helena was beginning to lever herself up.

'Give me a hand, Izaac; I must talk to your mother. Come, Lotte.'

They left the room. Louise, wondering if there was anyway that she could be included in this expedition, lingered. It was up to Izaac. He was staring into his glass ... perhaps he was thinking of Stravinsky. She was struck by how tired he looked. He had been working so hard; they both had. A weary smile crossed his face.

'You'll come too, won't you?' He said. Then, more seriously, 'You've ... you've ... been a bit standoffish lately.'

So he had noticed. Ever since that nearly disastrous concert when he had lost his place in his music, she had indeed been 'a bit standoffish'. That flood of affection that had swept over her that night might not have had anything to do with his losing his way in his music, but it had affected her deeply. Why, oh why aren't I able to love people just a little? she sighed to herself.

'I'd like to come, Izaac.' Then, with a smile, 'We can work on the Stravinsky together.'

'Not you as well!' he groaned. 'We will both go down on the Bim and we will walk in the Wienerwald, and listen to the birds singing, and pretend that we are working. Oh, will I have to bring your picture too?' he asked.

'No,' she laughed. 'There were whole weeks when Gaston and I rode out ahead of the troops, miles in front of the baggage train where my picture was, but I knew it was there.'

Izaac only had a rucksack and his violin to carry as they made their way around the Ring to where the tram for Mödling waited.

Louise was glad when they left the suburbs of the city behind. To their right were the wooded slopes of the Wienerwald. To their left, stretches of golden corn and dusty stubble. Carts piled with sheaves of wheat waited for them at crossings. Girls, wearing broad straw hats and bright dresses, sat on top among the upright pitchforks. Izaac, relaxed now, told Louise how the flatlands to their left stretched as far as Hungary.

She embraced the little town even as they tramped up the hill from the tramway below. It nestled into the side of the hill like a dog curled up in its basket. The dusty yellows of the fields merged with the orange glow of the tiled roofs. Pools of shade invited them in out of the searing heat. Above the town, craggy outcrops of rock showed through the trees.

'Look, Louise,' Izaac had stopped. 'Madame Helena was right, Beethoven did live here; it says so above the door: 1818 to 1820. Come on, we must go in.' Beyond the arch was a narrow courtyard, cloistered on both sides, opening beneath another arch into a tantalising garden at the end. 'Imagine the music that must have filled this place?' he murmured. 'Do you remember the sonatas we worked on? And the Violin Concerto? Oh, to have been here!'

At that moment a woman emerged from a door to one side. She looked Izaac up and down, saw his violin, his rucksack, and his awed expression.

'Looking for Herr Beethoven, love?' she called out. 'Well, you're a hundred and twenty years too late. My great-great-grandmother threw him out because of the noise he made. Roaring like a lion he was, and hammering at his piano till the strings broke. We haven't lodged musicians since!'

Before Izaac could explain that he wasn't looking for a room, she had disappeared with a genial chuckle. 'He was deaf as a post,' he explained to Luoise as they retreated, 'and used to get furious when he couldn't hear his piano.'

They got directions to their new address from the clerk in the town hall, a lovely little building with an onion dome. Ten minutes walk brought them to another court-yarded house, with Uncle Rudi's now dusty car waiting like a guard dog in the entrance. The windows had all been thrown open, and Madame Helena emerged, looking like an Arab dancer, with a gauze scarf across her face. 'There was a fire that destroyed the local sawmills a week ago,' she explained. 'The smell of smoke seems to have got in and lingered inside.' She plucked off her scarf. 'The first of my seven veils! We are going to have fun!' She led Izaac inside. 'I have chosen a room for you. It backs up onto the woods so you won't disturb anyone when you begin to practise later. However … my orders now are for no practising for at least a week!'

Louise, wanting privacy, went off to find a place for herself; the Abrahams family seemed to have expanded into every room available. Trunks and cases stood open everywhere. Helpless men waited for their loved ones, or Lotte, to unpack for them. Eventually she found her way up to the attic where she discovered what had probably been a servant's room. It reminded her of her attic back in Delft, so she furnished it in her imagination in the Dutch style and went on a welcome journey back into her past, thinking of Father and Pieter and of her home in Holland.

Madame Helena closed the door and Izaac was on his own. He shed his rucksack, laid his violin on his bed, and bent to undo the two clips that held it closed, but then stopped. Helena had been adamant – no practising – but yet the itch, the urge to take out his violin and start playing was overwhelming. If he couldn't practise, what would he do? And Louise? What about her? She had been on his mind recently. She and his music were bound together as his one great love in life, but, looking back, he'd made a slave of her, hadn't he? Now, for the first time he was become aware of her as a person. They were much of an age. He decided that they would explore Mödling together and perhaps venture up into the woods as Beethoven and the others had done. If Helena was right, it would still be part of their music together, but he would make it Louise's holiday as much as his. He lay back on his bed, closed his eyes, and promptly fell asleep.

Louise was delighted to be included in Izaac's explorations and thrilled with the lovely little town. They walked the streets and the courtyards, and when it got hot, they took refuge in the cool of one of the churches. The exuberant altars and the baroque decorations of the church, all trumpets and angels and gold, were so unlike the austere interiors of her native Dutch churches. Then she remembered the little Catholic church, hidden in an attic in Delft, where there had been colour and light like this. She smiled at the memory. Izaac, seeing it, offered her a penny for her thoughts, so she told him about the little town of Delft, its high walls and criss-crossing canals.

They went back to the Beethoven house on the following day and the fierce lady thawed and showed Izaac the room where the great man had composed what she called his 'Diabolic Variations'. Louise wondered what devil had got into him, but Izaac laughed and said that she meant the famous Diabelli Variations; Diabelli had written the tune and Beethoven the variations.

As they exhausted the sights of the town, they began, tentatively at first, to explore the paths and tracks that led up into the Wienerwald. The paths left the town wherever they could, threading their way between people's gardens and behind their houses until they joined a whole network of paths that spread throughout the woods. Coloured splashes of paint and little signposts showed the different walks through the forest. The first day, Madame Helena joined them, determined to walk the *Beethoven Way,* but soon decided that she could enjoy the company of the great composer perfectly well sitting on a rock overlooking the town.

To Louise's surprise, Izaac found he liked walking. He even went off and bought a pair of stout shoes. When he started worrying about remembering his Stravinsky, she suggested that he associate the music with their walks. Then when it came to performing, all he would have to do was to remember the walk. So he would stride along, humming to himself. Blisters on his feet were Izaac's only problem to begin with, but he soon became hardened to the exercise, and reports came back to town of the young violinist striding through the woods talking to himself, just as the young Brahms was said to have done; they understood musicians in Mödling.

A week later, Madame Helena announced that she had booked a table for them in the local vineyard. Izaac explained to Louise how the vineyards had their *Heurige* evenings on rotation, when they were allowed to sell their own wines and keep their customers happy with traditional dishes. As most of these were based on pork, including crackling and fat bacon, Helena had taken the precaution of ordering a special goulash for her predominantly Jewish table.

They were all there, even the baby, plus Lotte, for whom it was a welcome break from cooking. Helena looked down the table, pleased with her organisation. She could see Izaac at the far end of the table, alone but apparently content. The band began to play and people from the surrounding tables abandoned their wine glasses and their steins of beer to get up and dance.

Izaac had thoughtfully left a space for Louise on the end of the bench. She looked up at the dusking sky between the grapes ripening on the trellis above, and then watched the dancing. The men wore white shirts, lederhosen, and long white socks, while the girls looked enchanting in their lovely dirndls, brightly coloured skirts with matching bodices, white blouses with puffy sleeves, and aprons. They were quite like some of the costumes she had worn in Holland. The men did the vigorous dancing with a lot of stamping and thigh slapping; the girls joined in, but more sedately. Even though Louise knew how hot those costumes must be, she still wanted to join in. After so much classical music the four-square music had her feet tapping.

At a lull in the dancing, a group of youngsters began to chant; Izaac told her to watch. A boy and girl stood up, laughing with embarrassment. Each held a glass of wine in one hand. Then, careful not to spill a drop, they linked arms. While their friends sang, they drank a toast to each other from their linked glasses. Having done that, they kissed and sat down, laughing, to a round of applause from everyone present. Louise was a little bit shocked; they had kissed each other on the lips, in front of everyone!

'Are they getting engaged?' she asked Izaac, remembering how Reynier, her supposed fiancé, had tried to kiss her in the market place in Delft in order to shame her into marrying him. When she had let Pieter, a mere apprentice, kiss her once on the walls of the town, they both could have been denounced from the pulpit next Sunday for lewd behaviour.

Izaac laughed. 'No, it's called *Brüderschaft*. They are drinking to their friendship. It means they can now call each other "*du*" instead of the formal "*sie*" for "you". They are officially friends now, that's all.'

Louise absorbed this information slowly. How wonderful that a boy and girl could show simple affection for each other without a virtual commitment to marriage. She thought of Annie, dear Annie, she would never have understood. For Louise, on the other hand, it felt as if the chains and shackles of her upbringing were being finally loosened, and she could be herself.

*　　　　＊＊＊*

Madame Helena waited at the vineyard gate for Izaac to come up. He thanked her for the party.

'Izaac, I've been thinking that we might start on the Beethoven sonatas for your Austrian tour when I get back next week.'

'But Madame, we have a piano, but no pianist.'

'I have an idea about that; you should have a regular accompanist, you know, but we'll talk about it later.' She looked up. 'The harvest moon. Now's the time to walk, while the heat has gone out of the day, but I must be up early tomorrow. Good night.'

Izaac's moon-shadow stretched in front of him, an exclamation mark on the white track. He watched Louise looking after Helena, a slight smile hovering on her face.

'Louise,' he said. 'Let's walk; as Helena says, it is cool and the moon's bright as day. I promise I'll talk about nothing but Stravinsky!'

'Oh no!' she laughed and they turned away from the house and up the path leading into the Vienna Woods.

Louise, who had seen Izaac charm whole audiences in their seats, failed completely to recognise when she was being charmed herself. She didn't mind where they went, or what they did, she just felt gloriously liberated. All she wanted from Izaac was simple friendship, like she had seen between the youngsters at the *Heurige*.

He started off conscientiously talking Stravinsky, but soon abandoned it in favour of a demonstration of Nathan having a tickling session with his baby. Then, by some trick, he got her talking about Pieter, and they both laughed at her description of Pieter absentmindedly walking off into space when halfway down the steps from the wall in Delft. She told him about Gaston's father, who talked to his grapes as if they were schoolchildren. Then of Colette, who she had loved as the sister she had never had.

The black and white of their moonlit world made it easier for her to talk of things that had been taboo to her for years, like poor abused Jacquot, and the Count du Bois, though here she did not tell all. It was such a relief to be herself again. By common consent they made for a place in the woods that they both liked, where there were the ruins of a castle, and a semicircular clearing looking out over the town below. They stood looking down on the roofs, silver in the moonlight.

Louise turned back into the clearing to find that Izaac, attracted by any stage, had positioned himself in the middle of it. It wasn't, however, the familiar Izaac that she saw there but the 'General' from their Volksgarten days – the old tyrant after all these years still guarding the Emperor's precious grass from little boys.

He slipped effortlessly from one sketch to another, doing his duck act for her again, and then becoming Helena battling with her scarves in a wind. Finally he changed into someone she had never seen before: a pathetic little fellow with pointed-out toes and a walking stick. Who gave a shy smile, then plucked up courage, and blew her a kiss. Louise, charmed, returned this. So he plucked up courage again, came a little closer, and blew her another. Then he was holding up his cheek; laughingly she bent towards him.

CHAPTER 12

Evil Planting, New Growth

The shadows came on them from all sides, silently on gym shoes. Louise stepped back, terrified, as they formed a ring about Izaac.

'And what the hell do you think you are doing? Are you bloody mad, acting like an idiot? This is our place, our territory; you ask permission before you come up here on Saturday nights, alright!'

The voice came from a young man, seventeen perhaps, with striking blonde hair showing white in the moonlight. He was pushing his way through the ring of boys who made up the circle. He produced a flashlight and shone it full in Izaac's face.

'Well, damn me; we've got a bloody Jew. Hey, lads, we've got ourselves a Yid, a kosher bloody Yid. Erich, kick up the fire, we must entertain our guest here.'

Louise noticed a boy standing a little apart from the rest, a younger version of the blonde leader, thirteen perhaps, a brother surely. He uncovered some ashes and coals, added twigs, blew on them, and soon had a bright flame licking the thicker branches that he piled on top. The leader went on: 'Well, lads, this is special, let's be hospitable. Form a circle and let *Mr* ...?' he said sarcastically.

'Abrahams,' Izaac muttered.

'Abrahams! The very founder of the tribe, if I'm not mistaken. Now, *Mr Abrahams*, perhaps you would tell us what you were doing acting like an idiot in our forest?'

Louise couldn't hear Izaac's reply, but the young man declaimed it for the benefit of his own small audience: '"Acting" boys, he was "rehearsing", for one of his nasty little ceremonies perhaps. Widen the circle; Mr Abrahams is going to do a little acting for us.' There were nine or ten of them, all aged between eight and twelve, hitching back to widen the circle. Their disciplined silence was menacing.

'Mr Abrahams will now give us his impression of ... what shall we ask? How about a money lender, something familiar to him?'

Izaac was standing still, obviously trying to maintain his dignity. 'Run,' Louise willed, but Izaac didn't respond.

'Come on, boys. Mr Abrahams is shy. Show him your stings boys, just show.'

There was a lightning ripple of movement about the circle and a dozen scout knives glinted in the cold light.

Izaac had no choice. He made an unconvincing show of counting money.

'Not good enough, Mr Abrahams, we have seen you; you can do better than that. More Scrooge, please. Stings again, boys.'

Izaac obliged, he had to, and Louise turned away so he didn't have to be humiliated in front of her.

'Splendid, we have an evil genius on our hands.' Then the young man clapped his hands to his head as if he had just thought of something. 'What am I forgetting, our guest must be entertained. Food for the poor starving fellow, Anton. We have some nice pork rashers, I believe, run and get them.'

Louise, looking in desperation for any way for Izaac to escape, noticed that the boy, Erich, was standing back from the circle. He didn't seem to be enjoying what was going on; it was as if he was a little embarrassed by it. The fire flared up, lighting Izaac's face; the boy took a step forward and peered closely at him. Now he stepped through the gap made by Anton's departure and whispered in the leader's ear. The young man frowned, then shrugged.

'While we're waiting for his dinner to cook, Erich here would like to see Mr Abrahams play the violin for us ... Erich is very cultured.' The boys sniggered.

Louise could see Izaac looking, first at his tormentor, then at the younger boy. With a movement that reminded her of the day the great Fritz Kreisler had encouraged Izaac as a petrified youngster, he lifted an imaginary violin to his chin and laid his bow on the strings. The boy mouthed 'play' and he did. It was only a bar or two before the boy turned to his leader and drew him by the arm out of the circle. What was going on? Two fair heads leaned together. There was a moment of argument, then the leader turned; Louise saw a flash of anger on his face that chilled her to the core. However he soon got it under control.

'Game over, lads,' he called out. 'Mr Abrahams goes home hungry. Stand up and escort him to the edge of the clearing. Don't touch him, but make sure he knows how welcome he has been.' In a second the boys were on their feet, circling and jeering Izaac as he walked out of the clearing.

'Yid Yid, spit in your hood.'

Louise felt sick. It was as if a sewer had suddenly unblocked.

Izaac staggered from the clearing back onto the path they had come up. The boys stopped there but they continued to chant. 'Don't run,' Louise urged, though she guessed that the boys would do what they were told; they were like trained dogs. She could see Izaac shaking from shock. She took his arm and steadied him.

The boys scampered to heel at Klaus's command. They stood quivering with excitement, as silent now as they had been vociferous moments before.

'*Gut! Ins bett!* ordered Klaus. His arm shot up in the Nazi salute. 'Heil Hitler!'

'Heil Hitler!' they chorused, their small right arms rising like daggers. Klaus dropped his salute and they scurried off to their tent. Erich was impressed and a little frightened, but he realised that he was in trouble. He wanted to explain, because this new friendship meant a lot to him, but Klaus ignored him and walked stiffly past him to the edge of the clearing, where he stood looking out over the town. Erich followed, but halted a cautious few paces behind him. Then, without warning, Klaus span about to face him, his face livid with anger. Erich lurched. The moon was sculpting Klaus's face into a death's head; his eyes glinted cold and hard from smudged sockets.

'Never … never interfere with my orders again!' he hissed at Erich, stepping forward a pace. '*I* ordered the baiting of that Jew, and you interfered! *I* decide what the boys do, *I* tell them how to do it, and *I* order them to stop, without any interference from you or any milk-sop boy who hasn't the stomach for the task!'

Erich, frozen with surprise, wondered where his friend of only minutes ago had gone, but yet there was something familiar about Klaus's behaviour that held him. When he took another step towards him, Erich knew. This was what Grandpa Veit did: made one retreat till one's back was against the wall, so Erich held his ground.

'I just thought you didn't know who he was!'

'Get this into your head. It doesn't matter *who* he is, or *what* he is. He. Is. A. Jew!'

'Yes, but he's *our* Jew. That's what Mother says. She says he is probably the greatest violinist in Austria today. Don't you have respect for music in Germany?' This change of direction seemed to surprise Klaus.

'Why do you say Germany?'

'You have the kids saluting Hitler. You are Austrian, but you behave like you're a German.'

'I belong to the future, Erich, when Germany and Austria will come together to form the greater Reich, we have one language, therefore we are one people. *Ein Volk, ein Reich* – One People, one State, remember? Together we can conquer the world or enough of it to survive. The British, the French and even the Dutch have their empires and their colonies. We need room to live and to expand, *Lebensraum* is what we need, Erich. Listen to me, and learn.'

Erich felt a surge of anger. 'I know my own language, Klaus,' he snapped, 'and I know your *Ein Volk, ein Reich,* but do you really hope to achieve this by setting small boys to bait our greatest violin player?' He was surprised at his own vehemence, but saw his dart strike home. The cold stare in Klaus's eyes shifted, and he turned abruptly to look out over the town. Erich watched as the rigidity went from his friend's shoulders. When Klaus turned, the light fell more kindly on his face. Erich felt a flood of relief. The older boy reached forward and gave his shoulder a friendly squeeze and shake.

'You are good for me, Erich. We will need people like you in the new Reich. At the moment we haven't got time for culture; it's numbers that matter. Take the Brown Shirts – a thousand voices, ten thousand salutes, but they are like corn, easily cropped.' He dropped his voice. 'There's an elite growing about the Führer, Erich: men of iron, yes, but of culture too. They will be the new standard, you will hear more of them: they are called the SS.'

While he talked, he was guiding Erich over to a log, polished by the seats of lovers for over a hundred years, and they sat down.

'You wonder where my allegiance lies,' he went on. 'As I told you, I live in Germany with my father now. I just come here as a penance to see my mother and my brat half-sister who does nothing but play the piano. Father wants me to train for the SS. I like the uniforms – black as sin.' He chuckled. 'These boys of mine are just a hobby; they have their uses, but they, like the Brown Shirts, are scum. They'd have burned old Solomons's timber yard down there just for the fun of it without any help from me.'

Erich remembered the smear of yellow paint he had found on his hand after the fire. So that's where the paint had come from – Klaus – when they had shaken hands up here on the night of the fire. He didn't say anything. His feelings about the fire were confused. His parents thought that Mr Solomons, the timber merchant, was wonderful, while Grandpa Veit thought that he had started the fire himself to get the insurance. So Klaus was behind it; one in the eye for Grandpa Veit. Now Klaus was asking him a question. 'Tell me about yourself, what do you want to do with life, Erich?'

Even while he told him, Erich realised that he was making it up as he went along. He had never seriously thought about his future. The timber yard perhaps ... but now that had been burned, so he said the first thing that came to mind.

'I want to study art.' Why had he said that? It had never occurred to him before.

'What! Art *and* music! You *are* cultured.' Klaus was laughing at him. Erich felt his ears glow with anger; he didn't like his idea being laughed at; he had meant what he said.

'Yes. My mother is an artist, modern, but I like the old masters. I'd like to work in one of our big galleries.'

'Did you know that the Führer was an artist? A good one too. He wanted to study in Vienna, but they turned him down. He's not forgiven them. But you look fit, Erich. You wander in the woods on your own ...' He tapped Erich on the chest. Then laughed: 'There is a core of steel here, isn't there? I can sense it.' Erich wasn't aware of any core of steel, but he wanted to please his friend.

'I like climbing over roofs at night!' he chuckled, and Klaus gave him a resounding thump on the back.

'That's more like it!'

What was there about his using the roof rather than the door that attracted attention? First Grandpa Veit, though he said nothing, and now Klaus. Erich didn't much like his grandfather, and he was a little frightened of Klaus, but he wanted their approval. He was ready to go now, but Klaus anticipated him; Erich's education was not yet complete.

'You want to go, I know, but we have a little unfinished business ... about your Jew.' Erich's heart sank. He didn't want to talk about the Jew or anyone else – there was too much new going on in his head – but he realised Klaus would not be put off. He shrugged. Klaus went on, 'You know of the conspiracy, don't you, the great Jewish conspiracy? A worldwide movement designed to lead to the gradual destruction of the Aryan peoples by the Jewish race. Not by confrontation – they're cowards – not by war, but by infiltration, and ultimately by poisoning.'

'But Klaus,' Erich protested. 'Izaac Abrahams is a violinist, a musician. And, when you think about it, half our geniuses in any field you mention are Jews.'

'Precisely, Erich, don't you understand? How can one race suddenly produce these automatons? Think ... if you want to produce more milk you breed cows that produce more milk; if you want geniuses for some evil purpose you breed them.

How they do it we don't know, but go into any bank, and they are there behind the counter; go to a lawyer and he will be a Jew. We, Erich, we spring from the pure Aryan stock that spread civilisation across the western world. That was the first thing I thought when I saw you that night when you came up here. You and I, we have the stamp: the fair hair and blue eyes that show that we have been bred true. No virtue to us, but we have responsibilities. We are the inheritors, Erich, but our culture is being infiltrated, our genes are diluted, and our society polluted by their evil genius.'

Erich noticed how Klaus had clamped his hand between his knees with emotion. He reminded him of Grandpa Veit.

'Maybe you're right, Klaus, but calling them names won't make a difference, surely?'

'No Erich, that's true. We must *prove* that we are better than them. Excel, Erich! Climb higher, paint better pictures, excel, though the Jewish disease will need some other cure.'

Erich hadn't been thinking in terms of a solution, but he was stirred by Klaus's words. He *would* excel! He'd show Grandpa Veit that Austria wasn't dead; he'd be like Father that night at the fire before he'd collapsed. He'd tame Mother's disturbing pictures into something worthy of the great masters! Yes, he was stirred. Thanks to Klaus he had decided on a career for himself. He didn't give two hoots about the Jews, though when he thought about it, they indeed were everywhere.

CHAPTER 13

A New Hero, a New Beginning

Erich took the long way home, a loop that brought him several kilometres into the forest and then back, to cross over the high multi-arched railway bridge above the town. While he walked, daylight gradually invaded the forest, enriching it with more and more colour. Time and again he had the sensation of walking through the frame of a picture, just as he used to 'walk into' the pictures he pasted on his walls at home, only this time it was real. He stopped, fascinated by a chest-high layer of mist that filled a hollow on his path; it looked liquid, like cream in a bowl. He plunged through it, laughing, his arms above his head like a swimmer dashing into the sea. Then he ran on, enjoying the feeling of speed that running in the half-light gives.

Later, he froze while a doe, followed by her two fawns, picked their way through the mist-laden spiders' webs beside the track and disappeared into the forest. Each new experience felt like a new beginning. Finally he rested, panting, with his arms on the parapet of the bridge and looked out over the roofs and spires of the town to a horizon where the planes of Hungary began. Life seemed to stretch in front of him to infinity. Everything seemed more hopeful; he pictured how it would be: Father's health would get better, Mother would be happy and her pictures would be like her singing, pure and beautiful. He would show Grandpa Veit that he had become a man.

It had really started with Klaus, hadn't it: this liberation? He could smell the wood smoke from Klaus's fire on his sleeves, and thought of the past night. It was Klaus who had asked the question he had never asked himself: 'What do you want to do with your life?' Erich smiled. Fortunately he hadn't had time to think, or he would have thought of something much more macho to impress his new leader. That's really what Klaus was to him, wasn't it, not just a friend, but a leader, some one to live up to? He thought of Grandpa Veit with a slight shudder. He realised that he had been trying to impress the old man all his life, but now he had a hero of his own: Klaus Steinman.

But he was secretly proud of the way he had stood up to Klaus over the Jew, Abrahams. It had been generous of Klaus to accept that the baiting was not worthy of him. Sometime Erich would try to understand this Jewish conspiracy business, but just now he was happy to have a friend he could look up to, and aspire to. He crossed the bridge and ran down the path towards home.

⟨✦⟩

Veit was standing outside the back door, as he usually did in summer, shaving into an enamel basin, his mirror hanging on a nail in the wall. He used a cutthroat razor that he would strop on his old army belt. He didn't hear Erich until he saw him in his mirror. Good God, the lad's turned into a young man without me realising! he thought. After years of brutalising young recruits, his automatic reaction was to face about, razor to cheek, and demand, 'Where have you bee–'

'Morning Grandpa.' Erich stepped past him and went in, ignoring his demand. The old man's jaw dropped, he turned back to his mirror and found himself looking into a toothless chasm. He snapped it shut. A trickle of blood was spreading through the foam from a nick on his cheek.

'Now look what you've made me do!' he grumbled, but Erich was gone.

Having had a hurried splash in the bathroom to clean the soot and sweat from his face, Erich went into the kitchen, where they usually had breakfast. He noticed the changed atmosphere the moment he entered. Father was leaning back in his chair, beaming. Mother was reading a letter. On the table was an opened envelope bearing the familiar rubber stamp of *Solomons' Wood Yard.*

'What is it, Father?' Erich asked.

'Solomons, he's keeping me on,' he said.

'Charity!' said Veit from the door, holding a towel to his cheek.

'No, Father.' Erich's father said. 'I'm to supervise the summer tree felling in the company forest in the Lake District. It will be two years at least before the re-building here is begun, let alone finished. But he says there will be office work for me here in winter.'

'Summer in Altaussee … the Salzkammergut,' Mother was saying dreamily, clasping the letter to her bosom.

'And who'll look after me?' asked Veit, examining his towel.

'You could come too,' Mother said, while Erich prayed, no … oh no.

'Not on your life,' snapped the old man. 'Anyway, I'm wounded, isn't anyone going to do anything about it?'

While Mother tended the cut, Erich was able to quiz Father about the proposal. The summer holidays were half over, but still the prospect of spending the rest of the summer up in the mountains seemed like heaven. The delay in re-building the yard was because someone had said that the fire wasn't an accident, and there would have to be an investigation before the insurance would pay up. It was on the tip of his tongue to confess what he knew about the burning of the wood yard, but something stopped him; he wasn't ready to betray Klaus.

⸺✲⸺

The turmoil of the last two days had subsided; their family belongings selected, tamed and finally strapped down, were now safely contained in two large trunks. Only the tip of one of Father's belts showed like a tail. No one dared re-open that trunk in case they couldn't close it again; it would have to stay. Their 'Chalet' had been described as having all the necessities for a self-catering holiday, but the Hoffman family, Grandpa not included, would be there for close on a month.

Erich, keen to see Klaus before they left, was following directions to his home. It was a neat house on the far side of the town centre. Someone was playing the piano, running up and down scales at the speed of light. He would have to risk interrupting. He knocked on the door. The piano stopped and a few minutes later a girl of about his own age, with bright blue eyes and a tousled flood of fair hair opened the door. She looked at him, did a double take, then laughed. Erich smiled back.

'Is Klaus in?' he asked.

'I'll see–' she began but was interrupted by a man's voice calling from behind her.

'If that's one of Klaus's scouts let him wait outside.' The girl looked embarrassed.

'If you don't mind … I'll look for him.' She only partly closed the door and Erich heard her say, 'He doesn't look like a scout, more like Klaus's double.'

'Another damned Nazi!' came the rejoinder. Erich rather hoped the girl would re-appear, but it was Klaus who came out, jerking his head back to the voice behind him.

'My stepfather! As you can hear, this prophet is not welcome in his own country.' The scales started again, a cascade of sound. 'Bloody piano! Let's walk.'

'I've only got a few minutes,' Erich explained. 'We're going away. It will be for a whole month. I just wanted to ask you for your address in Germany.'

'I'm off too, duty to Mother done. There's a big rally in the autumn which I'd like to be at. I'd like your address too.' He fished in his pocket for a notebook and a pencil; they exchanged addresses. 'At least they want me in Germany, I'm *persona non grata* here.' He pocketed his notebook. 'So you're off,' he gave Erich a friendly fist on the chest. 'Remember what I said, Erich, we want men of steel. Good luck with your art. I'd give you the Nazi salute but people here aren't ready for it yet. Heil Hitler!'

Somehow Erich's tongue couldn't find its way to return this. '*Auf Wiedersehen. Klaus.*'

<hr/>

On the train journey from Mödling to Altaussee, Erich spent the entire time walking from window to window as the train wound its way up through the Semmering Pass, and deeper and deeper into the mountains. One minute he would be look-ing at rock rising sheer above him, next he would be gazing down into a foaming river, or into neat fields where miniature tractors, far below, were cutting the last of the corn. They were sharing their compartment with a family from Vienna. After a bit, however, Mother's excitement and little cries of joy embar-rassed him so much that he had to flee the compartment and stand at the end of the coach where he could move from side to side, even leaning out to watch the two engines belching smoke and steam as the long train snaked dutifully behind them. They had to change trains – trunks and all – to a branch line for Bad Ausee, a station close to Altaussee from where the felling was organised.

When they were met at the station, Erich was delighted to find not a car, but a forestry truck ready to take them and their luggage to their new home. As there was no room for him inside, he had to stand in the back, his feet spread, looking out over the cab. His feet stuck to the fresh resin that had bled from the timber that the lorry usually carried. For a while they followed the foaming Traun River. Then they turned up into smaller roads that led them eventually to the chalet that would be their home for the rest of the summer.

When they arrived they stood looking down in wonder at the little alpine village below, wrapped about the end of the bluest lake that Erich had ever seen; even Mother's exclamations of delight seemed inadequate. It was then that he turned and looked up … and up … and there it was, their own private alpine peak, the Kleinkogel, the driver called it. From here it looked every bit as high as Loser Mountain that rose straight up from the other side of the little blue lake, and Erich immediately decided he would climb it tomorrow.

The mountain was still calling him when he woke at first light the following morning, so he set out without even a bar of chocolate, following a path that the forester had pointed out to him. It curved around the bottom of the hill above the little lake, inky black now; only a single V-shaped ripple from some water bird broke its mirror surface. After a bit the path began to rise steeply, heading straight towards a vertical wall of rock. He had heard of people who climbed rock faces for fun, but this seemed too sheer for anybody. But the path looked well worn, so, despite a flutter in his stomach, he kept going. When it reached the foot of the crag, to his relief the path turned sharply left and followed the foot of the rock face. He stopped; a splash of paint and an arrow seemed to be pointing directly up the cliff. Erich examined it with alarm and then noticed a narrow shelf that climbed diagonally up the face. Scratch marks showed where other people had put their feet.

To begin with, he leaned in towards the wall and had the horrible sensation that the rock was trying to push him out into space. After a bit, however, he learned to stand up straight; miraculously his feet did not to slip. When he arrived at the top of the cliff he was panting, but more out of excitement than exertion. He felt as if he could conquer the world. Another half hour of climbing through trees and there was it was, the summit of his very first mountain peak, a crag rising above the trees.

He draped his shirt on a bush for the sweat to dry, and took out a map that he had found in the chalet. He lay down on his stomach, turning the map until the lake and the village were in their correct positions, and began to identify the peaks and valleys ahead. That was the Loser directly ahead, 1,838m high. There was the village; he could identify the church and the valleys radiating out from it. The forester who had driven them up had said that there were salt mines in the valley to the left of the Loser, and that deep under the mountains there were huge caverns, connected by miles of tunnels, where, over the ages, miners had dug rock salt out of the living rock. He said there was even a chapel down there dedicated to Saint Barbara, the patron saint of miners.

Erich took out a notebook that he had bought in Mödling before he had left; he had been impressed by Klaus's efficient little black notebook. He planned to keep a journal. On the first page he had written his name and address. Now he turned the page and wrote the date: *3 August 1928*, then he looked at his watch. He could hardly believe it, it was only eight o'clock; Mother would just be getting up, so he added: *08.00 arrived at the summit of the Kleinkogel, 1,201 metres*. He decided that the fact that his starting point, the lake, was at 712 metres was an unnecessary detail. The climb had taken less than an hour. Now what? Perhaps he should describe the scene.

Five minutes later he was still sucking his pencil. A sentence would start in his mind but by the time he had got to the end he would have forgotten the beginning. Without thinking, he began to sketch the view from the peak. His pencil just seemed to know what to do. He looked at the finished drawing in surprise; it was really quite good. The tops of the pine trees that were clinging to the rock face at his feet made a good foreground. There in the centre of the frame towered the Loser, which was just beginning to catch the morning light. Tumbling crags and tongues of trees led the eye down to the still lake, where he had sketched in the upside-down reflection of the glowing peak above. He had enjoyed that! When he got down he would ask Mother if he could have one of her sketchbooks.

He got up to brush away the little bits of lichen that were sticking to his front. Time stretched away to infinity all around him. There were mountains to climb, forests to explore, and salt mines to visit. Realising he was hungry, he cupped his hands over his mouth and shouted: 'Comingggggg!' as if his mother would hear him far below.

Suddenly there was a rustle and a deep croak. A raven as black as coal launched itself from the rocks beneath his feet. With a few deft strokes of its wings it rose up past him. He stepped back in surprise. On and up it rose to where it was joined by another. Again that deep croak; it was as if they were talking about him. Hastily he pulled on his shirt; it felt cold on his back. He hurried down, feeling a like a guest that has overstayed his welcome.

By the time he was running down through the meadow to the chalet, however, he was in high form again. Coming down had taken half the time it had taken him to go up. There was a smell of sausage in the air and he was ravenous.

CHAPTER 14

Uncertain Years

Uncle Rudi Makes a Purchase

The doorbell of the apartment rang insistently, as though someone were keeping a finger pressed on it. There was no sign of Lotte, so Izaac reluctantly put down his violin and opened the door. Uncle Rudi and Nathan were waiting on the landing. Uncle Rudi wasted no time on explanations but pushed past Izaac.

'Find Lotte and borrow her wireless,' he said urgently. 'I can't think why you don't have one yourselves.' Izaac's father was still at breakfast when they all trooped in. He looked up, puzzled. Nathan plugged in the wireless. 'Come, David, listen to this!' said Rudi. The set emitted a cacophony of hisses, crackles and pops while he searched for the English language station he was looking for. 'Let's hear it from the horse's mouth!'

The newsreader's accent was American:

'By close of trading last night, five billion dollars – I repeat – five billion dollars had been wiped off the slate in the worst crash in the history of the New York Stock Exchange. Friday, October 25th 1929 will forever be known as Black Friday. The Tickertapes have only just caught up. It was pandemonium on the floor of the Exchange; the shouts of traders trying to sell shares could be heard in the street outside.

Investors and brokers with now valueless shares on their hands face ruin. This is the worst crash since 1907 when America had to import a billion dollars worth of gold to support the currency. Ladies and Gentlemen–'

Click! Uncle Rudi switched the radio off. They all straightened up, looking at each other, and then at Uncle Rudi, their natural leader in matters of business.

'How serious is it?' Mother asked.

'They say that brokers have been jumping from the windows,' he said gravely. 'But it's the thousands of small investors I'd worry about.'

'Will it happen here?' she asked.

'Yes, indeed. London is in turmoil. It's only a matter of hours before it hits here, Judit, that's why I came. A bit of prudence now could save misery later. If people have to economise, the first things to go will be the 'luxuries', and those, I'm afraid, include the services of the piano-tuner – that's us – so let's sit down, list our resources, and decide what's best to do.

For a successful family business, their resources were modest enough. Their apartments, workshop and pianos were relatively safe, but the senior members of the family all had shares in companies just like the ones that were crashing on the stock exchanges.

'We must sell these, even if we make a loss!' Uncle Rudi urged. 'The question is, what to do with the money?'

'Why not bank it?' Izaac suggested. All the proceeds from his concerts were deposited in a small bank near their apartment.

'I'm sorry, Izaac, but you must get your money out of that bank as soon as possible. Small banks will be the first to go. Even the large ones are in danger of collapse.' Izaac had the horrible feeling that he was walking on quicksand that was about to engulf him.

'Well, what about banknotes – money?'

'Not worth the paper it's printed on.'

There was a pause, and then Mother said, 'What about gold?'

Uncle Rudi positively beamed on her.

'Yes, Judit! Gold never really loses its value. It's portable, and it's the one thing people want in a crisis. If I move fast – today – I will buy all the gold I can get before the price goes through the roof.'

Uncle Rudi reported back that evening, muttering darkly about scoundrels and sharks, but when Nathan pointed out that his investment had already more than doubled in the day, he polished his bald head until it shone.

'Can we see it?' asked Judit.

'I'm afraid I put it straight into a safe deposit. Ha, ha ... it's worth its weight in gold, you see!'

The Judging of Solomons

Erich could see a light bobbing towards him down the tunnel. He bent diligently to his work, bedding the sleepers of the small underground railway into the solid salt of the tunnel floor. Holiday jobs were hard to come by here, and indeed throughout Austria. The Great Depression that had followed since the Wall Street Crash two years ago was biting through-out Europe. His work in the salt mines was important and he wanted to make a good impression.

'Erich Hoffman?' A voice called.

'Yes?'

'I have a message for you.'

Erich put down his tools and hurried down the tunnel. The golden salt crystals glinted from the light mounted on his helmet. He couldn't see who was calling until his own light lit up the face of the mine supervisor.

'You're wanted in the office, Hoffman, something urgent. Follow the railway tracks, and don't bloody well get lost!'

The mine extended for kilometres into the hill here, with tunnels and caverns like burrows one on top of the other. These were connected by wooden slides so that the miners could get to work, whizzing down from level to level. The long walk back up was less fun. He assured his supervisor that he knew the way, and set off towards the mine entrance. What could be the matter? Spreading his arms wide he could just about touch the walls on each side. Clunk! His head hit the ceiling and his headlamp nearly went out. He felt in his pocket for his safety candle and matches.

He emerged into the blinding light to find one of his father's forestry workers at the entrance. The lorry was there, engine running.

'It's your father, Erich,' the man explained as Erich climbed into the cab beside him. 'He was trying his hand at tree felling when he collapsed; blue in the face he was. We didn't like to move him. He said you'd know what to do. It's only half a mile from here.' The lorry pitched wildly as the driver turned into a rutted forest road. 'He shouldn't be expected to do work that's too hard for him!' the driver worried.

Erich managed a wry smile. Typical – even now Father denied his condition; he hadn't told the men.

A minute or two later Erich was kneeling beside his father's prostrate form. 'Where's his lunch bag?' he demanded. They had it in a second; he snatched it and began to burrow frantic-ally for the little bottle of pills that should be there. He found it right at the bottom, and to his relief there was one left. With the help of the anxious men, he sat Father up. Erich placed the pill on his father's tongue and got him to swallow it with a drop of water. It took some minutes before the dreadful blue-grey drained from his face.

The men cheered when he opened his eyes. 'He should stay in the office and leave the hard work to us,' they whispered to Erich as they lifted him into the lorry.

As the lorry ground up the hill to the house, Father asked, 'Are we home, Erich? I'll be all right with a little rest. Don't let Mother get on to Mr Solomons.' He smiled. 'He might be cross with me.'

Erich felt his jaw tighten. He hated the thought that Mr Solomons kept Father on the payroll out of kindness; and being grateful didn't help him on these occasions. He wanted to be angry. Solomons *might* be a nice man but, according to Klaus, he was part of the great Jewish conspiracy. You don't get smoke without a fire, Grandpa Veit would say.

Mother hurried over, wearing her painting smock, and immediately shepherded Father to bed.

'No more heavy work, *ever*, Mr Hoffman!' said the doctor, once he was satisfied that his patient was out of danger. Erich saw him off but didn't go back into the house. He hadn't realised what a fright Father's collapse had given him. Grandpa Veit had always implied that Mother was, in some way, at fault for Father's weak heart, but Erich wanted someone else to blame. Damn Solomons for sending him up here into the mountains, and why hadn't the office in Mödling been re-built? Some nonsense about the insurance not paying up if the fire was deliberate. He remembered the speck of paint he had found on his hand when he had shaken hands with Klaus that night. But perhaps Solomons really had burned the yard himself for the insurance? Tomorrow was Saturday, if Father was out of danger then, there was a hike he'd been promising himself to do: a wide sweep right around Altaussee Lake, taking in as many of the surrounding peaks as he could. He'd walk off his depression. He went into the house, absentmindedly rubbing at his hand where the paint had been.

As Erich knew it would, his black mood had long lifted by the time he was swinging gratefully down the slope, having taken in his own little Kleinkogel peak on the way. The rhythm of walking, fresh air, and unfolding views had washed his mind. He could see the house now but was too pleasantly tired to run. Suddenly his legs stopped moving. There was a car outside the house. The doctor's? No, he had a Citroen. It was Mr Solomons' surely. His hands clenched. Someone must have told him about Father's attack.

He began to walk quickly and silently over the mown grass of the meadow. The curtains of his parents' bedroom were closed; the doctor had prescribed a sedative and Father was probably sleeping. But those in the living room, Mother's studio, were open. He paused to look inside. Mother was talking to Mr Solomons; it looked as if she had been crying. She wiped her eyes. Suddenly the Jew reached out his arms; Mother turned into his embrace and put her forehead on his shoulder. Confusion seethed in Erich. What right had this man, Jew or no Jew, to presume that just because he had been kind to Father he had any right to lay his hands on his mother! With bold strides Erich marched up to the house and opened the door.

In Marble Halls

Waves of relief and contentment swept over Helena. How perfect for her two protegés: Izaac, twenty-two, dark and lithe, and Gretchen, eighteen, a striking beauty, her hair tamed in coils of gold, to finish their Austrian tour here in the famous Marble Hall of Salzburg's Schloss Mirabell. While they had played a programme of Bach, Handel, Mozart and Beethoven, the light from the high French windows had faded, letting the glow from the glass chandeliers take over, first to pick out the gilt on the marble walls, then to catch the moving gold of Gretchen's hair as she bent to the final chords of the sonata. Helena waited through the four-second pause that the sophisticated Salzburgers allowed for the notes to die away, then relaxed. The applause was full and generous. Salzburg approved.

Izaac reached out for Gretchen's hand; she curtsied while Izaac bowed. How nice they looked together. At least here in Austria they could still play together. Helena seethed when she remembered the refusal she had got from a venue in Munich, just across the border in Germany: 'Due to racial considerations we regret ... ' If she could have got her hands on that Nazi! But something was happening here in the hall. People in the audience were turning towards her. Izaac was beckoning. Good heavens, he wanted her to come up on the platform! She gathered up her scarves and made her way up to join them. As she walked on stage, the audience rose as one; they were standing for her ... for them.

A last call, a last bow, Helena and Gretchen turned to leave the platform. As Izaac followed them, he turned and did something his concertgoerss had come to expect; he kissed his hand to the audience as if they alone were honoured. Helena knew perfectly well who he was kissing his hand to; she indulged him, and didn't object.

A Fateful Rejection

The last thing that Erich expected when he went to be interviewed for a place in the Academy of Fine Arts in Vienna was a full-scale row between his examining professors. There were three of them: Professor Boden, head of the Academy, Herr Komanski, master of painting, and a guest professor, Herr Frimmel, from the Academy of Art in Munich. It had all been going well. He had come into the interview room to find the contents of his portfolio scattered all over the table. They seemed to like his Altaussee paintings in particular. Professor Boden had hesitated over his only watercolour, a sketch of a bridge over the River Traun.

'This is pretty, but is it good? It is difficult to judge watercolours because they have to be done so quickly; it can be just luck.'

'You have made mistakes before!' said the German acidly.

Erich looked up in surprise. The man reminded him a little of Klaus, he was a lot younger than the two Viennese professors. Suddenly the air was crackling. Komanski replied, 'Ah! You mean Herr Hitler. We turned him down because he had no talent, I'm afraid.'

Frimmel went rigid. 'I am deeply offended by that, sir, where is your respect for our Chancellor?'

'Just as an artist, just as an artist he's ... well ... *scheiße!*' Herr Komanski enjoyed his reputation for bad language.

'Gentlemen, gentlemen!' interjected Professor Boden, but the damage had been done.

'If you wish to see his talents, Herr Komanski,' Frimmel said coldly, 'just look over your border to see what we are doing in Germany!'

Now Professor Boden tried to change the subject. 'As you can see, gentlemen, student Hoffman has undoubted talent in drawing and in oils. Perhaps you know of his mother, Herr Frimmel, Frau Sabine Hoffman? She created quite a stir at your Munich exposition on modern art.'

Erich was startled to hear his mother brought into the conversation.

'Not under my directorship, Herr Professor,' came the clipped reply. 'That exhibition should never have been allowed. Degenerate art, the lot of it! You just have to compare those daubs with what you have in your galleries here in Vienna to see how art is being degraded. You foster your Jews, you let in Negro jazz, and now you encourage paintings that could have been done by monkeys. No wonder your country is in a mess.'

Erich had been watching their faces like a spectator at a tennis match as Professor Boden tried to calm Herr Frimmel, and prevent Herr Komanski from exploding. The professor shot an apologetic look at Erich for the slight against his mother.

Fortunately Herr Frimmel looked at his watch. 'I must be going.' He turned to Erich. 'Stand up and be counted, lad, we need you. Stick to your classical style, a master race requires master painters. He turned to Professor Boden. 'Thank you, Professor, most revealing meeting.' He glanced significantly at Komanski. 'Heil ... pardon' he said scornfully, '... *auf Wiedersehen*,' and he left the room.

'Did you see him!' said Komanski, shooting up his arm in mock salute. 'Heil ... I'll Heil him.'

'Komanski ... order!' Professor Boden turned to Erich. 'Now, Mr Hoffman, so you wish to specialise in, let me see ... "History of Art with an emphasis on Dutch art in the seventeenth century?" That's going to be demanding. You see, we require that students develop the skills of their subjects...'

As the professor elaborated on the schedule Eich would have to undertake, he soon wondered if he shouldn't have chosen mediaeval flower painting.

Blood Must Flow

There had been no trouble during Izaac's concert in Berlin; Berliners love music almost as much as the Viennese, but he was delayed in leaving by people wanting autographs. The stage door, like most stage doors, opened into a dark alley. No sooner had it clicked shut behind Izaac than a disorganised mob of young men and women wearing red shirts and scarves tumbled into one end of the alley: Communists? They turned briefly to face some unseen enemy behind them.

Then he heard their attackers, singing, if singing it could be called: *'Blut muss fließen, Blut muss... '*

Nazi storm troopers!

'Blood must flow, blood must flow! Blood must flow, cudgels thick as hail! Let's smash it up, let's smash it up! That goddamned Jewish republic!'

It didn't seem to matter that these were not Jews but young Communists, running, terrified, towards Izaac. After them came the brown-shirted storm troopers, bats and bludgeons raised, smashing them down on the heads and shoulders of the young protesters. One of these, a lad holding a hammer and sickle, turned in defiance. In a second he was felled by a single blow. Izaac heard the boy's skull crack.

Terrified, he tucked himself back into the stage door and huddled over his violin. The tide had swept past before he dared to look up to find a middle-aged man in a brown shirt staring at him.

'Hey lads,' the man roared, 'a bloody Jew!'

Just then a girl's terrified scream came from further down the lane. 'Damn, I'm missing the fun!' and he was gone.

Izaac lost no time in getting back to his lodgings. When he recounted the incident to his host, he said, 'Izaac, you were very lucky. The Nazis are taking anyone who opposes them, beating them, torturing them, and leaving them for dead in the street. As soon as they have killed all the Communists they will start to kill the Jews. That concert tour you have lined up in America is your opportunity. Take my advice, when you get off the ship in America, stay there.'

Between the Mountains and the Sea

```
23 MAY 1933 STOP IZAAC ABRAHAMS
PASSENGER SS MUNENCHEN HAMBURG NEW-YORK
STOP USA AGENT REGRETS CANCELLATION TOUR
DUE ECONOMIC SITUATION STOP SUGGEST
DISEMBARK COBH IRELAND STOP NEGOTIATING
CONCERTS DUBLIN LONDON STOP MACCORMAC
MOUSTACHE WILL MEET YOU COBH STOP AGENTS
MEYER & MEYER VIENNA STOP
```

Izaac looked in amazement at the telegraph form the radio officer had just handed him. It was barely twenty-four hours since he had embarked from Hamburg for his first transatlantic crossing. Now he would have to go down and pack again, ready to disembark. His passenger liner was already nosing its way into Cork harbour. Wooded hills and pastures rose out of still waters. Gulls whirled and screeched above his head. He had never seen the sea until they had steamed out of Hamburg, and he didn't want to leave it. He hated Europe at this moment.

Now he stood on the quay in Cobh, in the turmoil of embarking and disembarking passengers. There were women in floods of tears and young men with cardboard suitcases tied with rope. There were beauties in hats and pearls, and gentlemen in suits. For the third time came the appeal: *Would Mr McCormack Moustache come to the gangplank where Mr Abrahams is waiting for him.* All at once Izaac was confronted by a man with a red face who was pumping his hand, flooding him with explanations and apologies in what might have been Gaelic but turned out to be English.

'I'm Paddy McCormack. God help me, I never recognised my own name as they were calling it. You see, I told your agent that you would know me by my moustache!' He roared with laughter, pointed to the luxurious growth that covered half his face, called a porter, and seized a couple of bags himself. Izaac followed in a daze. 'This is how it is, Mr Abrahams,' he said as they walked. 'We have the Gaiety Theatre in Dublin booked for you in a week's time. It's just between runs, so we're lucky. In the meantime I've been told to look after you. I have an allowance of a guinea a day for the two of us, which will be grand in the country. If it's the city you want, we'll have to go easy on the Guinness. What will it be then, the city or the country?' At last two words that Izaac understood.

'Herr McCormack, danke. Ja, I would like the country best, best of all the sea. We have no sea in my country, you understand?'

'God bless you, Mr Izaac, we'll give you a drop to take home with you. Now, we can fix your cabin case to the back of the car. The rest can go by train to Dublin for you. Will you keep the little fella there?'

'The little ... Oh, my violin. Yes, please. Perhaps first the telegraph office? I must tell my family and friends where I am and what I am doing.'

Izaac dispatched short telegrams to his parents and to Madame Helena, and a slightly longer one to Gretchen. Then Paddy McCormack and he set forth, neither of them fully understanding what the other was saying. When they came to a crossroads, Izaac would say, 'West, Paddy bitte,' or 'The Sea, Paddy bitte,' while Paddy would say, 'The pub, Mr Izaac, bitte.' It took them the best part of the week to travel up through the west of Ireland: Cork and Kerry, into Clare, and then out west to Connemara in County Galway.

On their last day Paddy drove him as far west as he could, beyond the mountains, until only the sea remained. Couldn't he stay here, Izaac wondered, safe beyond the mountains that now glowed behind him in the evening light? *They* would never get him here – the Nazi louts on the streets of Berlin; the poisonous children in the Vienna woods – they'd never find him here between the mountains and the sea. He would bring Gretchen and they would make music and Louise would be with them, and they would all laugh again. If only he could persuade his parents to leave Vienna, it would all be perfect.

He laid his violin case on the sand and began to play. Without thinking, he played Helena's *Humoresque*. The sun sank in a riot of colour and he heard Louise say quite distinctly, 'Your fingers are stiff as pokers, what have you been up to?' So he played the sun into the sea and then he told her all that had happened to him.

CHAPTER 15

Edelweiss and New Boots

Erich sat back in a corner of the wide wooden shelf that served for a communal bed in the mountain refuge. He looked down on a group of five climbers who were cooking their evening meal on a primus stove. Erich had arrived earlier, in time to stretch out in the evening sun and ease his feet. His new climbing boots had been stiff and uncomfortable. The crisp rim of toothed nails designed to dig in and hold tight to the rock made them heavy. He had been woken from a doze by the arrival of the new group as they had dropped their coiled ropes and equipment beside his boots at the refuge door. Now the smell of their cooking was tantalising; he had already eaten the little he had brought, and was starving again.

He listened to their easy chat. Two were about his own age, eighteen or so, the others were in their twenties. Erich wished he could join them, but felt shy. He imagined them connected by some subtle bond – their ropes perhaps – a bond that didn't include him. He had never been one for games and group activities; after experiencing Klaus's scouts he had decided that he was a loner, but this was different.

'Hey, I didn't see you. Come and join us,' the oldest of the group called out. Erich nearly said no, but they were all looking up at him.

'Thanks,' he said, and slid down.

'I'm Stephan.' He introduced the others.'I saw your boots at the door – not tourist boots – climbing on your own? Sausage?' Erich's eyes widened. Stephan was holding out a whole sausage on his fork. He accepted it gratefully and bit into it; the juice burst into his mouth.

'I'm just breaking them in,' he mumbled. Then he realised that this sounded like bragging, and came clean. 'They're my first proper boots. I might try the tourist route tomorrow.' To his relief, the conversation veered on to boots in general, soft nails versus hard nails, their plans for tomorrow, and then reminiscences of past climbs. Stephan had even been to the Himalayas. Erich sat like a mouse in a theatre, enthralled, hoping he wouldn't be noticed. He could go on listening to stories of snow and ice, and of vertical pitches on the sun-warmed rocks of the Dolomites forever.

In the morning, before anyone else got up, he took his breakfast – a heel of bread – outside. Having just bought his boots, he was literally penniless and didn't want the others offering him food again. He would let them go, and then take the tourist path to the top. It was cool and fresh, the rearing cliffs of the mountain rose almost vertically behind him. Would he ever have the courage to climb them ... certainly not on his own. He discovered a tiny white flower, an edelweiss, in a crack at his feet; its petals were like velvet. He heard a voice above him.

'One of our group couldn't make it. If we had an extra man we could make up two ropes of three, would you like to join us?' Stephan was standing looking down at him.

Like! Of course he'd like ... 'But I've never been on a rope before!' It was out now; his boots were all just a show.

'No time like the present. If you decide you don't like it, we will see you down.'

Erich nearly objected that his grandfather said that he must always be able to climb down what he had climbed up, but he held his tongue.

To begin with, Erich could have kicked himself for having agreed to come, but Stephan, the leader of his rope, was patient in showing him how to tie it onto his waist, and how to pay it out while Stephan climbed. Erich soon realised that the rope, far from being a quick way of pulling all three climbers to their doom, protected them and secured them to the rock. Just as he had imagined, the rope really was a living link between them all. His boots clicked neatly into the firm rock and he could feel the air under his heels. Gradually life took on a vertical dimension, a world where red-legged choughs did acrobatics and eagles soared.

His last lesson that day was how to coil up the rope so it didn't twist; the climb was over. They arrived back at the refuge in good time for Erich to start the trek back down into the valley. The others were staying on for another night. He wanted to linger, but he must be back in Vienna for classes on Monday. He said his thanks and was shouldering his rucksack when Stephan came up.

'We're not a club, just a group of friends, but any time you'd like to climb with us, this is my address; drop me a card. Some time I'll tell you how difficult that climb you did today was, not bad for a pair of new boots!'

Erich practically floated with pride all the way down into the valley.

Piano smugglers

Of all the bizarre expeditions! Izaac and Uncle Rudi were driving the breadth of Austria with a dismantled piano in the back seat of Rudi's car! When they arrived at the border with Switzerland his uncle joked so much with the customs officials that Izaac began to be suspicious that Rudi was up to something. Then when they pulled into a junkyard and sold the old piano for a few Swiss francs, he was sure. But what Rudi's game was he had no idea. It was only when they drove through the massive gates of one of the principal banks in Zurich that Izaac twigged. Sure enough, when Uncle Rudi lifted the floorboards of the car, there were the bags of gold coins that he had purchased for the family at the time of the Wall Street Crash.

'Sorry I didn't let you in on it, Izaac.' Rudi whispered as the bank managers wound themselves about them, like cats being served cream. 'I thought it better that you knew nothing about it. You might have given us away at the border!' he chuckled.

The money was counted, the bags carried off to the vaults, and the paperwork undertaken with Swiss precision. Then, amid assurances of confidentiality, an account was opened in the family name of Abrahams. A password was entered into a leather-bound ledger, and immediately locked away in a gigantic safe.

Izaac drove most of the way home. The bank had given them a hearty lunch with plenty of wine, and Uncle Rudi, unfit to drive, was prone to sudden fits of giggles. Izaac was justifiably worried that he might tell the customs men on the way back how he had fooled them.

It was, however, a cold sober Uncle Rudi who called the whole family together a day or two later and explained the situation and how they must handle it. Having learned that Jewish businesses were being targeted in Germany, he had thought it best that the family fortunes should be safe in a Swiss bank. He then gave them each a copy of the details of the bank, the account number, and, most importantly, the password. They were to memorise these before leaving the room. These were their passwords for a future. When half an hour was up he took their slips of paper, including his own, and burned them in the tiled stove that stood in a corner of the room.

A Puppet in Hollywood

Two years after Izaac's aborted attempt to get to America, he set sail again. This time the trip was uneventful and the tour had been a resounding success. His name was now almost as well known internationally as it was back home in Austria. Last night, after an eventful day, he had given his final performance in all the glamour of a Hollywood celebrity concert.

'Hey! Mr Abrahams sir, you have certainly hit the headlines today, sir.' The man at reception was holding out *The Hollywood Herald*.

'A review so soon?' Izaac was surprised. He began to read. *Austrian Violinist Quells Kids' Riot in Beverly Hills* ran the headline. So that was what it was about! *Yesterday afternoon, when Austrian violinist, Izaac Abrahams, came to prepare for his evening concert at the Beverly Hills Palladium, he didn't know that he would end up playing for five hundred excited kids. When puppeteer 'Peter the Piper' failed to show for his matinee performance, stage manager Shawn O'Dwyer thought he had a riot on his hands. Here is what the kids had to say:*

'*Cool! Great!' says Mark J. Sands Junior. 'This guy walked on stage just like he was a puppet. Jerky steps, he has this violin, see, but whenever he gets it to his chin his right arm drops, or flies up in the air, so he looks up and gives out in German like to the man operating him, so like fools, we all look up too. When he gets his puppet strings straight he begins to play tunes, from musicals I guess. That violin, it's only a little piece of wood, but the sound he can get out of it is something else.'*

Next I asked Amy Kit, whose dad works in the Disney studios: 'I liked the time he looked like a duck – not Donald Duck – a sort of wild duck,' she says, 'and I liked when his violin turned into a python. Wow... it nearly got him.'

So, today being the last day of Izaac Abraham's West Coast tour, I asked him if he was anxious about going back home with all the trouble facing Jewish people in Germany. He said that Austria was different and that they would hold out against Hitler. He laughed and said that, anyway, he had someone to go home to.

When the ship docked in Hamburg, Izaac took the train south through France and Switzerland; he didn't want to travel through Germany again. He got up as the train wound down through the mountains, shaving carefully in the tiny wash-hand basin in his sleeper compartment. Then at last came the familiar suburbs of Vienna. He felt his pulse racing. Why did the train have to crawl? At last, the Westbahnhof. Would Gretchen be there? He lowered the window, searching the platform, and there she was, by a pillar, stretching up to see him over the crowd. He hurried to the door, overnight case in one hand and violin in the other, and here she came, flying down the platform towards him.

Fear for Lives on the Adlerwand

Sabine Hoffman strained to hear the voice of the newsreader, her face anxious.

'Next, to news of Adlerwand, where fears are growing for the fate of the three men trapped on the face due to a fierce over-night storm.'

Erich's mother switched off the wireless. She would paint her way through this, as through every other crisis. The rest of Altaussee stayed glued to their sets.

'After two days and two nights on the north wall of the Adler

Mountain, watchers are beginning to fear for the lives of the three-man Austrian and German team who are attempting the first ascent of this awesome mountain face. 'Only the North Face of the Eiger presents a greater challenge,' opines a member of the Austrian Alpine Club, observing the climb from the alpine ski refuge at the mountain foot. The storm that lashed the mountain during the hours of darkness has left the face coated with fresh snow. Since daybreak there has been no sign of the climbers moving on the face. Local guides are preparing for a rescue operation, using the easier west face route. Despite objections from local alpinists, a German film crew is also planning this ascent. "We strongly oppose this ghoulish interest," a spokesman says.'

<hr/>

It had been the worst night that Erich had experienced on a mountain since he had begun serious climbing with Stephan three years ago. The storm had raged with demonic fury, lashing at the thin sheet of tenting that covered them. The ledge they were sitting on, a mere fifty centimetres wide, sloped out. Only short lengths of rope, attached to a single steel piton driven deep into a crack in the rock, prevented them from hurtling into the abyss below. During the height of the storm, lightning had struck at the face. Each strike had commenced with a terrible tingle, a blue light would hover about the steel piton, and then would come a jolt, and a flash that lit their terrified faces as the electrical discharge hit them. Then came the snow, hissing stealthily over their covering sheet.

The storm passed and the first light of day filtered through. Long before the reporters and watchers below began to stir, they had had their breakfast. They forced down the last of their cold sausage. Apart from some chocolate, and some loose raisins, that was the end of their provisions. It was time to review their position. Up or down, they must escape from this terrible face today, before their strength failed.

Their shelf represented a cul-de-sac. It was perched at the top of a vast, near vertical slab of smooth rock that offered no holds for hands or feet. Either they must go back, losing precious hours in the process, or they must find some way to cross this slab. Stephan was adamant.

'We can't go back, lads. If we do, we could lose half a day and won't have time to go up or down. We *have* to cross it! Let's give it a go; it might, just might, lead into a crack to the summit!'

It took them some time to arrange the rope to Stephan's satisfaction. Erich remembered doing something similar as a boy, using a rope that was tied to a lamp post as a swing. Having moved back along the shelf to get as wide a swing as possible, Stephan was nerving himself. A two-thousand-foot fall down nearly vertical rock waited him if anything went wrong.

Then he was off, hurtling in a wide downward arc, swinging across the slab, his feet half running, half scrabbling at the surface. He stretched out; a centimetre more and he would be able to grab the far edge of the slab with his fingers, but he was just that little too short, and swung back like a pendulum, spinning and bouncing off the rock, cursing and swearing. Then, without hesitating, and taking advantage of the momentum of his backward swing, he lunged forward to try again. The rope – stretched to its limit – crackled with the strain, then his hands were on the edge, and with a heave he pulled himself forward to straddle the edge like a rider on a rearing horse. He looked over the far side.

Erich and Herbert hardly dared to breathe.

'It looks good!'

Relief flooded through them. Erich pounded Herbert on the back in delight. Joining Stephan was easy; they would slide along the rope like a cable car, pulling themselves towards him. Once they pulled the rope after them, however, there would be no going back.

Light was just creeping into the valley below when the three climbers came together on a perilous ledge and looked up. A cleft, like an open book, soared above them. Clearly this was the way to the summit; the only trouble was that it was choked with fresh snow.

'Before we cut off our retreat I'm going to test that snow,' Stephan said. He probed ahead with his ice axe. Perhaps it was this, perhaps it was the sound of his voice, but at that moment they heard a snap and a rumble. While the others hauled Stephan bodily back onto the ledge and hunched over him, the whole mass of snow began to move. Compressed air from the avalanche snatched at them as the night's snow thundered past them down the cleft, to burst out over the face below.

Down in the valley the watchers rushed out. Could anybody on the face have withstood such an event? Two rescue parties got ready, one to search the avalanche debris, and the other to climb up by the west ridge to see what help might be given from the top. Against all advice, the German camera crew went too.

Out of sight from below, hidden in the now snow-free cleft, the three climbers began to edge their way up, rope's-length after rope's-length. For six hours they battled against gravity. As the day warmed, stones, loosened from the melting ice, rattled and crashed down the cleft, leaving a smell of gunpowder in the air. Fortunately it was so steep that the stones usually bounced clear, buzzing past them like dangerous bees. They reached their last obstacle at about the same time as, unknown to them, their would-be rescuers arrived at the summit. A huge overhanging wave of frozen snow – the cornice – hid them from above and blocked their exit from the face.

Stephan, exhausted, asked Erich to take the lead. Somehow he would have to burrow through this roof of snow without bringing the whole lot of it down on himself and his companions. Working with his ice axe above his head, snow pouring over him and down his neck, he cut into the snow above. Black spots of exhaustion danced in front of his eyes. When at last he could see light shining through the snow he knew that with one more blow he would be through, but would that last blow bring the cornice crashing down? Working delicately, he shaved through the last inches. Blue sky filled the opening circle above him. He dug in his axe and lifted his shoulders clear, one careful heave and he would be out. At that moment he heard a shout. There were people up here on the summit. Someone had seen him emerging, and was running towards him.

'Stop!' he roared. 'Get back! You're on the cornice!'

There were other warning shouts too. The man halted a few yards away, a hand out as if to help. Erich blinked; surely he was hallucinating. It looked like Klaus Steinman! Erich shut the hallucination from his mind and wriggled out of his hole like a seal on to ice. And like a seal he humped himself away from the delicate cornice. When he was sure he was on solid snow he drove the shaft of his ice axe deep into it, looped the rope around it, and gave two sharp pulls to tell Stephan it was safe to come on up.

Even while he was drawing in Stephan's rope, the Klaus figure was around him, trying to shake his hand, even to help pull on the rope. Then he was gone; the alpine guides had moved in to keep the area clear.

Stephan emerged, hardly able to heave himself over the edge, and then Herbert. Now the guides were all about them, shaking hands, offering hot drinks, and sincere words of congratulation.

Erich only gradually became aware that Klaus was real. He could see him now, talking animatedly to the lens of a camera, dressed head to toe in fashionable climbing gear. One of the camera crew came over to ask the climbers to pose for them. Love of the world and affection for his companions was flooding Erich: this was the moment of euphoria that made climbers climb. Let them do what they wanted. He had no idea what he was saying to the camera. Klaus posed the questions, and provided answers for him when he hesitated. He agreed that this was a triumph for the Greater Germany, after all Herbert was a German. He put his arms over the shoulders of his fellow climbers and they smiled as best they could with cracked lips and wind-stiffened faces.

None of them saw the newsreel film as it was shown in German cinemas, where the mountain appeared to be hung about with swastikas, and where it wasn't all that clear whether Klaus Steinman was or wasn't one of the party; he was certainly the best dressed.

CHAPTER 16

The Purity of the Race

'Louise,' Izaac said, 'I think I should propose to Gretchen.'

'And about time too!' said Louise in return. 'What have you been waiting for?'

'Perhaps I felt I was too old for her.'

'Nonsense, what is she now, twenty-three, for your twenty-seven? What's four years! When will you ask her?'

'I thought I would go out to Mödling. Perhaps I should see her father first. He might object.'

'Not from what I've heard her saying, but her half-brother Klaus would be another matter. Off you go then; you can do this one on your own.'

When Izaac had gone, Louise stretched her arms wide, then hugged hersel in pure joy at their future happiness together. She had grown very fond of Gretchen, just as she had loved Colette nearly a century and a half ago. Izaac and she would be perfect for each other. Gretchen might look as light as thistledown, but she had a steely quality that Izaac needed.

Every clang of the bell as the tram to Mödling swayed out of town had nice associations for Izaac. He hadn't telegraphed or phoned; he wanted this to be a surprise. His pulse was racing. He rang the bell and braced himself for Gretchen's father, as a man's footsteps rang on the tiles in the hall. The door was opened by a far younger man; after the bright light outside all Izaac could see was an outline, fair hair perhaps. Taken aback, he stammered:

'Is Herr Wachter at home?' He felt the man look him up and down.

'No. Would you like to speak to my mother?'

'Thank you.' The man turned and disappeared down the hall. This must be Klaus, Gretchen's half brother!

'Mother, there's a man at the door. One of Fred's Jewish friends.' Frau Wachter appeared, drying her hands on her apron.

'Why! That's Izaac!' She hurried forward and joined him on the doorstep. Izaac wondered why she didn't ask him to come in; she was usually most welcoming. 'Izaac, how are you? You're looking for Frederick. I'm afraid he has taken Gretchen away for the week, they ... ' She pulled the door discreetly behind her. 'My son Klaus is here, so they know I'll be looked after.' Izaac understood; Gretchen and Klaus were at daggers drawn, and she absented herself as much as possible whenever he came to stay. It was a huge disappointment. He realised that Frau Wachter didn't really want to ask him in. It was a pity; he'd have been interested to talk to the dreadful Klaus.

'Thank you so much, Frau Wachter. Please give Herr Wachter my regards; I will call again later.' As he turned he looked at his watch. It would be an hour before the next Bim.

⌒╶╫╫╫╴⌐

Klaus stepped back as his mother closed the door.

'Is that Izaac Abrahams, Gretchen's violinist?' he asked.

'Yes. We're all very fond of him.' It was bravely said. Frau Wachter was frightened of Klaus, the son who had been virtually taken away from her at birth by her former husband and had ended up living in Hitler's nest of loyal followers in Munich.

141

'I'd like to meet him,' said Klaus. 'Come to think of it, Erich and I are planning a visit to Vienna. I'll call in on Erich now and we can take the Bim in together. Perhaps I'll introduce myself to Herr Abrahams.'

'Remember, he's been very good to Gretchen!'

'Good *to* her perhaps, but not good *for* her, I think.'

Oh dear, thought Frau Wachter.

Erich was only too glad to interrupt his studies and join Klaus on a trip into town. They had to hurry to get the Bim and then Klaus seemed keen not to be seen by some other passenger in the front compartment. What was Klaus up to? He chatted away, but when they got off, Erich got the impression that they were following someone. There were times when you didn't ask Klaus questions.

Izaac walked home through the Volksgarten, as he did whenever he wanted to think. How would he propose? On one knee with clasped hands, or catch Gretchen during his snake dance and propose in its coils. He loved to make her laugh, the stars laughed when she laughed like that. He smiled to himself; he must think out something special for her. All at once he realised that there was someone in his path; he stepped to one side with a murmured apology. The figure moved too, blocking his way. Izaac looked up ... a friend perhaps? No, a stranger: tall, fair, good-looking in an Aryan sort of way. But there was something familiar about him.

'Pardon,' Izaac said.

'No, Mr Abrahams, no pardon, not for you!'

'Excuse me, I don't understand.'

'You will!'

'Have we met?' asked Izaac warily.

'Unfortunately, yes.'

It was coming back to Izaac now: wood smoke, small boys, a tall mocking youth. 'Yid ... Yid ...' it was all coming back to him.

'I think our dislike may be mutual,' he said, and noticed a flash of anger cross the man's face, but he had stood up to hostile audiences, he would stand up to this man.

'From now, Herr Abrahams, from this minute, you are to break off all relations with my sister Gretchen. That is an order!'

Izaac almost fell back in shock. This man, the man who had opened the door to him in Mödling, the murderous youth who had ambushed him and Louise up in the Wienerwald, were one and the same: Gretchen's half-brother Klaus!

Regaining some of his composure, Izaac asked what he now knew to be an unnecessary question, 'Why?'

'Because you are a Jew!'

'That's no answer, and anyway Gretchen can answer for herself.'

'It *is* an answer! It is *my* answer!' The man was pushing his face closer and closer to Izaac's. 'Because I care for the purity of my *blood!*'

'Only half, if I remember rightly.'

Klaus's face drained white with anger. 'I will not be talked to like that by a Jew. The very thought of your polluting paws on any girl of our pure race revolts and sickens me. You have corrupted her mind; you will not have her body. I would kill her before I let you near her, and I mean it! I don't care about you; you are *untermenschen* – subhuman – as far as I am concerned. It is she who I will drag through the mire for betraying our race.' With that, Klaus turned on his heel and srode off.

For a moment, righteous indignation rose like gall in Izaac's throat; he would follow that man and tear him apart with his hands, but in his mind he heard a mental *click*. It was the click that one domino makes when it falls against another. As a child he used to make long curving chains of them, and then when they were ready, give the first one a push: click ... click ... click. Down they would go until the last one fell. Ever since he had first met Gretchen he had been building this chain, domino after domino, while denying that anything could topple it. He had been an Austrian first, a Jew second. He had made himself part of the Austrian dream of music and civilisation. All it had taken to topple the domino chain was to reverse the names: a Jew first, an Austrian last. Klaus meant what he said; he would go for Gretchen, not him, and feel righteous in doing so. How could he propose to Gretchen now? How could he expose her to this? The last domino was down.

'Who was that you were talking to?' Erich asked when Klaus joined him at the circular fountain in the Volksgarten. He noticed that Klaus's face had that unpleasant death's head look that he remembered from their first meeting in the woods above his home.

'Never mind, a family matter. Come, we are going for a little walk. I have something to show you. It's time you had your eyes opened to what's going on in this country.'

They set off at a great pace towards the Hofburg palace, passing the statue of Archduke Karl on his prancing horse, and then plunged through the high arched passage into the inner city.

'Where are we going?' asked Erich.

'It doesn't really matter, Erich, *they* are everywhere.'

'Who? The Jews?'

'You're learning! Come, let's try a bank.'

Inside the marble interior he lowered his voice. 'Now, look at the tellers: Jews to a man, what did I tell you? Shh!'

A young official came up to them. 'Can I help you, gentlemen?'

'Yes,' said Klaus, 'I was wondering if you have any vacancies?'

'I can't say, sir; if you will follow me, I will consult with my superior.' He led them into an anteroom. 'He won't be a moment. To pass the time while you wait you might like to tot up the columns on this sheet; it won't take you a minute.'

'Bloody cheek,' whispered Klaus. Erich dug him in the ribs; there was a second candidate sitting in the room. Klaus ran a pencil professionally down the columns, entering the answers with a flourish. Erich was impressed. At that moment a more senior manager, every inch the Jew to Erich's eye, entered. With elaborate courtesy he collected the sheets of tots from the two candidates and examined them briefly. Then he turned to Klaus and explained that unfortunately they didn't have a vacancy at present, perhaps some other time. Then he turned to the other candidate.

'Herr Korngold, this way, if you please.'

'What did I tell you? A Jew, jobs for the boys!' hissed Klaus as they emerged. 'No Aryans need apply.' As they walked down the street, Klaus managed to find a Jew in every shop they looked into. 'Now we will have a cup of coffee.'

Erich held back; they were outside one of the most expensive cafés in Vienna. He hoped Klaus was going to pay. As they sat with their tiny *mocha* coffees they gazed at the well-heeled women at the surrounding tables.

'They look like overfed Vienna to me.'

'Yes, but, this is a Jewish café! Do you know why they are here?' Erich shook his head. 'This is where Freud, the Jewish psychoanalyst, comes. These women are his patients; he tells them that they are sexually repressed, and they love it. Don't you *see*, even the doctors are at it; systematically corrupting our nationhood. These women should be at home, breeding, and feeding the nation, not listening to filth in a Jew's surgery.'

By the end of the day Erich was beginning to see nothing but Jews. Jews with ringlets, black hats and greasy-looking clothes standing on street corners, 'whispering' and 'conspiring', according to Klaus. They had heard a strange barbaric wailing from inside a synagogue, and Klaus suggested a human sacrifice. Erich suspected that this was nonsense but he was now enjoying feeding his prejudices; he envied Klaus's air of superiority. What did little truths matter in the face of the great conspiracy? Just as Grandpa Veit had warned him, they were everywhere.

Eventually Klaus took him, footsore and weary, to an unquestionably Aryan *Bierkeller*, and ordered schnitzel and beer for them both. They felt private in the clatter and clamour of the cellar. It was then that Klaus leaned forward.

'Erich, my friend, you may not know it, but since your Adler-wand ascent you have become a bit of hero over the border in Germany. There is a call for men of steel and men with high ideals. What you said after your ascent has met with approval.'

What had he said? Erich wondered, but he was a little drunk now.

'I have a proposal to put to you.' Klaus said, 'have you considered joining the SS?'

CHAPTER 17

The Anschluss

'Izaac ... Izaac! Come quickly, the Chancellor is speaking.' Lotte's head appeared in the doorway and disappeared immediately. Izaac hastily laid his violin in its case and ran out to the kitchen where Lotte kept a watch on the world for them through her small wireless set. Louise didn't follow him. The whole family would be leaning forward, straining to hear, through the hiss and crackle, what was happening to their country. She was as anxious to know as they, but she would leave it to Izaac to tell her about it later. She heard a general gasp: '*Oh no!*' and then nothing until the radio was switched off. It seemed ages before Izaac reappeared, looking numb and shocked; he began to put his violin away.

'Izaac, what's the news ... bad?'

He took a resigned breath. 'You remember we were going to vote–'

'For a *Free and Independent Austria*?' Louise said, glancing out of the window. 'I've enjoyed the flags: *Rot Weiss Rot* – Red White Red – they look so brave.'

Izaac snorted. 'They can come down now. Our Chancellor's resigned!'

'No! Why?'

'Because Hitler has moved his troops up to the border, and said to Chancellor Schuschnigg that if he doesn't resign, and put Hitler's own man in charge, he'll invade Austria by force.

That's what was on the wireless just now – Schuschnigg announcing his resignation. He sounded close to tears, poor man. Now Hitler is free to walk in.'

'Will that be bad ... for you as Jews ... for us?' Louise asked. She had been a silent partner in many an anxious discussion as the family had watched the rise of Hitler and the progressive persecution of Jews in Germany. She knew it would be bad, but she didn't know how serious it would be here in Austria.

Izaac shrugged. 'We are Austrians first, Jews second, I'm sure the people will stand by us.' He didn't sound convinced. Louise held up her hand. 'Hush, Izaac ... what's that?' There was shouting in the distance.

Izaac went to the window and fumbled with the catch. A lorry was approaching from the distance. A huge swastika flag waved above it. It carried the most extraordinary motley of men, wearing literally any sort of uniform they could find. Some had helmets, some caps, other had old storm trooper jackets, even Hitler Youth uniforms. There were men in trousers, boys in shorts, but all of them were wearing swastika armbands, and nearly all of them brandished pistols or rifles of one kind or another. Now people were running out of the houses into the street to look, many to cheer them on.

'*Ein Volk, ein Reich, ein Führer!*' One People, One State, One Leader. The chanting from the lorries was being taken up by the crowd. More and more lorries streamed in to join the cavalcade. 'Where have they come from?' Izaac wondered aloud. Less than quarter of an hour had passed since he had been listening to poor Schuschnigg's last despairing message. Had these people been hiding like rats in the sewers, knowing that this moment would come? Hitler had won. This was the Anschluss; Austria was being sucked into the Greater German State. The people cheering below were his neighbours! Had they no idea what they were letting into their country?

Izaac watched in disbelief as lorry after lorry trundled past. Now there was a new chant; his stomach tightened, and his knees felt weak.

'*Juda verrecke! Juda verrecke!*' Die Jew! Die Jew! The chanting got louder and louder, the syllables spat out with machine-gun precision, '*Ju-da ver-re-cke!*' He drew back involuntarily. While others were throwing their windows wide, Izaac was struggling to close his. As the windows closed the sound was suddenly muted, he turned his back to the glass and looked at his hands; they were shaking with a fine vibrato.

'Oh Louise, I never dreamed that this would happen here.'

By evening, tales were spreading that, everywhere in the city, Jews were being dragged out of their apartments and being made to pick off with their fingernails, the posters advertising the vote that had never happened. Only Lotte, who was fair haired and clearly not Jewish, had dared to go out. Within a few minutes, however, she was back, panting. She rushed into the music room.

'Izaac! Open those curtains quick, quick! And a window or two!' She was struggling with a latch. 'They are looking up at apartments to see where the curtains are drawn and the windows closed. That's how they're trying to spot Jewish families or their sympathisers!' So, thanks to Lotte, and perhaps good neighbours who didn't betray them, there was no knock on their door that night.

The following morning Izaac began work as usual, feeling that this alone would blot out the madness of last night. He had a concert that hadn't yet been cancelled, so he set about preparing for it. He paused, his bow hovering over his strings. Suddenly he felt a sound so deep that it seemed to be rising through his feet. He noticed Louise look up too. It was as if a crack in the earth was opening ... a sound swelling louder ... and louder. He looked at the piano in amazement; a snow of white petals was drifting down from a branch of cherry blossom that Lotte had placed there yesterday. Now even the strings of the piano were resonating.

'What's happening, Louise? Is it an earthquake?' He moved to the window; when he touched the frame he could feel it vibrating under his fingertips. Immediately a line of black shadows swept overhead; he ducked involuntarily, like a bird below an eagle. A flight of German bombers was sweeping over, all in perfect formation; black crucifixes against the clouds. Another roar, and another line of crosses swept to join the massed tombstones in the sky. On they came, line after line. He could see the swastika markings clear on their wings, even the heads of the pilots. Suddenly it was all over and all that remained was a sky full of leaflets, fluttering and falling over the city like the petals from the cherry branch on the piano.

⟶ ⦚⦚⦚ ⟵

There had been real snow, a late fall, during the night. Hunched over Lotte's wireless, the family had heard the adulation of the thousands who welcomed Hitler when he crossed the border from Germany and drove in triumph into his home town of Linz. Now when he looked along the street, Izaac noticed a change; the black and red of Nazi flags had joined the red and white of Austria, 'Free and Independent' no longer. Overnight even these had been defiled: hastily stitched swastikas strutted over Austria's flags like crow's feet. Stitched in fear or in triumph, he wondered?

Lorries were approaching, grinding through the slush, but what a contrast to yesterday's rabble. These vehicles passed with military precision: lorry after lorry, their open backs crammed with soldiers all staring straight ahead, shoulder to shoulder, their rifles vertical between their knees, helmets looking like eggs in an egg-box. It was terrifying, but magnificent in its way. At least with the German army here, surely the rabble would be dispersed. There was nothing Izaac could do, so he turned back into the room.

'Where were we, Louise?' he asked, hoping to lose himself in music.

CHAPTER 18

Untersturmführer Erich Hoffman

The summer following the Anschluss passed in a strange limbo. Izaac still had professional engagements. When he crossed the border into Switzerland to play the Brahms Violin Concerto in Geneva, he found himself part of a stream of Jews fleeing west. They were all urging him to leave while the border was open; he would be welcome anywhere because of his talent. When he got home he tried to persuade his parents to go, but his mother, whose health was failing, wouldn't even contemplate moving.

'Izaac, you go,' she said. 'I am too old, too sick to face the journey.' The family discussions went on and on. Only Uncle Rudi seemed to sense any real danger, and he was voted down. Louise, listening to the family discussion, wanted to scream: 'Go, go. Pick the old lady up and carry her, but go!' She had been through a pogrom in France and knew its horrors. Time slipped by and a strange lethargy settled over them.

<hr/>

November 9th 1938 began like any other day but the hammering at the door was unlike any normal knock. Had the Germans found them? Izaac hastily placed his violin in its case and hurried towards the door. He didn't want his elderly parents getting a shock, but it was Lotte who got there first. She had just opened the door of the apartment, and was facing a German army corporal when Izaac arrived. Izaac noticed that the man had placed his foot in the door so that she couldn't close it. Behind him, in the dark of the landing, Izaac could see a tall figure in the all-black uniform of the SS. The two lightning flashes on the man's lapels glinted stark in the half-light. What could have brought one of Hitler's elite bodyguards to his door?

'Heil Hitler,' the corporal snapped. 'This is the residence of the Jewish family Abrahams ... Ja?' Izaac put his hand on Lotte's arm and drew her back.

'I'll handle this, Lotte,' he murmured. Then to the corporal: 'Yes. What can I do for you?' At this, the SS man stepped forward into the light from the door. So far, the peak of his cap had kept his face hidden. Now Izaac could see it; surely he had seen that face before? He remembered his encounter with Gretchen's half brother, Klaus, in the Volksgarten. There was certainly a similarity, but this wasn't Klaus. And when he spoke, this man's voice was different, tight but courteous.

'Thank you, Corporal.' Then he turned to Izaac: 'May I come in?'

'Certainly,' said Izaac, though he had no choice in the matter. There was a clatter of steps coming down the stairs, and Izaac had a brief glimpse of the Zelmans, the elderly couple who lived in the top flat, being half carried, stumbling and slipping, down the stairs by a group of militia men.

'Close the door, Corporal,' snapped the officer. 'We are not to be disturbed.'

Izaac felt he should protest about the Zelmans, but realised that there was nothing he could do for them; also he had his own old people to think about. He led the way into the music room and turned to face the officer who seemed to tower above him, his peaked cap rising like the prow of a ship. Izaac felt as if it was bearing down on him. He heard Louise whisper; *'Don't shrink, Izaac!'* He straightened himself up.

'To whom do I have the pleasure?' he asked formally. The officer clicked his heels:

'Untersturmführer Erich Hoffman.' Izaac guessed that this was equivalent to Second Lieutenant; a new recruit, in other words. The young man was unbuttoning the flap on his breast pocket; he took out a black notebook, which he flipped open and commenced questioning.

'Family name: Abrahams?' Izaac nodded. This was entered in the book.

'Christian name?' then he corrected himself: 'Forename?' as if remembering that Jews didn't have Christian names.

'Izaac.' For a moment the man hesitated, his eyes flicked up and made a quick search of Izaac's face.

'*The* Izaac Abrahams! Excuse me, I didn't recognise you. 'Occupation ... violinist, obviously.' Izaac was used to having his name recognized, but the information seemed to have upset the officer, who was now drawing himself up to make a formal speech.

'It is the intention of the Führer to acquire, on behalf of the people of the new Greater Germany, works of outstanding artistic merit. These will be displayed for the benefit of *all* Germans in a new gallery, the *Führermuseum,* to be built in the Führer's hometown of Linz. My information is that you possess a picture from the Dutch School referred to as ...' he consulted his notebook, *The Girl in the Green Dress?*'

Izaac's jaw literally dropped. What was the man talking about? It couldn't be Louise, nobody knew about her portrait outside of family and friends. She was private property. But the man had said *acquire.* The Nazis acquiring pictures! It just didn't fit.

Louise had darted behind the SS man and was frantically signalling 'no' to Izaac. But what could he do? Try to deny the existence of the painting? But there it was on the wall directly behind the man. All he could do was play for time.

'I don't think your information can be correct.' (But where *had* the information come from, he wondered.) 'The picture I think you mean was bought by a common pedlar in exchange for a few pots and pans over a hundred years ago. It's been in our family for generations. It is unsigned and quite worthless.' Perhaps he could divert him. 'We have a small Picasso which we might lend.' This was, in fact, true, the fruit of an unpaid bill accepted by Father to help an impoverished customer.

Surprisingly, the officer grimaced and shook his head. 'We have no interest in *degenerate art,'* he said. 'Kindly show me the picture I have asked to see.' Izaac turned to Louise but she was too distraught to be able to help. There was nothing else for it.

'It's there on the wall behind you.' Perhaps he would choose the wrong picture. The SS man turned, glanced at the wall and gasped.

'Liebe Gott!' He took a few steps forward and stood directly in front of the portrait while Izaac and Louise watched helplessly.

'Stop him, Izaac!' Louise was beside herself with fury.

'It's a pretty enough painting, officer, but it is just pedlar's junk from the last century,' Izaac said despairingly. 'If you look closely you will see that it has a bad tear in it.'

But his observations were falling on deaf ears. The man had whipped off his cap, as if out of respect, and was standing mesmerized in front of the picture.

'Herr Abrahams,' he said slowly; 'I must disagree. This is seventeenth century, probably from Delft. It is not a Vermeer, nor yet by Fabritius, and it is not rough enough for Rembrandt.

But yet there is something about it that reminds me of one picture in particular ... a picture of a beggar? I've got it: *The Singing Beggar*!' I could swear they're by the same artist. Rembrandt's the only other master who makes his white lead like that. Because he never signed his paintings, we don't know this one's name but we call him 'The Master of Delft'.'

Louise gave a whimper.

'He's right, Izaac. Izaac, you can't let him take me!'

'How can you be so sure?' Izaac challenged.

'I have just completed my thesis here in Vienna on Dutch and German Art.'

The young man turned. Izaac was more certain than ever that he had seen his face before, but where? It was Louise who made the connection.

'Izaac, remember that night in Mödling when you were attacked by a group of scouts up in the woods? He was the younger one; the one who spoke up for you, I'm sure of it!'

They watched the man's back as he took out a lens to look more closely at the brushwork. Then he stood up, clasped the picture, lifted it from its hook and examined the back. 'That canvas was stretched by the same apprentice as stretched *The Singing Beggar*. I'd know his style. And just look at this mend! What amazing work!'

'Izaac, he was decent to you once; work on him,' Louise pleaded. 'Say that you need me for your music; he'll understand.'

'I remember you now, officer,' Izaac said. 'You were kind enough to help me when I was attacked by scouts one summer in the woods. I know that you appreciate music. If I said to you that this painting is the principal inspiration behind my playing, I think you would understand.' Had he struck a chord?

The man had turned his back to them and was running his fingers over the mend in the canvas. He turned around, but his face was grave. 'It is my duty, Herr Abrahams, to acquire this painting and thus ensure its safety. God knows what will happen to it if the mob out there visits your apartment. Also, you are one person, while the German people are many. You don't play for yourself; you play to an audience. This picture should have a wider audience than you can ever give it here. Also, I have my orders.'

'I don't want to end up in a Nazi gallery, Izaac; I couldn't bear it!' Louise was desperate.

Izaac lost his temper. 'How dare you! You are a thief! This picture belongs to us. It's our property and you have no right to take it!' Even as he said the words he realised that this was a mistake. In this new Austria you didn't question a Nazi's right to anything.

The man's features hardened, his body went rigid. There would be no further argument.

'It is my duty to acquire this painting on behalf of the Greater German people. You will receive compensation in accordance with the laws of the Third Reich. This is your receipt.' He wrote in his notebook. 'You will see that I have made a generous valuation. I apologise that printed forms are not yet available, but this will be perfectly valid.' He tore the page from his notebook and handed it to Izaac. Then, taking up the picture, he called to the corporal. 'Bring the packing, Corporal!' So, they had come prepared. The corporal wrapped corrugated cardboard and brown paper around the painting. He tied the package firmly with string.

While he was working, the young Nazi walked uneasily about the room, looking at the other pictures. He saw Izaac's violin lying open in its case and touched it, then withdrew his hand quickly.

Louise, panic stricken, was being pulled in two directions.

'Izaac, if he takes my picture, I will *have* to go. I *daren't* lose touch with it. When we went to Mödling I knew where it was and I had you to take me back to it. But if I try to stay with you now, and he takes it, it will be like separating my body from my soul. I want to stay with you, Izaac, but I've no choice. I must go with my picture!'

Izaac looked at her in despair and saw the same beauty that the Master had seen nearly two hundred years before, but now it had a delicate transparent quality as if she was already fading from him. He gave a groan that made the SS man half turn towards him.

Louise was thinking ahead: 'Izaac, you may not see me again. But think of me when you play. Play for me, and listen for me. I will be with you in spirit. In that way we may still be able to work together.' The corporal was tying the last piece of string. 'Goodbye Izaac.'

The SS man strode towards the door, then hesitated. Izaac thought he was about to say something but he clearly thought better of it. He clicked his heels, and saluted.

'*Heil Hitler*,' and he was gone.

Izaac turned in dismay to where Louise had been standing and found that she was gone too.

CHAPTER 19

On Second Thoughts

Erich walked stiffly down the stairs from the Abrahams' flat. His uniform felt like a strait jacket across his shoulders. He had done it! He had acquired his first work of art for the Führermuseum, and an outstanding one at that. But yet he felt like dirt. The uniform that had made him feel like a god on their triumphal entry into Vienna that spring now stifled him. He thought longingly of the worn comfort of his climbing clothes; all he wanted now was to be swinging loose-limbed down the path from Montenvers to Chamonix after a week climbing in the French Alps.

What was he doing here? He stopped on the landing; the sweat that had sprung up during his interview with Herr Abrahams was cooling uncomfortably. Why, when Klaus had told him about the picture, had he not given him the man's first name? He must have known that this was the famous violinist. Was he testing him, or was Klaus getting his own back for the time when he had stood up for Abrahams in front of the boys? The Jew would, of course, be compensated, he consoled himself, and he was a musician, not an artist, but when Erich recalled touching the wood of the maestro's violin, he felt as if he'd burned his fingers. The arguments against the Jews seemed to lose their power when faced with someone like Izaac Abrahams.

Looking down the stairwell, he could see the corporal

waiting at the door; he'd better get on. There was a motley group of militia and civilians skulking under the stairs. A couple of them raised their arms and said 'Heil Hitler'. He ignored them and hurried out; what were they were waiting for here? The elderly couple he'd seen being dragged down earlier were on hands and knees scrubbing the pavement, their toothbrushes now bald, while a mixed group of local people, some carrying shopping bags, watched and chatted as though it was the most natural thing in the world.

He noticed two men in suits being made to paint anti-Jewish slogans on a shop, probably their own, surrounded by glass from their smashed windows. Erich stopped in disgust. In the distance clouds of smoke were rising from the burning syna-gogues. This has got to stop, he thought. The sooner the authorities get on with finding somewhere for the Jews the better. He strode on. A new thought crossed his mind. He stopped so suddenly that his corporal, walking behind, nearly bumped into him. Those militiamen under the stairs of the Abrahams' house ... who were they waiting for?

'Corporal! Take the picture back to my quarters. I have left something behind in the Jew's flat. I will follow you directly.' People stepped out of his way as he marched back, his SS uni-form clearing a path as effectively as a snowplough. Admiring looks added to his sense of disgust and urgency.

There was a bigger audience outside the apartment now. He quickened his pace. A policeman was holding back the crowd where someone had thoughtfully spilled white paint on the cobbles, and was making an elderly couple scrub at it with cold water. The more water was added the more the paint spread, and the more abuse they got. The woman, dressed only in a light kimono, had obviously been forced from her bed. Erich did not see Izaac Abrahams at once; he was sur-rounded by a big crowd of his own. They had invented a game. They were throwing tiny groschen coins on the cobbles and making Izaac pick them up, chanting: 'Yid, Yid, pick up a quid.' If he didn't try, he got a clip on the head; if he did, they tried to stamp on his fingers. Erich looked about for help; thank God, he saw the black uniform of a fellow SS officer in the crowd. He pushed his way over to him.

'Heil Hitler! Officer,' he said. 'I think we should stop this.' The man just laughed.

'Aren't they doing a great job?' he said, looking with interest as a man in working boots slammed one boot down within a centimetre of Izaac's hand. He grabbed Erich's arm, laughing, 'Hah ha! Go for it, get his greedy fingers!' he called out.

Afterwards Erich would not remember precisely what he had said to his fellow officer, but he did remember lashing out at him before he turned to the mob and shouted:

'Don't you realise who this is? It is Izaac Abrahams, one of our finest violinists! You ignorant Yahoos, if you break his fingers you deprive ...' A boy lifted his foot. 'Don't you dare!' In one lunge, he lifted the boy and threw him bodily out of the circle. That, combined with the ominous effect of his uniform, was enough for him to be able to clear the civilian scum from the corner. Herr Abrahams explained that the lady in the kimono was his mother and that she was unwell. Together they helped her and his bewildered father upstairs to their flat. Erich was too angry even to acknowledge their thanks. When he arrived at the ground floor door again he was greeted by the SS officer he had spoken to outside.

'Congratulations, *Untersturmführer,* you protected your Jews very well. Perhaps I could have the pleasure of your name?' Erich felt his tongue dry in his mouth; why this unexpected courtesy, the man had done nothing to help him? Why this sudden emphasis on his rank? Then he looked – as he should have done before – at the officer's collar. There, next to the three officer pips like his own, were not just one, but two silver bars! The man was a Captain, two whole ranks senior to him! Erich gave his name, which the officer wrote in his notebook. 'My name, if you wish to make an apology, is Captain Winkler,' he said, like a dueller dropping his glove.

⚬⚬⚬

Erich was marched into the room where he was to be charged with his offence.

'Left, right, left, right, left, right. Halt! Salute!'

'Heil Hitler!' Erich raised his right arm.

'Cap off!' He took off his cap and placed it under his left arm while the sergeant major who had marched him in took two steps back, saluted, and positioned himself with his back to the door.

Retribution had been quick. It was less than three days since the incident outside the Abrahams house. The charges against him read: 'Assault on a senior officer, insubordination, fraternizing with Jews, and disgracing his uniform.' His friends had told him he was lucky not to have been court martialled. Captain Winkler, the officer he'd confronted outside the Abraham's flat, was making his case to the judges; his accusations rising to a fanatical scream. Erich concentrated on the outlines of his judges, haloed against the light streaming in from the high windows behind them, trying to ignore the fine spray of spittle as Captain Winkler raved. In the centre would be the presiding officer, flanked by Erich's own colonel on one side, and the one representing Captain Winkler on the other. At the end of the table was a clerk, taking notes. At last Winkler was running out of steam.

'... this *officer*, gentlemen, is worse than the *crawling* Jew he tried to protect – no doubt for his own interests. He is a disgrace to his uniform, to his oath, and to the Führer. Heil Hitler!'

He snapped to attention, and stepped back. Erich noticed his fingers drumming against the side of his leg.

'Untersturmführer Hoffman,' Erich's colonel grated. 'You have heard Captain Winkler's accusations; what have you to say to the charges made against you?'

Erich knew he was in deep trouble; if this went to a court martial, not only might he be put in prison and reduced to the ranks, but he might be thrown out of the SS and end up as a private in the army. For all that he knew he could even be shot. He *should* be conciliatory, but fury at Winkler's ignorant tirade got the better of him.

'Fellow officers, I had not expected to hear the language of the Viennese gutter in this courtroom. It is my understanding that the uniform I wear is to uphold the highest standards of behaviour in our new Greater German State. It has been put to me that I am disloyal on the Jewish question, far from it. But if what I saw on the streets last week is the sort of behaviour we can expect from our citizens, the sooner the Jews are protected from them the better. If something has to be done, let it be done soon and with dignity and compassion. Stamping on the fingers of a great musician and artist is not the way. What Captain Winkler has described is substantially correct; but he, wearing the uniform of the Reich, not only failed to intervene but was actively encouraging this gutter behaviour by cheering them on. If I had seen that he held the rank of captain, frankly gentlemen, I would not have believed it. As far as my conscience is concerned, my oath and my allegiance to the Führer are unshaken. Heil Hitler.'

Captain Winkler couldn't resist intervening: 'You see, he admit–' he began, but the presiding officer rose.

'Silence!' As he had risen, Erich noticed the light shine for a second on the silver-on-black shoulder boards of a full general. Erich blinked. A general! He really must be for it!

'I think you have made your case, Captain Winkler,' he said. The voice was authoritative but neutral. 'You will both wait outside while the court considers its verdict.'

They were marched out and put to sit, one each side of the door, under the watchful eye of the Sergeant Major. A secretary, typing her way through a pile of forms looked up, caught Erich's eye, and smiled encouragingly. Angry voices rose inside.

'Just because he climbed the Adlerwand doesn't make him beyond the law!' A moment later the door flew open and they were being marched in again.

The general addressed them: 'Untersturmführer Erich Hoffman, you have been found guilty as charged. You will remain here for sentencing.' He turned to the captain. 'Hauptsturmführer Winkler, you may return to your quarters.'

For a moment Winkler stood, his mouth opening and closing like a fish; he wanted to hear Erich's sentence. 'Dismiss!' He had no alternative but to go.

The general then turned to the other two presiding officers. 'Gentlemen. I will now interview the prisoner on my own.' Erich's heart sank.

The general ushered his colleagues to the door, put his head outside, told the girl who was typing that they were not to be disturbed, and turned back into the room where Erich was standing ramrod stiff.

'At ease, Lieutenant,' he said. He came up with his hand outstretched. 'Von Brugen.' He clicked his heels. Erich shook his hand. He recognised the name as that of a general from the First World War, one of Grandpa Veit's heroes. He had a lined face and eyes set deep under bushy brows. Most SS men were young, ex-storm troopers who had been handpicked for Hitler's bodyguard. The general moved stiffly to a small table, extracted a file from his briefcase, waved Erich into a chair opposite to him, and fixed him with a penetrating look.

'You may not have been told, Lieutenant, but I am the head of the Art Acquisition Programme. I decided to involve myself in your case when I heard that you had applied to join this pro-gramme. You have not made the most auspicious start, have you?' Erich inclined his head. 'You understand that it will be my duty to punish you, no matter how much I may be in sym-pathy with your attitude. You struck a senior officer, and also countermanded his orders. If it was wartime I could have had you shot. Captain Winkler may be over-zealous, but techni-cally he is in the right, and will expect a maximum penalty. My job, however, is not to waste a good man over a silly argu-ment. In order to decide what I do with you I need to know a little more about you. I see that you are a graduate of the col-lege of art here in Vienna.'

'Yes sir. I specialised in art history.'

'Your thesis was on Dutch Art of the seventeenth century; good. So this is why you volunteered to work with the new SS Art Acquisition team?'

'Yes sir.' The general was running his finger down the sheet.

'It says here that your mother is an artist?' Erich nodded. Suddenly the general chuckled. 'Oh dear! "*Modern, degener-ate*" it says on your file. Would you say her art was "degener-ate", showing *Jewish or Negro* influences, perhaps?'

Erich's colour was mounting; he was, as always, torn between loyalty to his mother and his dark associations with her paintings. In his dreams Grandpa Veit, though years dead now, looked out at him from her pictures. Erich continued to be tortured with doubt about Mr Solomons and his influence on Mother. Were the catalogues and books he brought for her intended to corrupt her or were they to draw her into his arms?

'I'm afraid she *was* infected, sir. I don't like her work.'

'Well, never mind. Perhaps you will learn. And the Jewish

thing?' Erich gulped; he found these changes of direction confusing.

'If, as they say, there really is a conspiracy to establish a "Jewish Republic in Europe", to overwhelm the Aryan nations, then of course something has to be done. We need a solution. The British have supported the idea of a Jewish homeland in Palestine. We need somewhere for them to go.'

'But you don't approve of seeing old Jews scrubbing the streets, and a violinist having his fingers stamped on?'

'Of course not, that just degrades us.'

'How about acquiring their art?'

Erich winced. Ever since his visit to the Abrahams', he had been struggling with this. 'The Jews are bleeding our country of its wealth, sir. Art should not belong to individuals but to all the people. This is the idea behind the Führermuseum, isn't it? That's why I volunteered to work on the selection of suitable pictures for it. It's for the common good. Owners should, of course, be compensated,' he added lamely. His scalp was prickling, as it did whenever he was unsure about what he was saying.

'So you would be offended if people started taking these works of art for profit, or for their private collections?'

'Yes, sir, of course! I would be horrified. Who would do such a thing?'

'You'd be surprised, Lieutenant … very surprised. But we will come back to that.'

'Now, tell me a little about your ascent of the Adlerwand?'

This time the change of direction was welcome. Erich began his usual three-minute account of the climb, but the General was having none of it.

'You say it took you three days – so that means you had to carry food and water and something to sleep under?' So Erich had to give him a detailed account of their diet and their equipment. 'Did you have these new ice claws for your feet?'

'Crampons,' Erich confirmed. 'Yes, sir.' This was like being back on the Adlerwand, with a new companion on the rope. He began to relax, but again was brought to with a jolt.

'When did you become a Nazi?'

'Well, I've never actually joined the Party, sir. I was, well, swept in after the climb, as a sort of mascot.' Erich spread his hands. 'They wanted to make the climb a *German Conquest*. Before I knew what had happened I had a swastika pinned on me and a glowing career in the SS promised if I applied to join. It all sort of … happened.'

'So that uniform you are wearing, for example, does it mean *everything* to you or …?'

Erich supposed he should say 'yes' but he'd got the feeling that the general wasn't looking for easy answers. The eyes under the bristling eyebrows were as demanding as ever; he took a deep breath. 'To be honest, General, I'd feel more comfortable in my climbing gear.'

'Yes. I thought you would. For my part I would more comfortable in the grey of the Wehrmacht uniform. My career has been in the regular army, you see, but I didn't feel the SS should be left just to you young people.' The general looked at his watch. 'Time flies. So, what are we going to do about you?' He looked at Erich quizzically, then appeared to make up his mind.

'Let me explain. As I understood my orders, I was to have sole responsibility for seeing that works of art of all kinds were acquired, catalogued and stored in safety for the Führermuseum. Whether we agree with it or not, the great Jewish collections are going to be forfeit. My mission was to rescue their art so it is not dispersed or destroyed. My main reason for joining the SS was the promise that I would be responsible for this task. Now, however, the Führer has decided to create a new civilian

Art Administration Organisation to do the listing and cataloguing. The SS will have no jurisdiction over this organisation.'

'Surely there aren't so many Jews with art collections in Austria, that we need two organisations, sir?'

'It is not for me to read the Führer's mind, but I think Germany's search for living space, *Lebensraum,* is not going to stop with Austria. I think war is inevitable. If this happens, there will be a huge influx of items for the Führermuseum. Whatever occurs, I want to be sure that all these items end up in the museum, and not lining other people's pockets. I already detect signs of a feeding frenzy developing among our own people. People who have never shown the slightest interest in art are looking to grab what they can for their own private collections, and worse, to sell them for profit to the highest bidder.' The general's voice had risen. 'Now that we are to have two organisations I find myself with responsibility but no control!' He leaned back, narrowing his eyes. 'So ... I am looking for an agent, someone of integrity to penetrate this new Art Administration Organisation and to report directly to me on all illegal appropriations by anyone, and I mean anyone, from the Führer down. I may not be able to do anything to stop items being taken in the short term, but my ultimate aim is to see that every single item that is acquired ends up in the Führermuseum.'

He leaned forward. 'I'm used to judging men, Lieutenant, and making decisions. You have the qualifications, and I think you have the integrity. Think before you answer. But it will be marginally better than peeling potatoes in some remote SS barracks!'

Erich was flattered and a little nervous. 'But ... but Captain Winkler's complaint? And what could I do?'

'As for Captain Winkler, he will be delighted at having had you thrown out of the SS, at least until he finds that he has been posted to some obscure outpost in the Black Forest. When it is safe, you will re-emerge as a civilian looking for a job as an expert in the Art Administration Organisation. There you will make yourself a trusted member of staff and use your skills as you know best. You will, however, have one additional very secret duty. You will observe and report personally to me on every illegal appropriation and every theft that comes to your attention.'

Erich was thrilled. In the six months since he had driven in triumph into Vienna, he had lost all interest in his uniform and in his duties as an SS officer. The thought of being able to throw all this off and get back to his beloved pictures was like being offered his dearest dream, but there was something that bothered him.

'Wouldn't that really be work for the Gestapo to do, sir?' He shivered; everyone hated and feared the secret police.

'Yes, it is indeed their work. Because of this it would make a lot of sense for you to join the Gestapo; they will train you, help you with what you need by way of codes and communications and will protect you if you are discovered. However, you will still report to me and to no one else. You might end up with two salaries: one from the Gestapo, and one from the Art Administration Organisation!' Erich realised by now that he had little choice but to accept the general's offer. Perhaps rumours of the Gestapo were exaggerated. Anyway, as General von Brugen had said, it would be better than peeling potatoes.

Thanks, no doubt to von Brugen, there were no announcements or ceremonies. Erich simply handed in his uniform and insignia and walked out of the SS barracks in a civilian suit and made it known in his old art circles that he was in the market for a job. On the agreed day, a week or two later, he met General von Brugen 'by accident' in a side chapel in St Stephan's Dom Cathedral. Here, kneeling side by side, Erich was given and memorised a password that even the Gestapo would know nothing about.

'By the way, Erich, what is the name of your violinist, the Jew?'

Erich had avoided mentioning this before now. He told the general.

'I'll keep it in mind,' was all von Brugen said as he dusted off his knees.

Later that same evening, for the first time since the day he had appropriated it, Erich thought about the portrait that still stood wrapped up in a corner of his room. It hadn't occurred to him to mention it at his trial or even to the general. Perhaps he was better at keeping secrets than he realised. He would hold on to it for the moment. He could probably use it as an entrée to the Art Administration Organisation when he applied. In the meantime, he thought he would be nice to take it out and see if it was as good as he remembered.

CHAPTER 20

Limbo Years:
1939 – 1942

Louise hardly noticed her own gradual drift into timelessness. To begin with she had felt Izaac calling her, as ever, through his music. She would awake feeling tired but stimulated, and would guess that Izaac had been drawing on her to work on some new piece or programme. If, however, she tried to recall what it was, it would fade like a dream. She wasn't aware when the Nazi unwrapped her portrait and began his critical examination of it.

Erich, however, was looking forward to the moment when he would hand the picture over to the Führer museum. Possibly it would be hailed as the greatest art discovery of the century. But, somehow, there never seemed to be a right moment to reveal it. Also, the more he saw of senior officers of the Reich squabbling over pictures they didn't appreciate or understand, the less inclined he felt to risk it falling into their hands.

⌒≈

Over the next months, as the Nazi race laws became more and more restrictive, Izaac's performing career collapsed, and so did his playing. He felt debased by the yellow Star of David that all Jews were now forced to sew on their clothes. Even to go out on the streets was taking a risk. Normal life as he knew it ceased.

A year in this limbo had passed when Nathan appeared at the door of Izaac's apartment. His face was contorted with anxiety.

'Izaac! They arrested Father last night, and came for Mother in a lorry this morning. They said he was a criminal for tuning an Aryan piano. I've been to every office in town and can't find where they have taken him!'

Izaac joined in the frantic search for information until he was threatened with arrest himself. That was how Uncle Rudi went. Just like that. The head of the family gone, probably to a concentration camp! Izaac had to lie to Mother; she relied on Rudi, more even than on Izaac's father. Just to create an atmosphere of normality, he continued to practise, but he no longer had the will to play.

Having lost its leader, The Tuning Fork Quartet was soon to lose its viola player. Nathan and Krystal, together with their two children: Rachel, eleven, and Herbert, nine, were ordered to assemble in the *Juden Platz*. As Izaac walked with them he remembered how Rachel – the baby then – had been with them on their wonderful holiday in Mödling. He took her hand and pointed out the *Drei Mädel Haus*, where Schubert used to come and play to the three sisters who lived there. At the *Freyung* he had to show his papers and was turned back. Nathan promised to try to keep in touch. They would, of course, meet up again later. They were just being evacuated to … that was the trouble; the Nazis never said anything more specific than *'The East'*.

Izaac wasn't overly worried about Nathan and his family. The sort of camps they were being sent to were nothing new. Ever since the First World War there had been camps designed to house displaced people. It had been a humanitarian move.

There were rumours circulating that the Nazi camps were pretty rough, but then so were the ghettos that many Jewish people still lived in, even in Vienna. In some ways, Izaac wished he had been evacuated too. The waiting, the uncertainty, not being able to play, was wearing him down.

In February 1942 all that ended.

CHAPTER 21

Arbeit Macht Frei

'This can't be our train, Otto. These are just cattle trucks. I'm sure you have the wrong platform.' The high querulous voice ended in a nervous laugh. Izaac looked at the fur-clad lady who had spoken. Didn't she know that they were using cattle trucks to transport Jews?

He turned away, shifting his position on the platform to take a last longing look through the barrier to where Lotte, grey haired now, was waiting to see him off. 'I'm like a boy going to school for the first time,' he thought. They had had to sit separately on the tram as it clanged around the Ring to the Apsang station. By now he was resigned to the yellow Star of David on his arm, and having to travel in the *Jews Only* section of the tram.

Restriction had followed restriction, and when the Nazis had finally forbidden Jews to take part in any public performances he had formed a quartet, so that he could keep playing and try, as best he could, to keep the now everyday horrors of the streets from his mind. Madame Helena had always said he would never be a good quartet player, as he would bully the others, but it had worked out fine. She had gone back to Poland after Hitler walked into Austria; he wondered how she was now that Germany had invaded Poland.

He wondered too if he would find Uncle Rudi, or Nathan and his young family at the end of this journey. Perhaps they had already been resettled in the east. Lotte had seen him and was waving. Dear Lotte, she had promised to look after his parents until they could come and join him. His mother was very fragile now, and Izaac wasn't sure that she fully understood what was happening any more. It had been an easy task to convince her that they would only be separated for a short time. The SS would surely not transport them, he thought; they were old, they couldn't work, and couldn't breed, so what danger were they to the Aryan race? Lotte was signalling to him, drawing his attention to someone beside her; he raised an arm to wave, and then froze, seeing an unmistakable splash of gold. It was Gretchen!

A flood of emotions swept over Izaac. Two years ago Gretchen had married one of Izaac's dearest friends from the Opera Orchestra, Willie Henning. Izaac had been at their wedding. Ever since, as humiliation after humiliation had been piled on Vienna's Jews, Izaac had breathed sighs of relief that she, at least, was free of all this. He had so nearly proposed to her, and she might well have accepted. What a catastrophe that would have been for her! He visited the couple discreetly and delighted in their happiness. Then a little over a year ago, he had been at the christening of their little boy, Konrad, who Gretchen was now holding aloft so he could wave to 'Uncle Izaac'; he could see her mouthing the words. It was almost more than he could bear; she shouldn't be here, it was dangerous. He waved, and even as he did so, he saw a man in a trench coat come up to them – Gestapo surely – and turn them away.

'Stand back! Stand back!' SS men were walking down the platform, unbolting the doors of the cattle trucks. 'Leave your cases on the platform, and get in.' *One piece of luggage only* the transportation order had said and then came a long list of forbidden items, including *No musical instruments*. So, biting his lip with anger, Izaac had abandoned his violin case, rolled his precious instrument in shirts, and placed it in the very middle of the suitcase – it was an outside chance that he would ever see it again.

'Get in!' Nobody moved; it was as if the people on the platform still didn't really believe that the cattle trucks were for them. There were more shouts from the guards. Then Izaac heard screams and the sound of someone being beaten. This was SS 'encouragement'! Izaac took the hint. Whatever about the people here, Gretchen and little Konrad mustn't hear this screaming. He grabbed the hand of the lady who had been complaining about the transport, and heaved her, protesting, into the cattle truck. Her thick fur coat felt soft and luxurious on his hand. He bent to the task of helping people clamber up, knowing full well that he was just postponing the moment when he would have to follow them. He got no thanks for his trouble but the butt of an SS rifle in his back, as hands reached down to pull him in too. The door was slammed behind him and the bolts were shot. There was hardly room for him to stand. The shocked silence was broken only by the mounting wails of the woman in the fur coat. Then they were off.

As time went by, the cold became intense. Sometimes the train stopped for long periods and with no explanation. Izaac got the impression that it only moved when the track was free of more important traffic. Rest was impossible. They took it in turns to sit, propped against the sides of the truck, but there the icy wind sliced through the cracks like knives. It was better to stand and doze in the comparative warmth of the huddle, until one's legs began to buckle. Whatever Izaac had anticipated about transportation, he hadn't realised how excruciatingly uncomfortable and degrading it would be. From the voices and clothes of the people around him, these were well off, cultured Jews like himself who would hardly have used a public toilet, let alone a bucket within view of a hundred other people.

Morning was dragging itself into being, and Izaac was taking his turn sitting with his back to the door watching the tracks through a crack in the floor. The rhythmic click of the wheels was hypnotic, like a metronome. Terra tack, terra tack, terra tack went the wheels, and he found himself whistling one of the pieces his quartet had been practising before he got his transportation order.

'I bet you don't know the name of that tune,' said a voice beside him.

'Oh, but I do,' Izaac smiled, surprised; 'it's Beethoven's Razumovsky Quartet No. 1.'

The man reached across and shook his hand. 'My name is Julius Kohn, cello with the Kohn Quartet. I thought I recognised you – Izaac Abrahams, isn't it? Let's start at the beginning, but a little higher if you please.'

Izaac started whistling again; to his delight his new friend came in, whistling not just the cello part, but the viola and second violin wherever appropriate. The whole atmosphere in the carriage eased. There were murmurs of appreciation when they reached the end, even a clap or two. Outwardly they were frozen but had an inner warmth now; they kept close when they stood up.

'I'm terrified that they will confiscate my violin; it's in my case. What a shame you couldn't bring your cello,' Izaac commiserated.

Julius chuckled and leaned close to Izaac and whispered in his ear:

'Oh but I have!'

'Did they let you bring it?'

'No. I have a friend who is an instrument maker. He dissolved the glue for me and helped me take it apart. It's in my bag now, in bits. I even have clamps and glue to re-assemble it, though God knows if I will succeed. Apparently half the Czech Academy of Music are in Terezín, the camp we are being sent to.'

'You know something about this camp, then?' Izaac asked.

'Probably no more than you have heard yourself. That it's a Jewish-run ghetto, somewhere near Prague in Czechoslovakia. They are inviting musicians and intellectuals to come and work there.'

The train was slowing and they heard voices outside. The door was drawn back a foot or so. '*Brot!*' Five loaves of dark heavy bread were thrust in through the opening. '*Wasser!*' A bucket of water was passed in, no cup or anything to drink it with. '*Scheiße!*' The stinking toilet bucket was passed out to someone in the striped suit of a prisoner, and an empty one passed in; the door slammed. Inside the cattle truck, a man who Julius identified as a professor began organising the distribution of food.

There were fifty people in the truck, so a tenth of a loaf seemed very small. Someone had produced a cup and a shuffling queue snaked about the carriage for an allowance of one mouthful of water each; the movement was welcome too. 'I can't eat this,' the fur-clad lady exclaimed in disgust. 'I will complain!' That caused a few wry smiles. When an aggrieved voice said, 'To think I paid five hundred shillings for first class!' everyone, including the complainer laughed; the train jerked forward, upsetting the now empty water bucket. For some reason they found this cheering. At least they hadn't lost their water ration. One score for them.

It was evening before the train pulled into a country station and they were forced out to stand in a line, ready for a two-kilometre march to the camp. Rumours had been circulating about Terezín. One man explained that the camp was like a holiday spa, and that he had paid in advance for special accommodation. Izaac eyed the iron-faced SS guards marching on each side of them, rifles at the ready, and wondered what was really in store. Julius leaned towards him.

'Have you noticed; these guards have skull and cross-bones badges on their caps?'

'The "Death's Head squads". I've heard of them.'

When the tired column turned off the road they crossed a bridge and arrived at an arched entrance leading into what appeared to be a vast fortress. Vertical sided moats stretched out on either side. The words *'ARBEIT MACHT FREI'* curved over the gateway.

'So, work will free us!' murmured Julius. He looked along the moat. 'They certainly plan to keep us here.'

At that the gates swung open and the file shuffled forward. They found themselves in a small town with streets laid out on a symmetrical grid. Izaac's immediate impression was of an anthill, order and chaos. A squad of boys who had been sweeping the road, stood back to let a line of workers in the striped pyjama suits of prisoners march by on their way to the gate. Izaac noticed that, unlike them, they weren't flanked by guards until they reached the gates, where their SS guards were waiting for them. A long line of people stood patiently clutching tin plates and spoons. Steam billowed from a food kitchen and there was a strong smell of cabbage. Izaac wrinkled his nose and thought longingly of coffee and a crisp roll. Despite the bustle, listless groups of people moved aimlessly, their eyes unfocused as if unable to take in what was happening around them. No one paid much attention to the new arrivals.

The accommodation seemed to be made up of high brick barracks. Through an open door they glimpsed tiers of wooden bunks, some occupied. An arm hung listlessly from a top bunk. Outside the door of the barracks an old man and an old woman were squabbling over a potato that had fallen on the ground.

'I can't sleep in there!' the fur-clad lady was almost hysterical. She turned away in disgust only to stifle a scream. A handcart was being pushed past her towards the gate. A tarpaulin revealed the unmistakable outline of a human body.

It was too much to take in all at once. Whatever Terezín was, Izaac thought, it was no 'holiday spa'. Then suddenly, out of the misery and horror of this place came the sound of someone playing a flute. It was like a shaft from heaven. He gripped Julius's arm. They stopped short, causing the people behind to pile into them. The SS guard nearest them shouted, unslung his rifle and worked the bolt as if he meant to use it. They hurried on, took a left turn, and stopped in front of a once fine administrative building. The guards began to sort them into two parallel lines.

'Let's stay together,' Julius said, slipping in behind Izaac as the line began to inch forward. Just inside the entrance to the building there were two desks, one on each side. A girl looked up. She had a pile of pre-numbered cards, which she was filling in for each arrival. 'Name and forename?' Izaac told her. 'Occupation?'

'Musician.' She looked up, suddenly interested.

'Not *the* Izaac Abrahams, the violinist?' He nodded. She dropped her eyes as an SS man passed. 'I'm not supposed to talk; lean close.' She pretended to sort her cards. 'Have you a violin in your case?'

'If it hasn't been lost or stolen, yes.'

'Don't worry; it will be safe until they've had a chance to loot it. We're desperately short of instruments. Listen, there is an SS officer second from the left. You'll recognise him; he looks mean, he is mean – and he shouts at everyone. Find your case and get into his queue; it is always short. Tell him, "The statues still stand on Charles's Bridge" – he's a Czech from Prague – then put your head down and hope for the best.'

'So we have an honest SS man?'

'Don't be stupid! A well paid crook.'

Izaac went over to where prisoners in striped uniforms were helping the transportees to find their cases. Julius caught up with him.

'The girl at the desk told me to talk to you. I'm sure she's a viola player with the Philharmonic.'

'Yes. Apparently what we've got to do is this … ' Suddenly there was a commotion. An SS man, one of the searchers, was leaning over his desk, screaming like a maniac, trying to tear the fur coat off the woman from the train. She, foolishly, was resisting, struggling to hold onto her precious fur.

'Bloody Jewish whore!' A crack of his fist on her jaw and the woman slumped to the floor. There was a gasp from the new arrivals, but they all stood rooted. Only the woman's husband dared move, darting forward like someone coming within range of a chained dog, before drawing her back to safety. The SS man threw the coat into the tea chest behind him, and called for the next person. As the people shuffled forward apprehensively, Izaac began to question the girl's advice. Was this really the SS man he was to go to if he wanted to hold onto his violin?

Julius was obviously thinking the same. 'Can we trust him?' he asked.

'We have to, don't we?' Izaac went first, delivering his incongruous message as he leaned forward to undo the straps on his case.

'*Halt's Maul*, Shut up! Stop talking and stand back!' An open hand on his chest sent Izaac staggering back. All he could do now was watch helplessly as the man, muttering expletives, plunged his hands into his suitcase, apparently exploring every inch. The man stiffened. What if he and the girl at the door were in cahoots? He couldn't have missed the violin, but what else could he have found? As if pulling a rabbit from a hat, he held up Izaac's alarm clock for all to see: '*Verboten! Streng verboten!* he yelled. Then he turned and hurled it non-chalantly into his tea chest, where it landed with a soft thud on the fur coat. '*Raus!* Get out!' Izaac was fumbling nervously with his straps; '*Raus!*

Half an hour later, Izaac and Julius met up in a dormitory for new arrivals and compared the shaking of their hands. After the inspection they had been given a bowl of revolting soup, which they used to soften the single slice of black bread that appeared to be their ration. As nothing else seemed to be required of them, they lay down to get some sleep on the thin, straw-filled mattresses that bore the stains of many previous occupants. Exhaustion overcame squalor and sleep came quickly, almost as quickly in fact as the bed bugs that climbed out of the cracks in the bunks for their nightly feast.

⌁⌁⌁⌁⌁

'Psst … I'm Pafko!' It was early morning. Izaac opened his eyes to find a boy's face within inches of his own. 'You're Izaac Abrahams?' Izaac blinked and nodded. The boy glanced right and left. 'I'm not supposed to be in here, so I'll make this quick. I've been told to make sure you don't get put on a trans-port, or sent to work in the factory; else we might never see you again. Where's Herr Kohn?'

'That's him in the bunk above, but who sent you?'

'The Administration for Free Time Activities. I'm a musician. I sing in a choir,' the boy added grandly. Izaac smiled, but the boy was in a hurry. 'Listen, sir. First thing this morning, you'll get your number, a tattoo on your arm.' He pulled up his sleeve to display a not very clean arm with a blue number on it. Then the SS will hand you over to the Jewish Administration for your ration card and to be assigned to a work squad. You *must* get work in the town, not in the factory. The factory workers are the ones in the striped suits because they go outside to work. Go to Ondrej. He has a long drooping moustache, and he loves music; tell him you hope to work for the AFTA and he will give you a squad in the town.' There was a sound of someone blowing into a microphone, testing the loudspeaker. The boy stiffened. 'Got to go. That'll be the morning call. Tell Herr Kohn about Ondrej. Look for me outside.'

'*Raus! Raus! Schnell raus!*' but the boy had gone, in a patter of bare feet.

⚜

Izaac's ordeal was over. The freshly tattooed number on his arm felt no worse than the bed-bug bites that seemed to cover him all over. He stood scratching, guarding Julius's case with its precious dismantled cello, as his friend manoeuvred himself into the queue where the moustachioed Ondrej held court. When Julius came over, Izaac took up both cases, feeling that the sooner he got out of this building the better. They stopped at the bottom of the steps where Julius looked at the piece of paper Ondrej had given him.

'I wonder what this means?' he asked. '*EIII/6/10/107?*'

'Let me see.' Izaac looked down and there was the boy, Pafko, grinning up at him. The boy put down a bucket he was holding and held out his hands for their slips of paper.

Izaac laughed. 'I'd better introduce you. Julius, this is Pafko, messenger and go-between supreme. You were asleep when he came and told me about Ondrej.'

Pafko was busy examining their papers.

'Good old Ondrej, you're together. Block 3/ building 6/ room 10/ bunks 107 & 108. The good thing is that this block is just full of AFTA players. Come on, let's go.'

'Who sent to you look after us?' Izaac asked.

'Anna, who you met at the door yesterday, gave your numbers to Maria Thron who will be the head of AFTA when the Nazis agree. She sent me to find you to make sure you weren't sent off to make engines in the factory. I'm her *personal messenger*,' he took off his floppy cap and bowed. 'You see, the camp is segregated: men and boys on one side, women and kids under twelve on the other. Though I look older, I'm still eleven, so I can go both sides if I'm careful. The thing is to look busy.'

'How do you manage that?' Izaac asked.

'I carry a bucket,' Pafko grinned. 'Sometimes I put a brick in it. People think I must be doing some chore and so don't bother me.' They crossed a square outined with bare and tired trees. 'We call that building where you've just been the "Sluice"– open it and they pour in. More people come every day; Mrs Thron says the town was built for six thousand soldiers, guess how many people are here now? Fifty eight thousand!' The flow of camp information continued: 'That there's the boy's barracks, I'll be in there when I turn twelve. I'm with my mum and sisters on the women's side now.'

'Where do the musicians play?' Izaac asked.

'Anywhere for folk songs and things and solo instruments, then there is a hall in the Sudeten barracks; real concerts there, violins, flute, accordion, but no cello,' he winked at Julius. Did the boy know everything, Izaac wondered. ' … and no piano. AFTA are desperate for a piano. We have just one piano accordion for recitals, choir practice … everything! I found them a piano but it has no legs and it's in the part of the town where the Germans and their families live. The wimps won't go and get it.'

They had arrived at their destination. 'Here's your barracks, EIII/6.' Pafko announced.

⚊⚊⚊

Izaac sat drinking acorn coffee with Jacob Edelstein, head of the Council of Elders. This was an honour. To begin with, Izaac had been jealous of the almost normal apartment with proper furnishings and rugs on the floor. Now he was realising that these luxuries had their price.

'Izaac, when I agreed to run this ghetto for the Nazis, I just wanted to make it a refuge for our Czech Jews, to make life tolerable for them here in Bohemia until the war is over. We can wear our own clothes inside the ghetto, we largely police ourselves. Even when numbers rose to nearly sixty thousand, I thought, at least these people were safe in my care. Then last month I was ordered to select one thousand people for a transport out "further east", that was all I was told.'

'Why, what do they want them for?' Izaac asked.

'Dear knows. Labour in factories, perhaps. They talk about "re-settlement"… who knows the Nazi mind? But it was *I* who had to make the list, or to risk having to them do it for me.' He sighed. 'I kept the children where possible, I tried not to break up families, even so … ' His voice trailed away, lost in the loneliness of his position. 'All I can do, Izaac, is make life tolerable for those that remain. There are two classes of essential workers here: workers who keep our bodies together, and workers who feed our minds and our souls. They are equally important. I can't feed ten thousand properly on the food they give me, so I must feed the soul. This is where you and other 'essential workers' in the Administration of Spare Time Activities come in. Through your music you can liberate us, if only for an hour or two. We can leave this dreadful place in our imaginations, if not in reality. I need you for this work and will protect you if I can, but if the Nazis say that 'Herr Abrahams' must go on the next transport, I can do nothing but put you on the list. So, bring our people a little joy, who knows about the future. Now, I must go back to requisitioning: potatoes, cabbages and rotten meat.'

Talking to Jacob Edelstein opened Izaac's eyes to the way the camp was organised. Up until now he had been, like all newcomers, preoccupied with his own affairs: where to go for a meal ticket, which of the cooks was generous with what little meat there was in the inevitable soup, what toilets worked, where to get water to wash, and how to kill bedbugs. Now he started to look about him. His barrack was crowded, but at least they weren't two or even three to a bed as they were in the dormitories of the less privileged.

Driven by curiousity, he had visited one and been revolted by the stench of sickness, dirty bodies and incontinence that hung over the barracks. He climbed into the loft and found people lying and dying in total darkness. These barracks provided the gruesome daily fodder for the dead cart. It took him several days to rid himself of the fleas and bugs he had picked up on that visit and it brought home to him how priviliged he and the other musicians were. And it was only luck in their choice of profession that stood between them and the misfortunate others, he thought guiltily.

The Jewish Administration did their best to cope but it became impossible when more and more transports of dazed and miserable people continued to arrive. Little wonder that it was almost a relief to the administration when the Germans demanded a thousand for immediate transport to one of their other camps, where, hopefully, the people would find a better life.

Some people even longed to be listed for transport. 'Surely things will be better there,' they said. Others were apprehensive; at least here the camp was run by their own, not by the Germans. Rumours were rife of camps where people were worked till they died, slaving for the German war machine. Izaac would watch the pyjama-clad Terezín residents leaving to work in local factories, digging trenches or any other hard labour the Germans wanted. Inside the camp, women sewed uniforms or split great crystals of mica into paper-thin sheets for electrical circuits.

Within the more comfortable surroundings of Izaac's block, however, he found himself being greeted by a veritable who's-who of distinguished musicians from all over Europe, but there was little time for pleasantries. Izaac soon realised that there was a fierce work ethic in the ghetto. These musicians were here, not just to entertain, but to promote the cause of music as well. He would find groups huddled over plans for recitals, concerts, and plays. There were laments over the fact that there was so little printed music, and no ruled sheets on which to make copies. Musicians were writing whole scores from memory directly onto hand-ruled sheets of brown paper.

The lack of a piano was another great lament. When Izaac mentioned that Pafko said he had found a piano in the German part of the town there was immediate interest. Clearly, the Jewish authorities had vetoed Pafko's salvage plan as too dangerous; not so the musicians. Nobody ever revealed quite how it came to be there, but the miraculous appearance of an admittedly legless piano in the gymnasium of the boy's barracks was to become a turning point in music in the ghetto.

The great Victor Shek gave the first recital, a piano tuner in attendance to repair it between movements. As Mussorgsky's *Pictures at an Exhibition* marched on, the old urge to make music began to burn inside Izaac again. He thought of

Madame Helena, and felt ashamed. She she would never have given up as he had done. After the concert he heard two girls talking on the way out.

'You know, Greta, for one hour I haven't thought of hunger, or food tickets, or the black market, or passes to this or that. Tonight I will dream my own pictures and be a hundred miles away from here.'

Determined not to reveal how out of practise he was, Izaac made his way up into a loft at the very top of the block where he was housed. His hands were stiff and he felt as if he was starting from the very beginning again. He played the open strings: G, D, A, E, then again G ... D ... A ... E ... but so slowly that the sound turned to gravel under his bow. He was listening to the primordial sound of the violin again. Izaac let the horrible sound resonate inside him until he could bear it no longer. His bow moved faster; the gravel turned to sand, until finally pure sound emerged like a new shoot thrusting up through the soil.

Far far away, on the other side of Europe, Louise woke from her own hibernation. Izaac wanted her again and she would come. Day in, day out, Izaac played, clawing his way back, scale by scale, bow by bow, until he felt able to play with the cream of Europe's performers in the camp. He could feel Louise's presence, laughing, bullying, chiding, coaxing him as he played. He kept feeling that he only had to turn to see her there. But she must never see inside the camp. So he closed his mind to her image and kept it on his music; she must never see his emaciated face and this terrible place. And so they continued to share his music as they always had. In case she should pick up on his gloomy thoughts, he tried to concentrate on the few nice things about camp life: the cabaret about the lost food card, the children singing, and the swallows that swooped, chattering, about the square. In return he found, not only that he felt better, but that this began to show in his music. His audiences smiled more. So with Louise's help, in this way he plunged into the music of the camp, his repertoire increasing by the day: Vivaldi, Bach, Mozart, Tartini, Dvorak, Leclair, Franck, Paganini, Smetna …

Often the only musical score he had to go on was the one he carried in his head. Hours were spent ruling blank paper with lines to make music manuscript and then transcribing the notes from the one copy that someone had managed to smuggle into the camp. Izaac found himself leading orchestras for symphonies, musicals and operas. He played solo, and he played to the accompaniment of the legless piano. He would remember Gretchen then, and he would think of the little boy she had held aloft: the son that could have been his. Practising, rehearsing, performing and teaching were their work. There was something frenetic about their lives, as if every moment had to be consumed.

One day Julius joined him in the attic, carrying his reconstructed cello. They worked for a bit before Julius said, 'Izaac, where are they all going?'

'Who?'

'There was another transport out this morning. One thousand people crammed into cattle trucks. Two of my pupils were listed. They're too young to do useful work, so what are they wanted for? I sometimes think I'm playing my cello just in order not to think.'

'I think that's what we are all doing, Julius. But how would thinking help those who are going? While they're here we can do something for them; our playing makes life that bit more tolerable. At least, I hope it does; otherwise it is all for nothing. And I couldn't bear to think that.'

Julius went with the next transport, one name on a list of a thousand. Izaac realised that even the privileged few were not immune to the Nazi whim. His cello, however, went on being played for as long as music was played in Terezín.

CHAPTER 22

Jeu de Paume, Paris

'Erich, my old pal, tracked you down at last!' Erich looked up in amazement; the doors of the gallery had long been closed for the night and he had thought he was alone.

'Good heavens, Klaus Steinman! I haven't seen you in years!' He struggled to get up. Klaus looked formidable in his SS uniform. Erich began to raise his arm.

'Put that arm down, Erich, you were never any good at the Heil Hitler thing. Come on; give an old comrade a hug.' Erich hastened round his desk and they pounded on each other's backs for a moment.

'So, what is this place?' Klaus asked looking around.

Erich glanced nervously towards the safe in which he kept his codebook and spying materials; Every week he sent a secret message to General von Brugen about the dishonest dealings of certain senior Nazi officers. The door to the safe was open, but, after all, Klaus was an old friend, and what interest would he have in the safe anyway?

'It's the Jeu de Paume. Once the French King's indoor tennis court, I believe; now it's a picture gallery. This is where we collect all the art that has been acquired from the great Jewish collections; we sort out the best for the *Führermuseum*.' There were paintings everywhere, hanging from the rails, five deep, and stacked against the walls. 'I have a room here, it's free, I can work late, and can avoid the curfew. But sit down, Klaus, just move those books.' Erich was genuinely pleased to see his old friend. 'So, how long has it been?'

'Four years ago, give or take – *Kristallnacht*, 1938. And here you are, surrounded by your art, where you should have been all the time.' He chuckled. 'Perhaps the SS was not for you. I heard about your brush with Captain Winkler. Dear old Erich, you were no better at baiting Jews than you were at saluting.' Erich blushed deeply.

'I'm sorry, Klaus … I feel I let you down, especially after you got me a place in the SS. So you've come across Captain Winkler?' He was feeling his way; perhaps Klaus and Winkler were friends.

'Oh don't worry about Winkler, he was posted out east, ended up in my division; he's found his level. He's as happy as a pig in muck!'

'So it's tough on the eastern front? Where exactly are you fighting now?

'Would that it was fighting. No, it's an administrative job, trying to put in place the Führer's final solution for the old problem of the Jews. A matter of finding food, and work and – how shall I put it – a suitable future for them. The concentration camps get a bad press, but the Jews have been living in ghettos since forever. It's home from home for them. I've visited one in Czechoslovakia that's like a bloody holiday camp compared to … well, never mind. Anyway, half the Jewish musicians of Europe are in there, sawing away to their heart's content. Your friend Mr Izaac Abrahams is there, I saw his name on one of their handwritten concert bills. Now that the Jews are out of the way, our own German talent can make it onto the concert platforms. We'll show them!'

'And this *final solution*?'

'The code word is "evacuation". It's really just an innovative way of creating *Lebensraum* for our Aryan peoples. It's tough enough work though.' Then Klaus laughed. 'But that's quite enough about me. Good old Erich, I always think of you as my double. It's nice to imagine you working away, living a blameless life here in the heart of Paris.' Klaus waved his arm at the profusion of pictures. 'So, what will you be doing with this lot?'

'I'm separating the art wanted for the *Führermuseum* from degenerate art: the Picassos, van Goghs, Renoirs etc, which will be sold to buy finer works.'

'And that, on the table?'

'That's *Christ in the House of Mary and Martha* by Vermeer. Like it?

'Not very much.'

'That proves that you have better taste than Reichsmarschall Göring, and are more honest than most experts. If you were Göring you would see money, and the prestige of owning a Vermeer. If you were an art expert you would be lying through your teeth to prove it's genuine.'

'And it's not?'

'A Vermeer in which the figures look dead? No it's a fake, but I am junior to Göring's experts. It'll go off to his country house next time he brings his private train to Paris.' Erich would have gone on, but he realised that Klaus's mind had wandered; he was looking at his watch.

'I feel like a drink. There are some of our chaps meeting in a bar on the Rue Saint-Honoré; that's quite close isn't it? Come on, shake the dust off yourself, and join us.'

At this point Klaus turned as if to go, but in turning he found himself opposite the picture that hung on the wall facing Erich's desk.

'I don't believe it!' Klaus said under his breath. And, so quietly that only Louise heard, 'So this is where you are!'

Erich looked past him, and his heart nearly missed a beat. What Klaus should have been looking at was the usual

government issue portrait of the Führer. Instead he was looking at *The Girl in the Green Dress*.

Some time ago, frightened that some expert – and there
were plenty working in the gallery – would spot Louise's portrait and ask awkward questions, Erich had mounted a copy of
the standard Führer portrait on its back. In the evenings, as
now, when he knew he would be on his own, he would turn
the picture, frame and all, so that Louise's portrait faced out.
Then he would lose himself for a few precious moments in the
tranquillity of the Dutch interior. As he worked he would talk
to the girl in the green dress, Louise her name was, telling her
the news, and speaking about his work, even his secret work.
She was company and there was no one else he could unbur-
den himself to. Without his realising it, he was becoming
addicted to her presence. Tonight he had had no time to turn
the picture back, but after all, it was Klaus who had first told
him about the picture; he had a right to admire it.

'Well, well, well! So this is where she ended up, eh? I often
wondered what became of Abrahams's painting after I sent
you to pick it up. Must have taken you by surprise when you
realised who he was?' Klaus laughed; he had obviously
enjoyed the trick he had played on Erich. 'I hope you weren't
too cross with me, old chap. After all, I did have a score to
settle with you over that time in the woods.'

'So you knew who you were sending me to when you told
me about the picture. Why didn't you tell me?' Erich
demanded.

'Because if I had told you, you would have gone soft-
centred, as you did when my scouts had him cornered in the
Wienerwald, and said that because he was a "prodigy" he was
excused his race. And I was right, because you then com-
pounded the folly by going back to rescue the creep from the
mob, and ruined your chances in the SS.'

Klaus was still examining the picture, and something in his attitude to it made Erich feel uncomfortable. He got up and turned the painting to the wall. When Klaus saw what was on the other side, he laughed uproariously.

'Our Führer – a decoy! So you are keeping the young lady for yourself, is that it, Erich?'

'Of course not. I'm doing research on the origins of the painting. It's unsigned and I need time to check its provenance.' Erich hoped he sounded convincing. It was true, wasn't it? Then a thought struck him. 'How did you know that Abrahams had this picture in the first place?'

'Ah, did you ever meet my half-sister Gretchen? Probably not – she tends to avoid me – I can't think why.' Erich had a vague memory of a bouncy girl with a shock of fair hair; he'd thought she seemed rather nice, but Klaus was going on: 'She became rather good at the piano. Well, let me put it this way, I heard on the grapevine that she was developing a most inappropriate relationship with the man she accompanied, so I decided to investigate. In best Gestapo manner, I did a little recruiting, and got our maid to do some listening in for me.'

'You spied on your family?' Erich was shocked.

'Our party acknowledges that this is necessary when the purity of our race is at issue.' Klaus said primly. 'Well, one of the results of my little investigation was to find that the subject of my sister's affections was the owner of a very special picture. Gretchen told our mother that it was his inspiration, his muse, if you like. So, I thought, let's see how the Jew plays without his muse. And who better to get the picture than my old friend Erich?'

He glared at Erich suddenly. 'Damn it, man! You had the picture – why bother with the Jew?'

Erich tried to make light of it. 'Guilty conscience perhaps.'

'Jesus Christ, Erich. These pictures belong to *us*, understand!

Conscience is a luxury we give up when we take our oath!' For a moment Erich saw the face that had frightened him that night in the woods, then Klaus shook himself, as if throwing off his anger. 'Well, all water under the bridge now, eh? Come on, Erich, let's drink!'

'And don't forget to close your safe before you go.' Klaus peered inside. 'I see you still have your civilian passport.' He picked it up and flicked it open. 'Visas to everywhere, lucky man! They don't want people like me flitting the country.'

'We do some trading in neutral countries,' Erich said quickly. 'I have to be able to travel.'

The safe was a modest affair built into the wall with a simple three-ring combination; anyone could read the numbers while the door was open. Klaus closed it for Erich and spun the dial.

'Right then, Erich, Drink!'

For some months Louise had been rising from the depths of unconsciousness, drawn upwards by Erich's interest in her portrait. It was a gradual, even cautious awakening. When he had appropriated her picture she had recognised him as the boy who stood up for Izaac that time in the Wienerwald. She still resented having been taken from Izaac, but Erich talked with her naturally and this had given her confidence to listen, if not to respond, to what he had to say. In this way, she had become familiar with the gallery and his work there. Up to now, Erich had been meticulous about turning her picture to face the wall before anyone came into the room. Tonight he had been caught unaware and she was in full view.

As she listened to the suave tones of the newcomer, with his bonhomie and his *'Erich, my old pal,'* alarm bells began to ring. Where had she heard a voice like that ... Of course! The treacherous Count du Bois who had nearly destroyed both her and her portrait almost a hundred and fifty years ago. She listened in fear. Had she known Erich for longer she might have attempted a warning, but she had never tried to communicate with him before, and he wouldn't have understood anyway because what she was hearing from this apparent *friend* was a totally different story to the one he was telling to Erich. While he was teasing Erich about his salute, Louise could hear another voice mocking Erich's honest efforts to do the right thing. She was affronted: What sort of friend was this?

When the man talked about the Jewish 'solution' Louise was seeing through his mind a line of ragged people, men, women and children, their hands in the air, a machine gun trained on them. The officer in charge had his handkerchief raised to give the signal to fire. Before he dropped it he turned and winked. Louise broke her mind free before the handkerchief fell. If only Erich had turned her picture to the wall, but the voice, or the thoughts behind it, were too compelling to be ignored. Erich was rambling on happily about Vermeer, but Louise was seeing two chimneys belching black smoke, and bodies heaped like spillikins.

Perhaps she fainted because the next thing she knew was that he was facing her portrait. An evil emanated from him that made her shrink back. And something else … even while he was telling Erich how he had found out about Izaac and her picture, his real words were directed at her: 'I know a lot more about you than you think, young lady. More even than that poor sucker, Erich. You've cast a spell on him, too, haven't you? But Klaus Steinman is immune to your charms. I don't give a damn about art or about you. There is only one person I give a damn about and that is *me*. But that doesn't mean I won't take you, given half a chance. If you're worth half what I suspect, then you could be a nice little pension. And I might need a pension one of these days. So, remember me. I'll be back!'

The encounter with Klaus left Louise trembling and fearful. Then the hateful images that he had conjured up in her mind began to take over her thoughts and a new and violent energy stirred within her. This man had given her a glimpse of evil stronger than anything she had ever come across before. So this was the Nazi mind: a cesspit of real or imagined horrors. She had just one desire now, and that was to defeat him – and his kind – in any way she could. But she could do nothing on her own. She must recruit Erich as an ally; he was her only hope. She remembered how he had stood up to Klaus that night back in the woods above Mödling, saving Izaac from a beating, or worse. Also, according to what she had heard Klaus say, Erich had gone back to rescue Izaac from a mob in Vienna. And just now, when he had turned her picture to the wall, she had felt protected, defended even. But yet he had greeted Klaus as an old friend, and had gone out with him will-ingly enough.

At quiet times during the past months Louise would catch glimpses of another existence: a half-dream, half-real, world, where Izaac was calling on her to listen and to work with him on whatever pieces he had on hand. She would hear music, and occasionally get glimpses of drab audiences and strange places, but the minute she tried to grasp it, the vision would be gone, slipping away tantalisingly just beyond her reach. It was as if she was living in two parallel worlds with only the occa-sional dream-like glimpse to bridge the gap between them. The fact that Izaac was still making music should have been reassuring, but there was a desperate, almost frenetic feel to his playing. The snatches that she heard were superb, but why was she so often left with a nightmare taint, like a whiff of some dead thing passed on a country walk?

Recently, however, Izaac's playing had sounded more relaxed and the glimpses she was seeing were of pleasant things – a laughing audience, trees in a town square. Klaus had said that Izaac was in a holiday camp in Czechoslovakia. Despite her recent experience with Klaus, she allowed herself to be reassured.

Without any particular plan, she left her portrait, and for the first time began to explore her surroundings. At the centre of the room was a large square worktable piled with pictures, reference books, a huge lens for examining the paintings, and bottles containing various chemicals. It reminded her of the Master's studio in Delft. Ever since her capture, Erich had talked to her portrait, and she had heard about the progress of the war, and about the constant flow of art pouring into the Jeu de Paume from the great Jewish collections. Sometimes he would reminisce about his climbing and about a beautiful lake near the salt mines. He even told her of his clandestine spying into the activities of the senior Nazi art collectors. 'There will always be rotten apples, even in the purest of regimes!' he had said.

Louise halted in her prowling. Was that what he had said? Then, quite deliberately, she forced herself to listen again to Erich's voice. This time, as with Klaus, she heard another voice, hidden beneath Erich's self-righteous tones, a voice that said: 'What can you expect other than rotten apples in a rotten regime!' Louise's pulse was racing. She remembered how Gaston, the French hussar, had described his involvement in a 'glorious' engagement at the Pont de Chasse, which turned out not to have been a glorious battle at all, but a tragic encounter with a group of peasants armed with scythes! The more she thought about Erich's talk of the great *Führermuseum*, the more convinced she became that under this was a whispered voice of shame. Which was the real Erich? Could the lad who spoke up for Izaac above Mödling be the real Erich, the ally she needed? There was only one way to find out.

⟶∙𝕎𝕎∙⟵

Erich could never have contemplated an evening with an elite group of SS officers without Klaus's support. At the very least he could expect to be shunned. Most SS men would regard being dismissed from the force for rounding on a senior officer as a matter of shame. When he spotted a couple of colleagues from his training days he would have slipped away if Klaus hadn't stood up, drink in hand, and called order.

'Gentlemen, please! Let me introduce my good friend Erich Hoffman.' He put his arm over Erich's shoulder. If anybody says "Snap" I'll kill them.' There was laughter; they certainly did look alike. 'You've all heard of the climbing of the Adler-wand?' there was a murmur of interest, and heads turned. 'Well, young Erich here was not only on that first ascent, but he was first to the top. I filmed him myself as he broke through the... what do you call it ... the cornice, that's it. Let's drink to *"Erich and the conquest of the Adlerwand!"* Soon Erich had a small circle of officers about him, mostly from the Waffen SS, the fighting unit, who wanted a firsthand account of the climb. For a while then he felt part of the group, the old camaraderie sweeping him in. The friends from his training days came up, and they reminisced about old times.

'You were a star performer during training, Erich,' one of them commented. 'What's the civilian suit for?' He was evasive, and then felt ashamed. His oath had been to stand by these men, his comrades, to the death if needs be, and he had deserted them. What had he been doing over the last years while these men had been out there fighting for him? He missed the camaraderie they had shared in training, and when they began to talk among themselves of their fighting, and of the mad rush of their armies through freshly conquered territories, he regretted having talked about his own paltry climbing exploits. Since his training days these men had acquired a whole new vocabulary of words that meant nothing to him now, but had them nodding solemnly, or guffawing with laughter at some in joke.

Whenever the babble of voices dropped, there would be a call for a toast to anyone one from the Führer down, with 'bottoms up' to show that their glasses had been drained. As the evening wore on he became more and more conscious of the isolation of his work in the museum. He should be out there fighting with these men. Erich, now unsteady on his feet, wandered over to where Klaus and other officers of the Death's Head detachment were chatting and laughing. As he approached, he saw Klaus signal to the others to be careful of what they were saying. Erich would have gone away, but Klaus, as if to make amends, raised his glass.

'Here's to the Jeu de Paume and the Girl in Green!' Nobody knew or asked what he meant, but glasses were raised and the moment passed. Klaus, however, looked at Erich over his glass, and despite his smile, Erich knew that this toast was a challenge: *She's got you in her thrall hasn't she, Erich? Fancy, you – conqueror of the Adlerwand – losing your manhood to a girl in a picture!* With a shock Erich realised that Klaus was right; Louise had become part of his life. Tomorrow he would write to General von Brugen and explain to him that, with the dire state of the war, he would like to be relieved of his spying responsibilities so that he could volunteer for the Waffen SS, the fighting regiments of the SS.

When he arrived back in the Jeu de Paume he struggled to get his key into the keyhole, which, for some reason, seemed to be scuttling about the door like a mouse. At last he got to his room and stood braced against the doorjamb until the floor stopped tilting. Now he finished the SS song with which the company had ended their revels: '... *Diese gotverdammte Juden Republik!'* He began again: *'Blut blut–'*

'Don't you dare sing songs like that!' The voice came from *inside* the room. He let go of the doors and stepped in unsteadily, to be met by a vision in green. The girl, whoever she was, was berating him for being drunk, for singing Nazi songs ... His eyes were beginning to focus now. He recognised her now, of course! Who else, but the girl from his picture?

'Lou ... ise!' he said, having difficulty with the word. 'You look 'zactly how you look in your portrait.' He lurched forward and opened his arms, not quite sure of his intentions.

'Come to Erich.' The girl looked at him in disgust. Then, avoiding his grasp, she slipped behind his desk and headed for her portrait.

All evening Louise had been thinking about Erich, wondering how best to appeal to his better nature. Surely his Nazism was only skin deep? But now the fool had come in drunk; he hadn't even reacted to her presence. He was no use to her in this condition. She turned to her painting but it had disappeared! It *must* be there! What in God's name was a portrait of Hitler doing there, where she was sure her picture should be? Where could she go? She never left her frame unless she knew where her picture was!

'What have you done with my picture? Where is it?' she demanded.

Erich stopped, looked puzzled, and turned to the wall. Then he let out a roar of laughter and lurched over to the Hitler portrait, reached up and turned it around. Oh, joy. There it was – home – her own place, where Pieter had made a special room for her in the studio, and the Master had teased her about Galileo, and where Annie had sat sipping Kathenka's special brew. It had never occurred to her that there might be another picture on the other side. Erich was standing back, pleased as punch with his conjuring trick. He bowed; she was free to go.

Erich manoeuvred himself upright with care, feeling as though an axe had been driven through his head. He put on a dressing gown against the chill, went out into his workroom and sat down at his desk. He remembered his dream about Louise. Klaus had said he was in her thrall, perhaps he was right. He would hand her picture over to the archivist as soon as he had written his letter of resignation to General von Brugen. It was nonsense to think that a mere picture might influence him.

Making a conscious effort to smarten himself up, he washed and shaved with only one cut to the chin, and went out to the café where he usually went, under the colonnade on the Rue de Rivoli, for breakfast and a cup of the brown liquid that they called coffee.

Elaine Colville, the proprietor's pretty daughter, came over and sat with him for a while. She worked in the gallery as a cleaner, a job she had got through her father, who was a strong supporter of the Vichy Government of France that co-operated with the Germans. Erich liked her and flirted with her when he could.

When she had gone, he thought back to the events of last night and how he had felt with his old comrades. His route to the SS had been so different from theirs. It had really started after the climbing of the Adlerwand, when the Nazi propaganda machine had taken over, claiming that it showed what Germany and Austria could do together if they merged. When Erich was offered a commission in the SS, it had seemed logical to accept. In the months before the Anschluss, while he was at SS training in Germany, Erich had seen nothing but Germany's industry and prosperity. Autobahns streaked the country like arteries. Volkswagens – 'people's cars' – buzzed like bees, factories boomed, whereas in Austria everything seemed to be stagnating.

The disipline and the training had suited him; he was hailed as the model recruit, a man of steel when it came to route marches and assault courses. He was top of his class at the bookwork as well, but he glossed over that; for all their Aryan looks, his fellow recruits had not been the brightest.

He had been able forget his father's blue face and heart attacks, and his mother's strange disturbing pictures – degenerate art – as he knew now, with that Jew, Solomons, around her all the time. Grandpa Veit had had been right about that. In the SS it had been a relief not to have to think, but to follow orders, and to ride on the crest of the Nazi wave. Last night's meeting with Klaus and his old SS colleagues had brought it all back. Talking to that girl's picture just showed how far he had slipped; it was time to give her up. He paid his bill, forgot his change, crossed the Rue de Rivoli via the Metro underpass, and climbed the steps to the Jeu de Paume two at a time. He then spent the day tidying up until all he had on his desk was a blotter and a tray of pencils. The Führer stared down on him with intense blue eyes.

Élaine Colville came in. 'Erich, mon cher, you have something on your mind? You forgot your change.' She put the coins on the table, then sat on the edge of his desk, and fiddled with his pencils. Normally he would have enjoyed her company; she would ask questions about his work and didn't object if he put an arm about her waist while he explained. She asked endless questions about the odd collection of experts that worked in the gallery during the day. 'They are all pigs!'

she would say irreverently, and then give him a pat on the cheek before slipping away.

'I've a letter to write, Elaine.'

'Is she beautiful?'

'What? Oh no, it's a business letter.'

'Then I will go. But just in case you are lying to me, I will turn my little Dutch friend around so that she can keep an eye on you.' To Erich's astonishment she got up and turned Louise's portrait face out.

'How did you find out about her?' he asked, but Elaine just laughed and said, 'Erich, I know everything!'

He turned the key in the door, pulled out a sheet of paper, filled his fountain pen with special ink, flexed his fingers and looked at the ceiling. He would normally communicate with General von Brugen in code, but invisible ink was allowed in an emergency; he felt that offering his resignation did constitute an emergency. He was still looking at the ceiling when he realised that he was not alone. He lowered his eyes slowly and found himself looking into the level gaze of the girl in the green dress. So it hadn't been a dream.

'*Guten Abend,*' he said as politely as he could.

Louise noticed the change in Erich's manner. His acceptance of her, and a gaze as level as her own, was disconcerting and she found herself apologising.

'Excuse me, I hope I'm not intruding.'

'On the contrary, I think I was expecting you. Let me, however, say straight away that, whatever you have to say to me, you are wasting your time.'

'But I haven't said a word?'

'But you were going to. So, let me tell you first that I have taken my decision. I am going to join the Waffen SS. The situation in the world is changing. Our forces are struggling on the Eastern Front against the Russians, and there have been setbacks in North Africa. In time we must expect the British to try to invade. I have a duty to fight for my country.'

'And I suppose this was Klaus's idea?'

'Not just Klaus; the members of the Waffen SS – the men who are actually doing the fighting – who I met last night.' Louise felt a surge of anger. Damn all wars! she thought. First Gaston, and now Erich. She looked at him with disappointment.

'But you can contribu–'

'No! I don't want any more interference from you. I am sitting here to write my resignation from the Art Administration Organisation and at the same time volunteer for the Waffen SS. My country needs me, not all this bloody art. And there is nothing you can do to stop me. You have influenced me far too much already!'

'Influenced by me? How can you say that?'

'You have been influencing me ever since I first saw you on Abrahams's wall, I realise that now. Klaus opened my eyes to you. Oh, it's stupid I know; just some *look* that an artist a few hundred years ago captured in paint that had me besotted. If it hadn't been for you, maybe it wouldn't have occurred to me to go back to see what the mob were doing to Abrahams. And for rescuing him I got thrown out of the SS.'

Louise was desperate. She could feel herself losing him; soon he would be beyond any appeal from her. If he wrote that letter he would surely hand her over to the Art Administration, and she would have lost her one chance to strike a blow against Klaus and his like. She still had nightmares about the foul things she had seen in Klaus's mind. She liked this new, more positive Erich; she responded to his level gaze, but that just made it more urgent. He must not be allowed to march off to war and leave her helpless.

'Erich,' she said, 'I'm not going to try to make you change your mind; I can't. I promise I won't interrupt, but I want you to tell me what Nazism really and truly is. Then you can shut me out of your mind and go and fight your war if you must.' She waited with bated breath. All he had to do was shut his mind to her, stack her picture with all the others against the wall, and she would be powerless. Two seconds ... three ...

Erich sighed, got up, and went over to the door. He took a '*Bitte nicht* stören' – don't disturb – sign and hung it over the handle. He smiled ruefully; the night watchman would guess that he was 'entertaining' a girl.

'The principles of National Socialism are ... ' he began. Carefully and precisely he laid out them out, omitting nothing, from the theory of racial superiority to the Jewish conspiracy. The girl listened, intent and silent. Apart from the occasional request for clarification she said nothing. It was past midnight when he said, 'Do I believe in all this? Well, the answer is it doesn't really matter what I believe. We are at war. Either I act without thinking or I think without acting. The time has come to act, and for me the SS is the obvious means. Now, if you'd be so good as to leave, I will continue with my letter.'

CHAPTER 23

Brundibár

Jacob Edelstein, Elder of the Terezín Governing Council, leaned back in his chair. This was a joint meeting of the Elders and the Free Time Activities Administration. Jacob looked tired. We don't know the half of the load he has to carry, Izaac thought.

'Gentlemen, ladies, before we proceed to our free time activities, at our last meeting disturbing rumours were circulating that the transports to the east were of a more sinister purpose than just for resettlement and labour. Recently we have been asked for lists of over a thousand of our people for transport that include whole families. Yesterday I requested a meeting with the camp commandant, Hauptsturmführer Anton Burger.' There was a stir of interest about the room. People leaned forward; 'I told him frankly that rumours were circulating in the camp that the "labour transports" were nothing but a cover for annihilation.' There was a general gasp; one did not talk to Germans like this. 'I am glad to say,' Jacob went on, 'that he appeared shocked at the suggestion, and that he has since come back to me to assure me that these are just that, merely rumours.' Relief rippled though the room. I wonder? Izaac thought to himself.

'Now, we have a long list of reports to get through: the *Ghetto Swingers* are in need of a drummer, I believe. The cabaret, *The Lost Food Card*, has been doing well. The *Czech Folk*

Singers say that they are getting too many people for their loft performances and want a better venue. Also the camp commandant says he wants to attend the lecture on Einstein's Theory of Relativity, so it will have to be in German. I think you have an elementary version which might be translated for the Commandant, Herr Brandovski?' Everyone chuckled and Izaac dropped into a pleasant daydream of playing musical games with Louise back in Vienna.

'Izaac! Izaac Abrahams. .. calling Izaac!' He shot up in his chair to laughter all round. 'Izaac, we have just volunteered you as leader of an orchestra!'

'Not another! I am already leader of two...'

'Wait till you hear. Herr Krása will explain. It's a children's opera, but the music is difficult and modern. Herr Krása ... ?' The composer then explained to Izaac: 'The opera is a simple story of two children pitted against a wicked organ grinder called Brundibár. The opera is called Brundibár after him. It is sung by children and I hear you are good with children, but your role will be to lead a small adult orchestra. I am writing it now but I need to know what instruments you can find for me so I can write the proper parts.'

Izaac had hidden himself away in order to study the music score, the black notes still almost wet from the composer's pen. He heard a soft footfall and looked up from the manuscript.

'Pafko!' he said. 'It's after curfew, and I bet you haven't a pass.'

'What's that, Mr Izaac?' asked the boy sidling forward, his head at an angle, to see what Izaac was working on.

'Brundibár, a new children's opera. I have to learn it for the auditions.'

'What's it like, Mr Izaac?' Pafko asked, coming around behind Izaac and looking over his shoulder.

'So you want me to go back to the beginning?' sighed Izaac, as he turned back to the first page.

'I'll test you on it, sir.'

'Cheeky! Here the choir is introducing Aninka and Pepíček. They have no father and their mother is sick. Only milk and rest will cure her, but how will they get milk without money?'

'The music looks modern, doesn't it?'

'If you interrupt, you go, young man.' Izaac said severely. Pafko just reached forward and turned the page. Izaac went on, 'Here the two children are singing of their plight, as the street gradually fills with citizens: the ice cream man, the baker and the milkman all shout their wares. When Aninka and Pepíček ask the milkman for milk for their mother, they are told in no uncertain terms that to buy milk they must have money, and to make money they must work! The children watch as people buy and sell but notice that one old man is making money without having to sell anything. This is Brundibár, the organ grinder. All he has to do is grind out a tune by turning the handle of his organ and people fill his cap with coins.

'Aninka and Pepíček decide that they will try this, and they sing a pretty song of ducks and geese and a flying machine, but no one pays them any attention. Then they imitate the organ grinder and begin a crude dance. Brundibár is furious, and encourages the people to chase the children from the square.'

'I like Brundibár!' murmured Pafko.

'You would!' said Izaac. 'At any rate, during a night spent on a bench, the two children are visited by a sparrow, a cat and a dog, who reckon that with the help of the three hundred children they know, they can defeat Brundibár. The three animals sing the children to sleep. That's the end of Act 1.'

'Go on, sir.'

'In the morning, the choir sing about the people getting up to do their morning chores, and the animals, true to their word, recruit the children to help Aninka and Pepíček against Brundibár. When Brundibár begins to play, the cat mews and the dog howls; Brundibár tries to drive them away, but the dog gets hold of his pants and Brundibár is silenced. Now Pepíček conducts the children's choir in a beautiful lullaby and the people fill Pepíček's cap with money. The children think their troubles are over until suddenly Brundibár darts in and steals the cap and their money. A huge chase begins; the children recover the money and hunt Brundibár away. The opera closes with the choir singing a triumphal march.'

'Turn back sir, please, to before the lullaby, when Brundibár sings last.' Izaac turned back, and Pafko began humming, then singing. 'Ty pra – ši – vý, sta – rý čok – le ...' it was a typical edgy Czech voice. He made only one mistake.

'No Pafko! it's B flat on the dotted crochet. I didn't realise you could sight read?'

'Turn the page ... ' Izaac could feel him vibrating with excitement. 'Look, Mr Izaac, this is where I steal their money!'

'What do you mean *you*?' Izaac asked.

'Me! Mr Izaac, I came tonight because I wanted a part ... any part, but now I want to play just this one, this Brundibár,' he hummed. 'See, I already remember his tune. I know my voice is rough, but I can be the worstest villain ever!' Izaac glanced at the eager face beside him and imagined him in the part. Here was a rogue that could be lovable as well, but Izaac had two worries. Every child singer in Terezín would be auditioning and Pafko would have to audition with the rest. Secondly, could he ever handle an opera of kids with Pafko in the cast?

'Pafko,' he said. 'You will have to take your luck with the rest. This is the only manuscript, and it is like gold. It must never leave this room, but now that you know where it is here, I can't really stop you glancing at it from time to time.' Pafko reached out. 'But with clean hands!'

'Oh thank you, Mr Izaac!' and he was gone.

The noise in Block L417 was deafening.

'Children! Children! Order please.' The choirmaster was holding his head in despair. The excitement of the first rehearsal, and the fact that boys and girls were allowed to mix together for once, had created a near riot. Izaac walked across the stage behind the choirmaster but in full view of the children. Suddenly, he hesitated, then carefully stepped over something. A couple of the children stopped shouting and began squinting this way and that trying to see what it was that Mr Abrahams had stepped over. Izaac was walking back across the stage now, this time carrying a chair. At exactly the same place, he took another careful step over the invisible object and walked on. The clamour of voices subsided; everyone was watching, fascinated.

'Is it a wire?' someone whispered.

'There must be, but I can't see it!' observed another. Suddenly Pafko stepped forward.

'I'll show him!' he boasted. 'Mr Abrahams sir! It must be a trick of the light, there's nothing there, no wire, nothing.' Izaac looked puzzled and scratched his head. 'Look, sir, I'll walk straight through it!' said Pafko marching towards him. There was a sudden gasp. At exactly the spot where Mr Abrahams had been making his step, Pafko tripped, somersaulted, and landed with a thump at Izaac's feet. Izaac picked him up, pretended to cuff his ears, and they both walked off the stage together. Some of the smaller children even went over to assure themselves that the wire really wasn't there.

'Did you rehearse that with Pafko?' Rafík, the choirmaster asked later.

'No. He did it off his own bat.' Izaac chuckled. 'You've got to use that talent. He's your Brundibár!'

From then on, Rafík had them at least partly under control and Izaac relaxed. The music was difficult, not just for the ten principal child singers, but for the two choirs as well: the 'School Choir' that sang on stage, and the 'Through the Windows Choir', whose singing would be heard coming from the cottage windows on the set. At rehearsals the accompaniment was provided by a wheezy old harmonium, but Izaac soon learned to imitate the young Czech voices on his violin and would play along with the weaker sections or show them exactly what Rafík really wanted them to sing. Izaac's little orchestra grew too: a flute, a trumpet, a guitar, an accordion, a piano, drums, four violins and a bass, with Hans the composer busily writing parts for the new instruments.

They are like a flock of birds, Izaac thought to himself. One minute they would be still, next they would be off in a whirl of wings, circling, landing, and chattering. Sometimes it seemed as if they had an unseen companion forming a focus to their game, someone who made their eyes dance with excitement? Izaac often thought of Louise during rehearsals; she would have enjoyed the children, but he kept to his resolve to only think of her through his music, and so spare her the squalor and misery of the camp.

It was Pafko who nearly brought the whole house of cards tumbling down. They had been discussing costumes when Izaac suggested that Brundibár, the tyrant, should have a moustache, Pafko was small, and a bushy moustache would make him look older. Nobody noticed when he slipped away, until suddenly he appeared, strutting purposefully across the stage with an unmistakable Hitler moustache! In seconds he became the Führer himself, the walk, the head pressed forward the right arm jutting forward. There was a shout from the door.

'The Camp Commandant's coming!' A shocked silence filled the rehearsal room.

'Pafko! Hide! Hide!' But there was nowhere to hide. The room was bare except for the harmonium. Izaac gazed at him stupidly, the moustache had been put on with burned cork, there was no getting it off. They could hear jackboots approaching. Suddenly Aninka, the heroine in the opera, rushed at him, dragging two other girls with her. She was wearing a long dress.

'Down, Pafko!' As he dropped to the floor she lifted the skirt of her dress, threw it over him, and sat down on him. The other girls rushed forward, one threw herself down in front of Aninka, while two more knelt in decorative poses on each side; the other girls crowded around. Now what? Izaac realised the next move was up to him. He shouldered his violin and slipped straight into the introduction to the lullaby that comes at the very end of the opera where the mother rocks the cradle and wonders how things will be when time has passed and her little birds have spread their wings. Just as the door was thrown open and the Commandant strode in, the girls began to sing. For a second Izaac thought he was about to call everyone to attention, but there was something about the scene, and the young voices, that melted even him. He raised a finger for them go on. When they came to the end Izaac skilfully led them into a repeat.

'*Schön!*' was all he said, beautiful. The door closed; the sound of boots on the cobbles faded, and suddenly Aninka leapt to her feet with a shriek.

'You ungrateful little worm! After me saving you from death, no less!' She rubbed her behind. 'Wait till we're in stage with a whole audience in front, I'll show you.' Pafko emerged,

smudged but defiant. Izaac told him to apologise. Not only had
Aninka's quick action saved him from punishment, but it had
possibly also saved the whole opera. Pafko's offer of a kiss was
indignantly refused. He thought for a moment and then dug
deep into his pocket, took out a small notebook and extracted
something precious. It was a special meal ticket, the kind that
people only got for exceptional labour. He gave it to Aninka
and her eyes lit up.

The dress rehearsal had gone so well that everyone now
expected a disaster on the night. Behind the scenes, Izaac's
unruly flock of performers were sitting like hunched fledglings
lost in the misery of first night nerves. As the hall of the Magdeburg barracks began to fill, curiosity began to replace nerves.
When the small orchestra, with Izaac as leader, stood up for
the conductor, they were ready. Rafík, concealed behind the
painted houses of the set, had his hand up. Count eight bars,
breathe in, nine bars. 'Tohle je malý Pepíček...' and they were
away, introducing the two children and their sick mother.

Marie had bargained and cajoled in order to get a bunk beside
a window, partly because she wanted to be able to read, partly
because she kept a journal and she needed light for this. She
read through yesterday's entry:

22 September 1943
*I thought that by working in the kitchen I would get more
food. But you can't eat raw rotten potatoes or meat that
already stinks. Will this hell never end?*

Now she sucked her pencil; a lot can change in a day. She
enjoyed making entries by the beam of the searchlight because

she liked the feeling that she was using the German's light for her clandestine activity. She wrote:

23 September 1943

And then waited for the searchlight to creep across the window again.

What an evening! Klara, bless her, came up with tickets for the new kids' opera in the Magdeburg tonight. The place was packed but we got two seats when some boys moved up on their bench for us. Even that was nice for a start, not segregated for once; I'd forgotten what it was like to sit beside a boy. That was the only missed opportunity of the evening because, as soon as the little orchestra struck up, we forgot all about them. You'd think it would be silly, two children wanting to get milk to make their mother better, getting help from a sparrow, a cat and a dog, but within seconds I was back five years to when I was ten and Michko and I would put on plays for the family. It was all very nice until Brundibár the organ grinder came on. He is the villain. He's quite a little fellow, and he doesn't really do very much, and he doesn't even sing very much, but I just couldn't take my eyes off him. He has this ridiculous sticky-outy moustache, like straight handlebars and has a special twitch for every situation. One moment I wanted to hug him, next I was as frightened as Aninka and Pepíček, and at the end I was standing up with everyone else cheering his defeat, but yet sorry to see him go. I'd love to meet the boy that plays him. We all stood and clapped and clapped, and cheered, even the Germans. When we all went out it was strange; it was as if we were walking on air. The whole sordid town looked like a stage set made of cardboard, we could puff and it would blow away. A group of German officers passed, laughing at Brundibár and his

moustaches. For them it was just a young boy in a kids'
opera. To us it was a victory over tyranny. We saw Hitler with
a dog at the seat of his trousers and three hundred children
chasing him away. We will defeat them in the end ... surely
we will.

Izaac was being jostled and pushed like seaweed in an ebb
tide as he stared at the transportation list. Pafko had given him
the news; he just had to see it for himself. There it was at the
top of the list, a name clearly added by the Nazi administration:
Jacob Edelstein. Izaac thought back; it was barely two months
since Jacob had taken the unprecedented step of asking the
Nazis about the transports, and what was at the end of them.
Well, Jacob was about to find out.

CHAPTER 24

The Turning of a Nazi

'Damnation!' Erich said to himself as he thrust the sheet of paper away from him and dropped his head on to his arms. 'Why did I talk to her? Blast her!' It was well past midnight now, and every attempt to draft his resignation to General von Brugen and request his transfer back into the SS had failed. His waste paper basket was half full of frustrated attempts, all of which would have to be burned because the ink and the process that he used were top secret; no one must know of his Gestapo connection. He emptied his waste paper basket, and, following his instructions to the letter, he burned the drafts in an old enamel basin, crushed them, and then washed them down the sink in his room.

―◦◦◦◦◦―

At times of quiet, Louise would listen for sounds of Izaac's playing, a faint vibrato to reassure her that somewhere out there she was participating in his music. Her waking dreams would be more vivid, but harder to interpret: sudden laughter and the impression of children circling about her, or bright young voices singing in a language she couldn't understand. Had Izaac become a chorus master? Then she would see things that made her shudder: cockroaches on a floor, a cart covered by a cloth, a foot sticking out. But these soon became confused with her Klaus nightmares and she would wake, sweating, unable to disentangle what she had been seeing.

She woke this morning with a feeling of despair. Her dreams had been bad, and she was certain that Erich had written his letter to General von Brugen. She could hear him moving about, with abrupt angular movements. He walked towards her picture; she felt a surge of hope, but then he moved away humming tunelessly. The door banged.

Erich had gone out to get something to eat, when Elaine, on her evening cleaning round, knocked on Erich's door and, getting no reply, used her master key to come into the room. Evening light glowed through the high gallery windows. She walked over to Erich's desk, reached up and turned Louise's picture about, hesitated and then sniffed.

'I smell burning. Paper?' she said. She sniffed again. 'What has Erich Hoffman been doing burning papers in here?' She ran her duster over his desk, examined it, and rubbed the small flakes of grey ash with her finger. 'Oh Erich,' she said. 'I hope you are not a naughty boy. Only people who have secrets burn papers – Gestapo people – and we don't like Gestapo people here.'

When the Germans marched into Paris, Elaine's father had decided that it was best for France, for him, to co-operate with them. Elaine, on the other hand, had chosen resistance. Father and daughter lived together happily, Papa knowing full well that Elaine was in the Resistance. Because she spoke some German and could use her father's influence, she had been able to get a job in the Jeu de Paume. 'We believe there is a Gestapo member there. We need you to find him for us!' Her resistance leader had ordered her.

Surely Erich couldn't be the one she was looking for?

'Perhaps you lied to me and were really writing to your

Fräulein, saying that you had fallen in love with a little French girl called Elaine?' She dusted thoroughly, as if to remove the evidence, but paused again at his wash-hand basin. There too were signs of ash having been washed down the plughole. When she had finished she sat in Erich's chair for a moment and let her eyes roam over the wall. Then, with an anxious smile at Louise she whispered, 'Tell me that it was just a love letter.' Then she turned the picture back to face the wall.

⌐₩₩₩⌐

That evening it was Erich who turned her picture about. He glared at her, but his look told all. He had not sent his letter of resignation to von Brugen! She realised she had won. She felt a surge of relief; she hadn't realised how her helplessness had been weighing on her. But what had she won? A little time, perhaps, until he was put to the test again? He had admitted that he didn't believe in the Nazi cause, but he had been a Nazi long enough to steal her picture from Izaac, and to volunteer for the SS after a drunken night out! Louise shuddered. There was something insidious about the Nazi doctrine. Klaus knew all about it and exploited it to his own ends, but Erich was trusting. Was it lying dormant, like a worm inside him? She needed to know for her sake, but also for his.

Erich's scowl softened as she emerged. He got up and cleared some books from her chair and then sat down himself. She wondered how to start, but then decided that the direct approach was best.

'Erich,' she said, 'I know very little about you, apart from what you told me while you were talking to my picture. You never sent your letter to General von Brugen, did you?' He shook his head. 'So we have a little time. When you remembered happy times, you talked about a village up in the mountains; I'd like you to tell me about it. Were the salt mines there?'

Erich had felt unusually flat since he had burned his last draft to General von Brugen. He had enjoyed the thrill of action again and had dreaded another evening of inactivity. Now the girl was challenging him and this fitted his mood. He made himself a cup of barley coffee, sat down opposite her and began to tell her about Altaussee. As he talked, the Jeu de Paume developed a misty quality until eventually it blew away and he was facing into a stiff breeze on the Loser Mountain. Surprised, he faltered, but Louise's voice was with him, like a companion urging him to pick up the thread again. After she had done this several times, she said simply, 'Wouldn't it be easier to take me with you?' and somehow she was there, walking, talking, and climbing like any other congenial companion.

⎯⎰⎰⎰⎰⎯

If Louise had known in advance where Erich would take her, she mightn't have been so keen to come. He tested her mettle. She found herself added to the rope on his first real rock climb, and later even on sections of the first ascent of the Adlerwand. She found a whole new dimension, where eagles soared and fixed her with tawny eyes, and the thrill of having what Erich called 'air beneath your heels'.

He told her about the salt mines, taking her into caverns and lakes deep under the mountain, where he showed her where the miners had cut out a chapel and built an altar out of solid salt. She listened to the timbre of his voice and liked it; she could trust this man. But then one day, Louise was suddenly alert. She realised that what he had been telling her was not in fact what he was showing her. It happened one evening when they had been on a long walk, returning over the top of the Kleinkogel and running across the meadow towards the chalet.

'Look, there's a car at the house, I wonder whose that is?' he had said. As they passed the window they paused and she saw Erich's mother, Sabine, crying. There was a man with her, Jewish looking, who was comforting her. Sabine moved towards him and momentarily rested her forehead on his shoulder. Erich had said with relief, 'Oh, good, Herr Solomons has come!' He hurried around to greet the man like an old friend.

Now Louise stared across the table at Erich in disbelief; the image she had seen and the words Erich had used bore no resemblance to the account he had just given her, here in the Jeu de Paume. What he had said was: *It was that bloody Jew, Solomons, making a pass at Mother, so I went around, burst in, and gave him a piece of my mind!* This was like Klaus, but in reverse! Had she found the worm?

'*Erich*! Do you realise what you have just said?'

'About Solomons making a pass at Mother? Yes, I was disgusted!'

'But Erich, that is *not what happened!* I was beside you, just seconds ago, when you saw Herr Solomons with your mother. What you really said was, "Oh good, Herr Solomons has come," and you went round and greeted him like a friend!'

A sudden chill came over the room.

'You shouldn't interrupt,' Erich said angrily. 'How can *you* know what happened?' It was on the tip of her tongue to say, 'Because you showed me,' but she kept quiet. He got to his feet and, angling his shoulders, strode away across the room. 'I'm not going to waste my time talking if you start making things up against me. Go on, fade away, or do whatever you do when you're not wanted.'

Down in his tiny bedroom, Erich banged about, washed his face, combed his hair; then feeling suddenly tired, he sat on the edge of his bed with his head in his hands, the defiance draining out of him. She was right. He had been pleased and grateful to see Solomons comforting his mother. It had only been later that Veit's poison had crept in, twisting poor Solomons's concerned smile into a wicked leer. Oh God, he wondered. How much more had he distorted in his mind, and where was Solomons now? In a concentration camp, most likely. It was almost a relief to find that Louise was no longer there when he went back into the room; he needed time to think.

⌒─✴╫╫╫─∽

As Izaac's audience and critic, Louise had learned how to deal with him when he had convinced himself that he was playing something right – when he knew deep down that he was wrong. Erich was, if anything, more willing to have his false notes shown to him: he had found something in himself that he didn't like. She never told him about her theory of a 'worm' but she became adept at spotting it in the memories that he told her about. They found it in Grandpa Veit, but also in the poverty Erich had experienced after the first war. They found it in Erich's father's sickness, and in poor Mr Solomons's charity to them. But above all they found it in Klaus. When she saw the way Klaus had skilfully manipulated Erich on his 'eye--opening' tour of Vienna's Jewish banks and cafes, she thought, poor Erich, he didn't stand a chance.

⌒─✴╫╫╫─∽

'Erich,' she said one day after one of her disturbing dreams. 'I'm worried about Izaac. I hear him playing in my dreams. But I see all sorts of nightmare things as well.'

'We all have nightmares. If he's playing his violin I think you can take it he's all right. We've got to believe Klaus on this; he should know, he's out there. The camps are just temporary

223

accommodation for the Jews until the war is over. He even said the place where Izaac is, is like a holiday camp. They say the first class carriages are all being used to take the Jews east.'

Louise was still uneasy, although, when she thought about it, the images Izaac had been showing her recently were mostly of good-natured activity.

CHAPTER 25

The Embellishment

Christmas 1943 brought a strange proposal from the Germans to the Jewish Administration.

'No! No! No! I will not cooperate! This is Hanukah, the time when we, as Jews, celebrate *independence* against tyranny!' Rabbi Ishmael brought a bony fist down on the table.

'But if we cooperate, conditions will improve, Ishmael!' the leader of the Council of Elders appealed. 'The Commandant calls it his Christmas present to us.'

'Fiddlesticks! Beware of Greeks bearing gifts. We stood up to the Greeks two thousand years ago ...' Izaac wondered what this had to do with the Germans, but he could see a religious lecture a mile off. With a deferential bow he cut across the quavering voice, 'Excuse me, Rabbi, but can someone explain exactly what it is the Germans want us to do?' He got a grateful glance from the Elder.

'The Danish government, Izaac, are worried about their Jews, the ones that have been arriving here recently from Denmark. They want the International Red Cross to visit Terezín to certify that conditions here are adequate.'

'But they aren't adequate!' said Izaac in indignation.

'That's the point, if we agree to cooperate, the Germans have promised to reduce over-crowding, improve our food rations and support our free-time activities. Our role will be to clean the place up; they will provide paint and materials. It will be a chance for us to show that we are capable of policing and governing ourselves! Hopefully the Red Cross will see this, and insist on the same standards in the other camps.'

'Pah! Another Potemkin village!' snapped old Rabbi Ishmael. Nobody paid any attention to him; the idea of improved conditions was tempting them all. Izaac was trying to remember what a Potemkin village was. It was coming back to him ... General Potemkin, a favourite of Empress Catherine II of Russia, worried that the Empress would see the dreadful poverty of her rule, had special villages built before the Empress's visits, and filled them with 'happy peasants' singing and dancing. Old Ishmael had a point, but the Red Cross would never be fooled, they would see through the ruse. Anyway the concessions would be worth it.

<hr />

'Hey there, Pafko!' Izaac shouted. Pafko had a clipboard in his hands and was looking up studiously at the windows of the Magdeburg building as if surveying the paintwork. The boy took a pencil from behind his ear, appeared to jot something on to his clipboard, and walked on. Izaac lengthened his stride and caught up with him. 'Pafko, where's your brick and bucket? Have you been caught for a job at last?'

Pafko gave a broad grin. 'I've promoted myself. Look!' he held up his clipboard. 'It's a lot lighter than the bucket and brick, and it works just as well. I bet you thought I was doing something official. See, it's even got a swastika on the back,' he held it up.

'You shirker! So I've been on my hands and knees digging up the grass from between the cobbles while you wander about pretending to be the town surveyor.' Under the Embellishment everyone had to work, even those exempted for other reasons, it was an all-out effort.

'Surveyors can go anywhere,' Pafko said with a wink. 'If it moves, move it; if you can't move it, paint it; if it moves on its own salute it. The Germans just love clipboards!' he grinned. Izaac changed the subject.

'How many performances of Brundibár have you done so far?'

'Over forty. You know they are putting up a special stage for the Red Cross visit? Have you noticed, the food is getting better?' Pafko prattled on. Izaac wondered what would happen if his voice broke; he must be nearly fourteen. They all agreed that if he couldn't sing, they would have to cancel. It wasn't just that people loved him and his moustache; he had made the villain, Brundibár, human, and human villains can be defeated. Izaac thought of the Terezín March they all liked to sing:

> '*The time will come to pack our bags*
> *And home we'll joyfully depart.*
> *We will conquer and survive*
> *All the cruelty in our land,*
> *We will laugh on ghetto ruins*
> *Hand in hand!*'

There was a feeling of optimism throughout the camp. Transports continued to leave, but as long as your name wasn't on the list you didn't have to worry. If they hadn't been so busy with what the Germans called 'The Embellishment', they might have noticed that it was the old, the sick, and even the ugly that were being magicked away. They left in the early mornings; old couples united briefly for yet another train journey to God knows where. The Germans were everywhere, planning the exact route that the Red Cross delegation would follow.

Sub-standard buildings were locked up. Mock washing facilities were put in. Fresh paint hid squalor. Teams of gardeners worked in the wide moat to bring on a lush crop of vegetables. A café was opened. There was nothing in it, but it was fun to sit there and pretend. A group of girls with rakes and spades practised the song they would sing as they passed the delegation on their way to work. Women were rehearsed to sit in the barracks knitting and talking among themselves about menus. In the café a little boy was to complain: 'Not sardines again!' He didn't know what a sardine was. A football team began cautious training on increased rations; they mustn't fall over from hunger on the pitch. Orchestras, bands, choirs, and plays went into rehearsals. Like everyone else, Izaac was far too busy to wonder why on earth they were all doing their utmost to help the Germans deceive the Red Cross.

In the midst of this came a rumour that the British and Americans had landed somewhere in France; Normandy, the rumours said. Suddenly there was light at the end of the tunnel. Then, for the few days before the delegation arrived from Switzerland, the quality of food improved dramatically. The Germans didn't want people who were used to starvation rations throwing up in front of the delegation because the food was too rich. Everything was ready.

Marti Bochsler looked down on the coloured strips of land – golden corn, green grass, blue green kale – as the plane of the Red Cross Delegation circled Prague airport. His hands were sweating, he didn't like flying, and even though there were massive red crosses on the wings and fuselage, flying over war-torn Europe was always risky. He was a junior clerk with the delegation and had never been on an international inspection before. Like everyone else on the delegation he had heard terrible rumours about the conditions in the concentration camps. What if they found that these were correct? Would he be able to take it? He had heard of delegates coming home nervous wrecks from examining prisoner of war camps, and this was the first concentration camp the Red Cross had been allowed to see.

The plane bounced, bounced again, and trundled along the runway to where a group of staff cars were waiting. Marti stared through the small window at the SS men in their black uniforms. These Teutonic giants would never lose the war! He thought with momentary pity of the Americans and British fighting their way through Normandy.

The drive to Terezín took about an hour. Marti enjoyed the fresh air in the open car, even though the dust of the cavalcade fell thickest on the last car where he sat behind Dr Elser, a junior doctor, and between two stony SS privates. He felt like a prisoner himself. 'Remember, delegates,' their Chef de Mission had said in Geneva, 'we are here to record what we see, we want facts, not rumours. You are forbidden to talk to the ghetto inmates. Our role is to see that the living accommodation in the camp is adequate, that they have proper sanitation, and a sufficient diet. Forget the rumours, collect the facts.' Marti felt for his notebook in his pocket and checked his pencils in his top pocket.

In the end he enjoyed the day. The camp was clean, the food was good. Dr Elser estimated the calories of the meals they saw being put down for the inmates, all of which Marti entered in his notebook. The bunks and the spaces about them were within international standards. There seemed to be a musician in every room. They happened on a jazz band, playing to a small audience, and a quartet was playing to old people sitting in the café. Dr Elser tasted the bread in the dining room and declared it excellent. They were even invited to watch a football match, and the barracks overlooking the pitch were crowded with children who made a healthy lot of noise. The highlight of his day was a performance by the children of an opera composed by one of the inmates. He noticed that even the Camp Commandant was amused by the Hitler-like antics of the wicked organ grinder.

~※※～

It was only when Izaac turned, aglow with pride for his young performers, and found himself face to face with the beaming faces of the Red Cross delegation and their flanking SS minders that he realised how their cooperation with the 'Embellishment' had backfired. Those fat faces showed no penetration, no conception that everything they were seeing was a paper-thin facade; that it was sham! The cockroaches would flood the kitchens after dark. The dead cart would resume its rounds, carrying the bodies of the starved and the shot, and he and all the others had gone out of their way conceal all this from the only people who might be able to help them. He packed his violin with trembling hands, and exited by a back door so he could intercept the party on the way out. The delegation had talked to no one, not one single ordinary camp inmate. Now they were going to!

~※※～

When the party was being led back towards the cars at the end of the inspection, Marti got separated from the main group. A first-aid team, followed by a hurrying doctor in a white coat, crossed their path, carrying a stretcher.

A voice directly behind him said, low and urgently, 'Don't believe what you are seeing. Believe none of it! This is a Potemkin village! It is all a sham. There is no First Aid, or even Second Aid. Tomorrow the food will be gone and we will be back to soup and rotten vegetables.'

Marti turned. Like most educated Swiss, he spoke German as well as French. He recognised the speaker as the man who had led the orchestra in the opera. He still carried his violin. 'Every week there are transports out of here to Auschwitz. What are they doing with us there? Work or death, we do not know. That's where you should be, not here.'

There was a hoarse shout; Marti's SS minder had seen him. The soldier rushed up and thrust the violinist back so that he staggered and nearly fell. Marti watched, shocked at this unnecessary violence, while the soldier took the violinist's name and inspected a number that the man had tattooed on his arm. The soldier raised the butt of his rifle threateningly, but saw Marti watching him and lowered his arm.

'Please, back to your barracks and don't bother the visitors.'

⁓·ⅢⅢⅢⅢ⁓

The following day, back in Geneva, Marti Bochsler asked to speak with his Chef de Mission. He sat on the opposite side of a vast polished desk, and described his encounter with the violinist.

'What is a Potemkin Village, sir?' he asked.

'Mr Bochsler, thank you for your report. You must not forget, our mission was to inspect what in the end turned out to be a well-run concentration camp. There we saw the actual conditions under which those people live. We recorded what we saw, and our mission is now accomplished. Thank you for your comments but I don't think we need concern ourselves with obscure Russian villages.'

When young Bochsler had gone, his superior tapped his teeth with the top of his pen. What would be the result if their first concentration camp visit came out with an unfavourable report? They would never be invited again. So he closed his mind like an oyster around a pearl, which in his case was the letter of the law.

⁘

Izaac forgot about the incident. The SS man was not a camp officer; he had been brought in to accompany the visitors. He'd even been polite for once, and was probably on the other side of Czechoslovakia by now. He didn't even bother to check the next transportation list for his name; it was one of the longest yet but Spare Time Activity members were normally exempt. He had a student at nine o'clock and was hurrying to the practice room when Pafko appeared.

'Mr Izaac, sir. Your name is on the transportation list.' His face crumpled like tissue paper. For a second he looked like a little old man, and then he threw his arms about Izaac's waist and hugged him like a drowning sailor holding on to a floating spar. Izaac could feel the boy's shoulders shaking.

It was after that that Pafko took Izaac in charge. He had been talking to men working in the underground factory close to the camp and finding out how they had come to be selected for work, and now passed this information on to Izaac. The day before Izaac's transport left, Pafko said something that struck Izaac as strange.

'We'll miss you both, sir.'

'Both?'

'Yes, you and your ... spirit girl; the younger ones call her Mr Abraham's ghost. She appears on the set and plays tag with the little ones. Oh, that's the curfew. I'd better be off.'

'What does she look like?' Izaac called after the fleeing figure. Just before he went out of sight Pafko turned and called out, 'She wears green.'

⁘

After a night standing on the moving floor of the cattle truck, the ground seemed to tremble under Izaac's feet. They stood in the blazing sun, a thousand of them: young and old, men, women and children, shuffling forward slowly in lines twenty across. To their left and right, row after row of black wooden barracks stretched into the distance, merging in the heat-shimmer like blobs of lead melting on a hotplate. Nobody spoke much; nobody tried to escape; dogs and guns and a feeling of security in their numbers held them together. Izaac, trying to remain alert, reached into the pocket of his tatty dungarees and fished out the last of the sand Pafko had given him to roughen his hands. He ground it onto his palms and up under his nails, before scattering it as a small libation on the ground.

'Just look at those hands – uncooked sausages – if you'll forgive me, sir,' he'd said. 'There's people in the factory here who've been through selections and they all say: "Tell them you're a worker," that's what they want. It's good that you don't wear glasses and haven't red hair, cos they can't stand them neither.'

Izaac had gone along with Pafko's instructions just to please him; now as he approached the front of the queue he was grateful. Parting with his violin had been a terrible wrench, but he had given it a good home with his best pupil in Terezín; it at least would play on. He squared his shoulders and walked briskly up to the selection officer, who looked him up and down. Izaac's stomach muscles tightened; the man's eyes, cold as a snake's, had stopped at the red weal under Izaac's chin, a callus from a lifetime of cradling a violin; it was a dead giveaway. Izaac swore inwardly.

'Where did you get that?' the man demanded.

Think, Izaac. Think. 'Carrying boards, sir!' he growled.

The officer flicked his thumb to the left and Izaac was sent off towards the barracks building. He saw the women and the children, the old, and, presumably, those with glasses and red hair, filing off towards a clump of young trees in the distance. They looked strangely pastoral, like families setting off for a picnic in the park on a Sunday. He wondered where they were being sent.

It was the hairdresser, or rather people-shearer, who spotted the weal under Izaac's chin and knew that it hadn't come from carrying boards. He was either new to the concentration camp system, or, at a guess, from Terezín where they weren't shaved.

'You're a violinist!' she hissed as Izaac's hair fell from his head in chunks. Izaac nodded carefully between snips. 'Me too. I'm Deborah, by the way.' Snip ... snip ... the scissors were clipping air now, playing for time. 'What's your name?' Izaac responded. 'Abrahams! Of course I've heard of you. There are six orchestras here. Ours needs a new leader.' Snip ... 'I'll tell our conductor.'

'But I've left my violin in Terezín!' Izaac exclaimed.

'Shhh. Don't look as if you're talking. Just listen. We have more violins than violinists. The important thing is not to lose you. Once you leave reception you're in the machine, consigned to God knows what, and finding you will be the problem.' There was a bellow from across the room. 'That's for me to stop talking.' Snip, snip, snip. The last of Izaac's hair fell in a flurry. 'Go quickly, we'll find you ... somehow.'

CHAPTER 26

Platform 14

The raucous screech of the klaxon horn rang through the Jeu de Paume. Erich looked up, one, two, three blasts. Not a fire ... almost worse, Reichsmarschall Herman Göring's private train had arrived, unannounced as usual, at the Gare de l'Est. The fat man was coming!

There were shouts now from every corner of the building. Erich dashed to his room, struggled into a suit, and ran for the door. Downstairs in one of the main galleries were all the pictures that might be of interest to Germany's most senior officer. The experts, of whom Erich was one, would have to be there ready to answer his questions. Göring's lackeys in the Jeu de Paume would guide him skilfully to the pick of the collection and suggest ridiculously low prices for the pictures, which he would then whisk off in his private train to Karinhall, his palace in Germany. While Göring swore that every picture he selected for his private collection was paid for, everyone knew that no money ever actually passed hands. The only person outside the Jeu de Paume who knew precisely what was going on was General von Brugen, and that was because Erich's coded messages got to him almost as quickly as the pictures got to Karinhall.

⌒⟋⟍⟋⟍⟋⟍⟍⟋⌒

The shouting and running stopped; a sudden hush fell on the

Jeu de Paume. The great man was down in the gallery making his selection.

The door of Erich's room opened and Elaine Colville slipped in. She had her duster with her but she didn't use it. She went to Erich's desk as a matter of routine to check what might be there. A clerk had just placed an order on his desk authorising him to go to the Gare de l'Est to supervise the loading of pictures into the Reichsmarschall's private train. She looked up, and noticed that the cord on Hitler's portrait was twisted. The cord was a dead giveaway so she got up and turned the picture half about. At that moment, there was a round of applause from below.

'The pigs!' she said under her breath. Then to Louise: 'Do you know what the other "Special Train" in the Gare de l'Est is today?' She prodded the order on Erich's desk. 'Cattle trucks crammed with Jews: men women and children being sent to concentration camps in the east. It is hidden away on platform 14. The locals can smell it! God help the poor creatures! The pigs down below know what's going on, but they don't care. I wonder if our Erich knows?'

'No. I'm sure he doesn't.' Louise exclaimed. Elaine leapt back from where Louise had appeared close beside her.

'*Mon Dieu!*'

Louise wasted no time on introductions. 'But he *should* know. I want him to know!'

Elaine was recovering from her shock. 'Wha ... what do you want me to do?' she stammered.

'Couldn't you show him, somehow ... take him there?'

'Take him to the train? No, no ... it would be suicide. But, maybe ...' She picked up the order from Erich's desk. Then she smiled. 'So, Göring's train is at Platform 1; that's handy.' She sat down at the table, picked up Erich's fountain pen and unscrewed the top. Then, her hand shaking slightly, she simply added the number 4 to the platform number. She returned the pen and wiped away the sweaty marks of her fingers with her duster.

'It's a slim chance,' she said. 'But we have to take it.'

Erich arrived at the Gare de l'Est early. The lorries would not be here for a quarter of an hour. He went, as usual, to Platform 1. To his surprise, the guard pointed out that his pass was made out for Platform 14. Security was tight when the Reichsmarschall's train was in. He hurried across the station. When he arrived at Platform 14, however, a soldier on guard there tried to turn him back.

'This is a special train sir, not for the likes of you!'

'I know a special train when I see one, that's why I am here,' Erich snapped crossly, and showed the guard a piece of paper with enough swastikas on it to impress his simple mind. The man shrugged and let him pass. The train had not pulled right in. As he walked towards it, it looked unlike anything the Reichsmarschall would ever use. These were cattle trucks surely.

And there was an appalling smell. He looked up as he reached the first of the trucks and there, to his astonishment, were eyes, dozens of eyes, looking over the top of the door. People were looking out at him. As they became aware of him they started to call out, asking for water, for food. Who were these people? Prisoners of war? He walked down the train in a daze, unwilling to pluck up the courage to ask. Then he saw a slip of paper being pushed through a crack towards him. He glanced left and right to see if he was being watched, but if there were any guards they were out of sight. He took the paper. A voice spoke from the cattle truck. Could he post this note? The voice was French.

'But who are you, where are you from?' Erich asked.

'We are Jews, of course. I am from Lille; my wife is not Jewish so they did not take her. She doesn't know where I am. I want her to know I am well. I've been in Drancy, the Paris concentration camp, for three months. Now they are closing it and taking us east. I heard the guards talking; we are waiting for some special train to leave. You're German, do you know what they will do with us?'

'No ... no,' said Erich hurriedly. 'But I will post your letter.' He blundered on down the train, his mouth too dry to speak, a growing sheaf of letters, cards and notes in his hands. Some were in envelopes, obviously prepared in advance. Others were hurried notes clearly scribbled on any scrap of paper they could find. Some people wanted him to listen to their stories; he didn't want to know. So this was a 'transport'. Terms like 'final solution' and 'sub-human' were exploding in his mind, drowning out the pleas behind the slips of paper that wriggled for attention in the cracks. He went on taking them until he heard shouts from behind him.

Soldiers were running towards him; one of them dropped to one knee and levelled his rifle at him; a guard dog was hauling its owner by its leash. Erich stood there with the notes plainly visible in his hands. The guards would certainly take them from him, but he had crossed his Rubicon: he had said he would post them, and he would. He opened his shirt and stuffed the sheaf of papers inside.

He saw railings in the middle of the platform, and steps leading down. Perhaps he could get out that way. He lunged forward, and half fell, half ran down the steps. A shot rang out. A bullet pinged off the railings above him. Metal gates blocked his way at the bottom. He seized them and shook, but they were locked fast. Then he noticed a bunch of keys hanging in the lock on the outside. He reached through, the key turned and the gate swung open. He had just time to close the gate, lock it, and pocket the keys before the soldiers arrived at the top of the steps. As he stepped out of the line of fire he saw that there was a tunnel at right angles to the steps, obviously connecting all the platforms. It was dead straight but as long as the gate held, it was out of sight of the soldiers.

He was sure now that the 14 on his order had been a mistake. Göring's special train would be at Platform 1 at the far end of this tunnel. If he could reach it, there were plenty of people who would vouch for him. He sprinted the width of the station until he reached the gate to Platform 1. He rattled the gate, it was locked. The keys, the keys – what had he done with the keys? He felt in his pocket; thank God, they were there. The lock was stiff, but the key turned. He slipped through the gate, relocked it, and was standing out of sight in the well before he heard the sound of running behind him. Walking up onto the platform as casually as he could, he found himself beside the Reichsmarschall's gleaming locomotive, hissing loudly enough to drown a whole battle below.

⚜

Erich and Louise sat late over the scraps of paper that he had collected from the transport. Some were in addressed envelopes, but many had been written in haste on scraps of paper, or card, whatever was to hand. They had to read these in order to find and transcribe the address. One brave little note after another: 'I am well ... We are well looked afte r... The train is quite comfortable ... Don't worry ... We expect great things in the east ... Little Marie, alas, has left us ...' Sometimes they couldn't find an address, or even a name. Wherever they found an address, no matter how brief, Erich wrote out an envelope. In the end he lowered his head on to his arms.

'Oh Louise, the inhumanity, the cruelty; how can we be doing this to human beings? What can I do, Louise? What can I do?' His shoulders were shaking.

Elaine got no reply to her knock the following morning and let herself into Erich's room with her master key. She found him lying face down at his desk.

'Erich, *mon chou!*' She hurried forward anxiously. Was he breathing? Then she smiled in relief as she saw the gentle rise and fall of his chest. She tiptoed forward. Envelopes were scattered over his desk. She glanced at them, puzzled; they all bore addresses in France. Then she noticed that his arm was resting on a number of handwritten scraps. Careful not to wake him, she eased one out from under his arm and read it. So this was what he had been doing. She put back the note, her eyes pricking with tears. She bent low and whispered, '*Merci*, Erich,' as she tiptoed away.

Erich came back from an early dinner to find Elaine sitting on the edge of his desk, apparently lost in thought. She looked nice like that, quiet and pensive. He approached, half expecting one of her little flirtatious looks, or some banter. What he saw was affection, even respect. It nearly disarmed him. He wanted to talk, to tell her about yesterday, and how it had changed him, but shame held him back; anyway she wouldn't know what he was talking about.

A murmured '*Guten Morgen*,' and he sat down at his desk. He had meant to look busy but found himself just gazing at the polished surface, seeing again the notes laid out as he had read them last night. Not one of these notes had spoken of the misery, the hunger, the stench, the uncertainty; they had lied in order to spare the people they loved.

Elaine came around the desk, and stood close; he breathed in the clean smell of her body. He longed just to turn and bury his face in her softness. She put her arm over his shoulders and drew him towards her. Suddenly Erich was revolted by himself. He pulled himself away and stood up, keeping her at arms length.

'*NEIN!*' He shouted at her. '*Ich bin schmutzig!* I am dirty, dirty, dirty!' He felt Elaine watching his back as he strode down towards his room, where he sat shaking, trying to recall the feel of her arm across his shoulders and the whisper of her breath against his cheek. It represented something he had lost the right to.

Elaine didn't flirt with him any more after that; something good had happened between them and he wasn't sure what it was. With Louise, however, Erich was like a lion chained. The last shreds of his Nazism had disappeared on Platform 14 of the Gare de l'Est.

'Just tell me what to do Louise and I will do it!' But Louise was too stunned to think. Whenever she tried to get her mind to bear on what he had told her, all she saw were the brave letters, and the torn and scribbled notes. They scrolled behind her eyes like Izaac's music as he played, each with its own sad tale.

CHAPTER 27

Frenetic activity at the Jeu de Paume

It was a time of frenetic activity at the Jeu de Paume. Rather to Louise's surprise, Erich was throwing himself into it with as much energy as the others; hastily packing pictures that hadn't even been catalogued. She envied him this preoccupation.

'What's the hurry, Erich?' she asked when she could get him alone.

'The British and the Americans are advancing and will be in Paris in a few weeks. Everyone here is trying to save as much as they can for the Führer museum. The whole collection is to be got out of Paris and hidden in the salt mines in Austria. The atmosphere in the mines is perfect for preserving pictures, indeed almost anything. Also, being underground, they'll be safe from bombing.'

'But why are you helping? Let the British and Americans come. I bet they'll take better care of your pictures than the Germans.'

'They might, if they ever got them. General von Brugen has signalled me to say that Hitler plans to order the total destruction of Paris if our troops are driven out. Do you realise what this means? It means blowing up the Louvre, Notre Dame, the Jeu de Paume, and everything that's in them. On top of that, Göring and the others are already gathering like vultures to snap up anything they think they will be able to sell after the war. I've got to save what I can!' Louise felt a wave of panic on her own behalf.

'What will happen to me, Erich? I don't want to fall into the hands of someone like Göring. But I can't expect you to go on hiding my picture for ever.'

'I'd never let that happen to you, Louise. I have a plan. You remember I told you about the salt mines in Altaussee?' Louise nodded.

'Well, that's one of the main repositories chosen for storing the pictures. Using the excuse that I worked in that mine, I've asked for permission to go there to help store the art. I'm going to take your picture there; it's the one place I know you will be safe and where I will be able to find you again.'

~~~

Louise could hear thunder … or something that sounded like thunder. But it was sharper, more rhythmic. A train, that was it, the clack of wheels on a railway track, followed by the manic shriek of brakes. She heard wooden doors being thrown open, there were harsh shouts, and the barking of fierce dogs; a child cried in terror. Someone announced an unfamiliar name – Auschwitz – a station perhaps? She thought of Erich's description of the transport of Jews in the Gare de l'Est and an icy chill gripped her heart. Suddenly the truth burst upon her. She had been deluding herself. Those images that Klaus had shown her were not just the foul imaginings of a deranged mind, they were real! So too then were the nightmare images that Izaac had accidentally let her see!

A silent scream rose in her mind, 'Are you all right, Izaac? Tell me you're all right.' Nothing. Time passed, days, weeks, a month, and still there was no response. Was it all over with him? Then just when she was convinced she had lost all contact with him, he sent her one small message of hope – the unmistakable sound of a violin being tuned. He was still able to play. He must be all right! Those few notes evoked a deep memory in her. For a moment she was back in Vienna, watching little Izaac turn, riveted by the sound being produced by the Cloud Lady, Helena Stronski.

⟨✺⟩

'Erich, I think Izaac's been moved. I heard a train, dogs, the name of a station I didn't know. I never told you of the horrible things that Klaus showed me: corpses, death. I thought they were just in his mind, but they are true. We've got to rescue Izaac. Take me with you, or leave me in your salt mine and go alone. We've got to do something now! Please Erich!'

Erich paused in his work. 'Believe me, Louise, I'd go off and find Izaac for you this very moment if I could, but I can't, I really can't. I would need travel documents, tickets, high security passes; it just can't be done. With the Americans and British advancing on Paris, let's hope it will be over soon.'

Louise sighed, he was right. She was powerless; all she could do at present was hope.

⟨✺⟩

When the klaxon started wailing they both looked up, Reichsmarschall Göring! Another surprise visit! And, as if that wasn't bad enough, a familiar voice, that neither of them wanted to hear, was ringing down the corridor.

'Erich! It's *him*, Klaus! Don't let him near me! He'll see me, I know it!'

Erich, already on his way to his room to smarten up for Göring's visit, stopped in his tracks.

'Klaus! What's he doing here? I'll run him out of the place!'

'No, Erich, please be sensible. Be civil and find out what he wants.' Resisting the temptation to fade into her picture, Louise stepped back out of the light. She wasn't going to miss this encounter.

'Erich, my friend! I come by special train all the way across Europe to see you and I find you busy.' Erich made a choking noise in his throat. 'Don't *worry*, old son. Run along and change, you can't go down to the fat man like that. I'll be good and read the paper quietly until you get back.' Erich hurried into his bedroom and emerged seconds later adjusting his tie. 'See you when you're done,' Klaus called. 'We'll chew the fat then and talk about old times.' He leaned back in Erich's chair with the air of someone who was there for the day, but as soon as the sound of Erich's footsteps began to recede, he laid down his paper, walked to the door, looked left and right, and closed it.

'Perfect timing!' Louise heard him mutter.

To her surprise, Klaus went straight down to Erich's bedroom. She heard drawers being opened, a cupboard door creaked, and a tap was run briefly. In a few minutes he re-emerged, slicking down his hair. Louise covered a gasp. Klaus was dressed in Erich's one good suit; the likeness was uncanny. He walked past her, humming, and went straight to the wall opposite Erich's desk, turned her picture face out, ran his eye over her portrait and said, 'Good, you're still here. I've been doing some research on you: "The Master of Delft's finest work", value astronomical, according to one expert, conveniently deceased. So Erich and I are the only ones who know that you are here, and dear old Erich can't talk because he would have to explain why you have never been catalogued for the Führer museum. Food for thought, isn't it? But now to more urgent matters.'

He turned away and dropped to one knee; Louise realised with relief that it was really Erich's safe that interested him. She stepped forward. He hummed as he turned the dials on the combination lock. Then he sat back on his hunkers, looking pleased with himself. 'Klaus never forgets,' he said as the door swung open. 'So this is the moment when Klaus Steinman becomes Erich Hoffman.' He reached into the safe.

Don't be a fool, don't be a fool, Louise thought, but she could contain herself no longer. 'How dare you take Erich's things! Put them back!' Klaus froze, but only for a second. Then he raised his hands in mock submission and turned to the point in the room where he'd heard her voice. She saw his eyes lock on to her like a stoat on a rabbit, and felt about as helpless.

'So there you are. Louise, isn't it? I knew you wouldn't be able to resist me for long. Don't look so surprised. My brat sister, Gretchen, told her mother and her father all about how you used to appear to Izaac, so why shouldn't you appear for me? Perhaps you'd like to help?'

'Don't you dare!' she said again, but she could have spared her breath. He turned back to the safe, withdrew a packet of documents and began to examine them. 'Damn me, Erich, you old fox! So you've been working for the Secret Police all this time. Well, Louise, we don't want these, do we? I want to be Erich the art expert, not Erich the spy.' He put the incriminating papers away. As he did so a small object fell from the packet, a coin perhaps, and rolled away; Klaus didn't notice it.

'Now, here's what I'm after.' He took Erich's passport, kissed it, and put it on the desk. Then he reached into his pocket and took out a small wad of papers. 'Fair exchange, no robbery. My identity in exchange for his. Now he has my uniform, my Death's Head Squad identity papers and even my travel passes to Auschwitz in September.' Auschwitz – why did that name sound familiar? Louise wondered. But Klaus's next words grabbed her attention. 'If our mutual friend, Abrahams, survives that long, no doubt he will play for him. I'm just sorry I won't be there to show him around.'

'What do you want with Erich's passport? Why, you've even taken his clothes!' Klaus smiled, popped his SS papers into the safe and slid Erich's precious passport into his pocket.

'Haven't you worked it out yet? Has Erich not been keeping you up to date, then? If our incompetent armies lose the war – and it looks as if they may – what do you think is going to happen to the elite SS? Our efforts to solve the Jewish question may not be appreciated, so a group of my colleagues decided to set up an escape route, with safe houses for ourselves in Brazil where we can re-group before disappearing into the South American continent. I, my dear, am the pathfinder, the chosen emissary, I have their money, I have Erich's passport ...'

'You rat! You're going to cheat on them, aren't you?' Louise exploded.

'Clever, isn't it? If by any chance my colleagues escape the hangman's noose and come looking for Klaus Steinman and their life savings, all they will find is a cooling trail leading to a blameless soul called Erich Hoffmann, a retired art expert.'

There were barked commands below. The noise level was rising. Göring would be leaving. Louise glanced hopefully towards the door. Klaus caught her glance.

'He's coming, is he? It's the back stairs for me then, but I've not forgotten you; I'll be back.'

And Klaus was gone.

⚜

Elaine saw Erich's figure hurrying down the corridor ahead of her; why wasn't he seeing Göring off?' The room looked bare now that most of the pictures were gone. She would miss Erich, and wandered round unhappily, remembering where they had had their little flirtations. She crossed over to his desk, gave it a desultory swipe with her duster and then spotted something lying on the floor. She bent, picked the object up, and then she stood staring at it in a state of mental paralysis. It was a small metal oval showing the Nazi eagle holding a swastika. There was a hole punched in it for a lanyard to hang around the neck. She turned it over, *Geheime Staatspolizei 7942*. A Gestapo identity disk. 'Oh, Erich, no,' she said. 'Not you! Please, it can't be yours!' She looked up, and there he was at the door, smiling, relieved that the ordeal over.

'Well, thank God that's over, Elaine, the Reichsmarschall's last visit I hope.' He walked over to her, his face open and happy. 'How will I manage without you, Elaine? A little kiss?' He stopped.

Against all rules, against all training, Elaine slowly opened her hand. Erich didn't notice what she was doing immediately; she had to glance towards it to get him to look.

'Oh dear,' he said, 'I'm afraid I have been careless.' She wanted to scream. Didn't the idiot realise the danger he was in? Didn't he realise that all she had to do was take the disk to her commander, together with his name, and he would be found floating in the Seine tomorrow? But, of course how could he, she was just little Elaine, the cleaner, who was here for him to flirt with. By revealing her hand to Erich, she had probably blown her cover. So she decided she had nothing to lose now.

'Erich,' she said slowly, 'you may not be all you seem, but neither am I. And I want to know what you are doing with this Gestapo disk.'

Erich looked at her in surprise. 'Are you *interrogating* me?' There was a slight smile on his face still, but it vanished when Elaine said, quietly: 'Yes. That is just what I am doing, Herr Hoffman. I am a member of the Resistance. Kindly sit down ...'

In a way it was a relief to tell her – about his work with General von Brugen; about the secret reports. Elaine listened in silence, then she said, 'What were you doing on Platform 14 of the Gare de l'Est last time Göring's special train came in?' She made it sound like an accusation. Erich stared at her, how did she know that? He had told nobody, literally nobody, about that incident. Only Louise knew. As he stumbled through his description of what he had seen and how he had collected the notes and letters of the people on the trucks, he relived the shame he had felt on that day.

Elaine had seen some of those pathetic scraps of paper on his desk. It had looked as though he were posting them, but she had to be sure.

'These letters,' she said sarcastically. 'Were they full of State secrets that the Gestapo must know about?' Erich, now close to breaking down, remembered those scribbled notes; he looked up at Elaine. Her outline was becoming blurred. He couldn't stop the tears.

'What *were* you planning to do, Erich, before I found this disk?' He noticed the past tense. He spread his hands so that they lay palm up on the desk, the white rope burns from his climbing exploits clearly visible.

'Would you believe me if I told you that I was planning to do some small thing to resist the Nazi monster I have helped to create?'

Élaine stood up, slipping the incriminating Gestapo disc into the pocket of her apron. His tears had been real, she was sure of that. But when she spoke her voice was hard.

'Herr Hoffman, I have no choice. I will hand this disk to my superiors. I will, however, delay doing this by exactly twenty-four hours. By which time you must be out of Paris, preferably out of France. Go then and tackle your monster.'

It was one o'clock on the following morning when Erich's train crossed the border into Germany, and the last Frenchman left his compartment. It had been a frenetic day, making excuses for his sudden departure and acquiring a temporary passport. He had had no time to talk to Louise about the theft of his clothes and his papers. It had to be Klaus, but why he had done it, he had no idea. The German border guards accepted the temporary passport and he relaxed. Louise's portrait, carefully wrapped, rested on top of his suitcase. With the hostile Frenchmen gone, Louise joined him in the carriage. The lights were dimmed and the windows were blacked out. Trains were favourite targets for enemy bombers. To the measured clack-clack of the wheels on the track, she told Erich about Klaus's visit, and how it was Klaus who had dropped Erich's identification disc.

'Fortunately I had my identity card in my pocket when he came. All he seems to have been interested in was my passport, and of course the visas. I don't fancy changing identity with Klaus Steinman.' Erich poked distastefully at the papers Klaus had left for him in the safe. 'What are these?'

'He called it his present for you.'

'All this SS Death's Head squad stuff makes me sick now. So, what have we here? A leave form, travel passes, security passes, all to a place called Auschwitz. I'm finished with this Nazi *Scheiße*, I think I'll just throw the lot out of the window.'

'No, Erich, don't! I've got a feeling about it. I'm almost certain Izaac is in this "Auschwitz" place. I heard the name when I dreamed about him being on a train, and then Klaus mentioned it, and how Izaac might play for you there. Oh, if only you could turn Klaus's trick against him!'

Erich shuddered. 'I've already nearly been turned over to the French Resistance because of him. Anything to do with Klaus is bad news. I've got to get some sleep now. We can talk about it later.'

Erich settled back. Louise tried to think ahead. In the morning they would arrive at some huge picture depot in Munich, where her picture might easily be discovered and taken from him. But she needed Erich to rescue Izaac. More and more she had a feeling that time was running out for him. She would give him an hour or two's sleep and then tackle him.

───※────

Back in Paris Élaine was serving in her father's cafe when the familiar figure of Pierre came in and sat at a small table tucked out of sight in the back of the café. She shivered. Thank God Erich had got safely away. Pierre, the executioner, was bad news. She went over, in her own time, and stood ready to take his order. He wasted no breath:

'We got him, your Gestapo bugger; the boss wants you to identify him. Absinthe please.'

───※────

Élaine stared incredulously at the familiar suit, the face – none the better for a bullet hole in the middle of it. How could this have happened? She had actually *seen* Erich climb into the car to be driven to the station. One half of her wanted to run screaming from the filthy cellar where his body lay, the other half stayed cool.

'The hands,' she demanded. 'Turn over his hands.' She looked, and looked again. Those hands had never held a falling climber; they were as clean and unscarred as a babe's. She turned to Pierre.

'That's him, that's Erich alright,' and her smile had a look of triumph that chilled even Pierre the executioner.

'Did you see her smile? She's a tough one, that Élaine!' he said to his colleague. 'You know, we all thought she was sweet on him!'

───※────

While Erich slept, Louise had come up with a plan. But was it preposterous to expect him to risk everything, life included, just to rescue her friend, one Jew out of thousands? Clack ... clack ... time was running out. She was jerked awake by shouts outside.

'Erich, wake up! Open the blinds, I want to see.' He unhooked a blind and it shot up, revealing crazy images of wrecked carriages, cranes, and a half capsized engine.

'Must have been bombed.' He reached up to pull the blind back down again.

'Erich, we've got to talk. We've only got an hour or two.'

He looked at her through gummed up eyes. 'All right,' he said eventually. 'Tell me.'

When Louise had finished, Erich took out Klaus's papers and examined them closely this time. Together they went step by step through what he would have to do if he was to get to Auschwitz.

'There is one problem I can see no way around. How I will persuade them to release Izaac to me? I will need some compelling reason.'

'You know, Erich; there is someone you've told me about who I've always liked the sound of ... ' she looked at Erich, her head to one side. Would he have the same idea?

'Von Brugen! Of course!' He thumped his knee. 'He's the one person I could ask. That very first time, after the Winkler affair, von Brugen asked me for Izaac's name, almost as if he would try to do something for him. All I need is an order from him for the "release of Jew Izaac Abrahams into the custody of the bearer for the purpose of interrogation. Signed, General von Brugen." No need to involve him in the details.'

'Then what will you do with Izaac if you rescue him? Hide him in the salt mines?'

'Not a bad idea. If I could find one of the old entrances that hasn't been blocked off, but I have another idea. My mother moved to Altaussee when Father died. There is a loft there that could be made habitable. I will check it out.'

Erich was too busy, and there were too many people around for any fond farewells when he finally brought Louise to the salt mines. However, Louise did manage to see the place where her picture was being stored, in an alcove behind the chapel altar. The altar was made of salt and it glowed with a honey light when the lights were on. Her portrait was packed exactly like all the other pictures: corrugated cardboard, brown paper, string, and a label. The only differences were that the number on the label was bogus, and that Erich had 'accidentally' spilled a blot of red ink on one corner. His last words to her were: 'Don't expect too much, Louise. You have no idea of the security surrounding the camps.'

She heard his footsteps retreating, and a silence deeper than anything she had ever experienced closed about her. On every side were piled the priceless art treasures of Europe. From time to time there would be a hum from the pumps deep in the mine, otherwise nothing. Out of sight, out of mind – had they effectively died – these beautiful works that had given so much pleasure and love, fading from the memories of the people who had given them life or dying as those people died somewhere above? Gradually, however, Louise realised that there was life still within the cavern surrounding her. She thought of them as tiny candles of light around her, springing into life as they were remembered by former owners, families, servants, just as she felt herself flicker to life when Izaac played, or when Erich thought of her waiting in the mine. Ominously, as the weeks went by she realised, that these tiny lights were getting fewer and fewer around her.

CHAPTER 28

Auschwitz Concentration Camp

Within hours Izaac had been sucked into the mad system that ran the enormous concentration camp, feeling like an insect crawling through some vast machine. There was no escape from the daily routine: identity parade, march to work, dig a drain, be yelled at, kicked or punched, fill in the drain, march back, queue for food, stand in line for the toilet, wash in an inch of water, and never, never leave property unguarded – another day over. Cogs – black-uniformed SS men, guard dogs, Kapos (collaborators) who were worse than the dogs, foul food, dysentery – waited to crush the unwary. Nobody knew or cared who or what Izaac was, nor did they want to know about music or orchestras. The man in the bunk above him died, probably of despair. Help carry the corpse to the mortuary, nearly full today.

What looked like a well-oiled machine was, in fact, chaos, everything was out of sync. Buildings were built and never used; roads were laid that were never finished. When you arrived at work, exhausted, it was time to turn for home. Only by throwing the lives of people at a job was anything ever achieved, and all the time smoke poured from the chimney in the little wood. *Don't listen to the stories about the gas chambers and the crematoria. Don't think about them! Stay alive!*

f it, then he picked up the violin, and ran his fingers over the
rings. It was still almost in tune. Perhaps it was only days
nce … he checked himself. He suddenly felt very much
one. He wanted Louise, he needed her, but he had managed
keep her out of his mind for the last month; this was no time
share his experiences with her.

Perhaps if he just tuned Helena's violin, Louise would pick
s up and know that he was thinking of her. He put his bow
the strings. The notes swooped and settled as he turned the
gs, tuning the four strings closer to each other until they
rged in perfect harmony. Then he drew his bow and played
brief scales and runs that he always played after tuning, fin-
ing on the high delicate harmonics. Instantly he was back in
past, playing the Dvorak Violin Concerto and listening to
wild harmonies that Louise had accidentally released to
that day.

e began to play, and out it came, like water breaching a
, a trickle, then faster and faster as all the bottled up fears
misery of the last weeks flowed out of him: the transport,
camp, all the things he had carefully concealed from her.
e was nothing he could do but let it go, as helpless as Pan-
when she opened her box and accidentally released all its
into the world until there was nothing left in her box but
. Poor Louise, had he sent her all that misery without hope?

⚜

gin with, playing Helena's violin was like riding a thor-
bred. Ramon, his conductor, would look down kindly at
nd Izaac would apologise.
ry, Ramon, did I cut loose a bit?' But Ramon didn't mind
se since Izaac had come, he found himself looking down
ty alert and interested faces, all wondering what their
ader would do next. In order to discipline himself, Izaac

But Izaac was no good at not thinking about things; he
couldn't sleep, he got dysentery, his hands bled, raw from the
unaccustomed work; he no longer cared; within a month he
was on a downward spiral into despair.

He nearly missed the shout when it came. 'Izaac bloody
Abrahams!' Exhausted after a day carrying bricks, he struggled
to the door where the kapo in charge of his barrack was standing. 'I have a message for you. You can have it for one bread
ration.'

'What do you mean?'

'Do you or do you not want to hear the message?' Izaac's
stomach was writhing with hunger, but he had no choice.
Reluctantly he handed over his quarter loaf.

'Report to barrack C28,' the kapo instructed. 'And go now,
before I change my mind!'

⚜

As Izaac sidled between the bunks in his new barracks, hands
reached out to shake his. He swapped names and found himself talking to musicians he had heard of from all over Europe.
Some he recognised joyfully from Terezín. The barracks was
identical to the one he had left, except that this one was clean.
The food was the same, but because the kapo – also a musician – was honest, there was no thieving. The morning bustle
started even earlier here because the various bands and
orchestras had to be ready to play at roll call. They would play
stirring marches and gay waltzes as the work-parties marched
out.

The barracks, like all the others, were segregated, but he
met his young friend Deborah in the rehearsal room; even with
her shorn head she looked pretty. He thanked her profusely
for rescuing him from the hell of the main camp. As he did so
he was shocked to realise that the sense of purpose, the desire

to entertain and to perfect his music that had driven him while in Terezín, had been subtly replaced by a more primitive urge – the urge to survive.

'We must get you a violin, Maestro,' she said. 'Perhaps I will be allowed to take you.'

It was a long walk past interminable barrack buildings to a place where groups of young women, working in the open, were separating vast piles of clothing into smaller piles. Suitcases were stacked in mountains. Inside one shed Izaac saw piles of shoes spilling towards the door.

'Where *does* all this come from?' he murmured in amazement.

Deborah looked at him, and he followed her eyes to where a chimney belched black smoke into the hot summer air. Izaac winced. Despite grudging confirmation from his former workmates, he still could not take in the reality of the gas chambers, and the crematoria. Deborah took his arm briefly; she understood. They all had to go through this dreadful moment of realisation.

She opened the door to a smaller store and they stood there, peering into the comparative darkness. First to come to sight were the brass instruments, gleaming like coiled snakes. Gradually Izaac realised that the four walls were literally piled high with musical instruments. Most of them were still in their cases, but others, gypsy fiddles for example, that had possibly never had a case in their life, were uncovered. Two double bases leaned together like drunks in conversation against the wall. He walked in. Where do you start, when faced with a six-foot pile of violins?

They were as different and as uniform as the players in an orchestra. Izaac ran his eyes over the heap and realised he was counting not just violins, but the lives of violinists. All these lives ... Suddenly he felt a chill that began at the back of his

disciplined them.

'Go on, go on,' Deborah told him in private. 'We love it, it's good for us.' The players would now linger in the rehearsal room and listen while Izaac took the legendary Stradivarius for a gallop. He would imagine himself back in Vienna being wrestled with by Madame Helena as she tried to mould him into a proper playing position. Instead of Louise shouting at him to 'go back. Get it right!' he was doing just this with his orchestra.

Members of the orchestra played in the mornings and evenings, for roll calls and while the working parties came and went. In between these times, many, like Deborah, had to do part-time work, but they also had to be available for two hours practice in the afternoons. There were camp concerts for inmates, and sometimes public concerts for the Nazi officers' friends and guests. The orchestra even wore dress clothes on these occasions, suits salvaged from the piles of garments that Deborah had shown Izaac on his first day with the orchestra. Izaac's health improved, his dysentery subsided. Of all their duties, the one they dreaded most was having to play during the selection process, when exhausted people from the transports were divided up, the 'lucky' ones sent to join work gangs, the others directed towards the grove of trees, and thence, as they all now knew, straight to the gas chambers. 'Don't look, don't listen, just play; it's the only thing you can do to help them,' Ramon advised on each of these occasions. So far Izaac had been spared this ordeal.

He now felt 'secure in the saddle' when playing the Strad, but that didn't mean he had complete control over it. It was as if Helena's rebelliousness was wrestling to get out and make some statement about the monster that was devouring them.

In the deep silence of the salt mines, Louise Eeden was wide awake. She had felt Izaac drawing on her, working with her, fighting some technical battle with his violin, and had wondered at the memories of Helena Stronski that this had invoked. Could it be Helena who was playing? She listened for her characteristic style, but no, this was definitely Izaac.

Louise would 'return' after these sessions, tired but triumphant. Perhaps there was a major concert coming up? Izaac was certainly playing at concert pitch. Then there were periods of silence when she was out of Izaac's mind. It was during one of these that she began to think about Erich, or perhaps Erich was thinking about her? She wondered where he was, and to amuse herself began to picture in her mind the compass points from which Izaac's and Erich's messages were coming. She imagined them as two steady beacons in the blackness of the mine. Then, quite suddenly, she was alert. Surely one of the beacons had moved; they were no longer so far apart. They were converging. Erich had set out for Auschwitz.

⌁〰️⌁

Ramon looked with deep misgivings at the order sheet that had come from SS headquarters. Not only did it demand an orchestra for a selection, it listed specific players, most of them from Terezín. Izaac Abrahams's name had even been underlined! Ramon had survived the camp longer than most, and had come to understand the Nazi mind. They loved to spring surprises. It was as if, bored by the daily quota of death, they needed to spice it up with special events, 'entertainments', which were invariably at the expense of their victims. He wondered if he should share his misgivings with Izaac; after all he was the leader of the orchestra. Then he decided against it. Ramon hadn't survived by taking risks.

When he saw where they were to play, Ramon was even

more suspicious. Though out of doors, it was like a stage set. The orchestra had been placed so that the players were on a slight rise facing the barbed wire that would separate them from the people arriving from the transport. It looked to him as though they had been placed there not so much to play, but to see. A transport had arrived earlier and the last of the people were filing past when they arrived to set up.

'We are Hungarians!' one of them had shouted up to them, but Ramon knew that his orchestra had not been called out to play for the Hungarians. Ramon looked to the right, to where the SS men in their black uniforms were standing, casually laughing and talking among themselves, boots and leather gleaming. What went on in their brains that they could laugh and look so normal, knowing where these starving, broken, people were going? As he watched, the SS men became alert; two trucks were backing up. Ramon got the impression that these were what the SS men had been waiting for. Several of them looked up towards the orchestra to see their reactions. Get the orchestra playing, quickly, was his solution. The busier they were, the less upsetting it would be. He tapped on his music stand to call the orchestra to attention.

~*~

Izaac had been sitting in his place in the front row of the orchestra, trying to keep his hands warm enough to play. It was October and the air was sharp. He was trying not to think, fixing his gaze on a clump of thistles that grew a few metres away, their downy seed-heads sticking up like white shaving brushes. There was a whirr of small wings and the thistles sagged and bobbed under the weight of half a dozen goldfinches. Izaac smiled, but at that moment Ramon tapped on his music stand, and the birds were gone in a flash of colour and a puff of thistledown. Louise had always said she loved goldfinches; he wished she was here, and then almost immediately was glad she wasn't.

He looked up at Ramon, his thoughts still full of little red and gold birds, and raised his violin to lead the orchestra into 'The Blue Danube' waltz. While he played, his eyes settled on the two trucks that were now unloading their human cargo. *I'm not looking,* he persuaded himself as the tailgate of the first lorry dropped with a distant clang. *At least the soldiers are offering the people inside a hand down.* The trucks were high; too high for some of the smaller children to jump from. Some of the older children lifted down the little ones. *Just keep playing, even though it's still too far for them to hear us.* There are boys in one lorry and girls in the other. They seem delighted to see each other again. *Look, they are hugging; that's nice. They must know each other.* At that moment the impact of what he was watching hit Izaac like a fist below the belt, leaving him gasping for breath. Of course the children knew each other. Hadn't they been singing together in the opera Brundibár for a year?

This then was the 'treat' the Nazis had planned for him and for the other Terezín players: they were to play their own young friends into the gas chambers. There was Pepíček, one of the two children who had gone off to buy milk for their mother. Where was his sister, Aninka, Izaac wondered? But the ice cream man was there and the sparrow, and the cat. And there was Pafko – Brundibár himself. No clipboard or bucket could save him now. Izaac could feel himself rising in tribute to his young friend. Ramon shook his head, so Izaac sank down, recognising more faces from the two choirs, boys and girls mixing together for the last time.

The orchestra played through 'The Blue Danube' again. The children were nearly below them now, looking more subdued. Their first greetings over, they were beginning to look about them, beginning to wonder. Izaac turned the page. What had they been told to play for them next: 'The Trish Trash Polka'. *The Trish Trash Polka!* Sudden rage exploded behind Izaac's eyes. He could control himself no longer, and neither, it seemed could he control his violin. They rose together. Ramon coughed, his eyes blazing a warning, willing Izaac to sit down and not to be a fool; they could all be shot. He saw that one of the officers had indeed detached himself from the group of smirking SS men, delighted at having got a reaction from the Terezín players.

With a curt nod of apology to Ramon, Izaac walked away from the orchestra. Let them shoot him if they must, there was no need to endanger the others. He walked to the edge of the raised platform and looked down on the children. They looked up and saw him. He could see the relief in their faces; here was someone who would look after them. Their false trust ran through him like a sword. Without a smile or a wave he signalled to them to line up, just as their choirmaster would have done. Immediately, and to the astonishment of their guards, the children ran and formed themselves into their choir groups. Izaac raised his violin and played the first bars of the Terezín March, the defiant cheeky march that was performed at almost every function in Terezín. He could hear the noise of the little orchestra behind preparing to play too. One ... two ... three ... the high clear voices of the children rose as if to heaven and the audience of SS officers shifted uneasily as their 'little entertainment' began to go sour on them.

> '*We will conquer and survive*
> *All the cruelty in our land,*
> *We will laugh on ghetto ruins*
> *Hand in hand!*'

Izaac glanced behind him; the SS officer who had detached himself from the rest looked strangely familiar. Afraid of reprisals, he stepped forward and urged the children to walk on; he didn't want any shooting. Pafko was the first to move, grasping the situation in one. With a cheeky grin up at Izaac, he set off in a wonderfully exaggerated goose-step.

Izaac watched them go, their voices still ringing in his ears. Despite Pafko's efforts, they looked small and so vulnerable. This was monstrous! They must not be allowed go alone! He wanted to rush after them, but what good would it do them if he hurled himself against the barbed wire? Was there no way he could go with them, was there nothing he could do to support them on their journey?

As if it had waited two hundred and fifty years for this moment, Helena's Stradivarius rose to his shoulder. Yes, he did have something to give them: his music. He drew his bow. For a moment the violin seemed to gather its breath; then the bow bit into the strings and the music poured out. Rising, it seemed to fill the vastness of the open air about the children as Izaac played the composition that had exploded in his three-year-old head in Vienna all those years ago; Helena's 'Humoresque'. The children knew it because he had often played it between rehearsals to keep them happy; they turned to wave. Watching them down the length of his strings, he noticed that they were beginning to dance, a whirling movement that seemed strangely familiar. How often he had seen them playing like this on the Brundibár set and wondered what they were dancing about.

Then in the very vortex of the dance he saw a flash of green, and Louise was there, reaching out as if to catch their hands and swing the little ones as they swirled about her like a flock of birds. So this was the origin of those games! Despite his efforts to shield her from the horrors of the camp, she had been there, invisible to him but not to them. For a second his resolve faltered; he would give his life for those children; he would sacrifice his music for them, but Louise – was she his to give?

'Louise,' he called out silently, just as he would have called to during a performance: 'Louise, you shouldn't be here. Do you know what you are doing? Do you know where you are going?' Her reply came back to him as clearly as if she was beside him. 'Yes, of course I know, Izaac. I've been with you all along. These are my children too, you know. Just play on, and we'll see them through this together.' And so they did.

Then they were gone. Izaac's arms sank slowly to his sides. He turned to face his fate. The members of the orchestra were standing, staring after the departed children, applauding them by tapping their instruments with their bows, a tiny rattle of sound that swelled and faded. Behind the orchestra the small group of SS officers was breaking up, drifting away, kicking at thistles, tasting perhaps the first bitter taste of defeat. Izaac stood, wondering what to do with his violin; it still throbbed with fury in his hands.

He found himself staring into the face of an SS officer who must have walked up while he was playing. He handed him the violin and waited for the shot. The officer took the violin but his eyes were focused on where the children had just vanished. In an awed voice he said, as if to himself, 'Dear God, what are we doing, what have we done? At least they had Louise. It's what she would have wanted.' Then he looked at his hand and saw that he was holding Izaac's violin. He pulled himself together visibly. When he spoke next it was a prepared statement.

'Izaac Abrahams,' he said. 'If you recognise me, I would ask you to keep quiet about it. If we get away safely there will be time enough for explanations.'

CHAPTER 29

Between the Mountains and the Sea

Erich and Izaac sat facing each other in silent animosity as their train inched its way across Poland towards Austria. Erich had given the Jew a brief account of how he had come to Auschwitz specifically to rescue him. The Nazis had thought that they were entertaining Klaus Steinman, who for them had an enviable reputation for brutal efficiency, so they had invited their guest to observe their own little display of Jew baiting. Now that the fear of discovery was receding, the sheer horror of what he had seen was beginning to take effect on Erich.

'At least the children are safe in heaven now,' he sighed.

The train clacked mechanically on; the Jew appeared not to be listening. He was looking out of the window. Erich watched him in his reflection. When he did reply it was to the passing fields.

'You know, Herr Hoffman, I think heaven is the one thing that you have denied them. What is heaven but a promise, and a comfort for those of us who are left behind? Perhaps it exists, perhaps it doesn't, but you know, even in your concentration camps we found heaven ... little bits of it, scattered on the ground; we picked these up and treasured them far more than any promise.'

Someone, lugging a suitcase, passed in the corridor, looked

in, saw the SS uniform and what looked like a Jewish prisoner, and went on. Erich looked down at his jack-booted feet.

'Can we ever be forgiven?' The train plunged into a tunnel, smoke swirled against the windows and the rotten smell of brown coal caused them to catch their breath. When the train emerged again into the weak autumn sunlight, Erich got up to open the window.

'Don't look to me for comfort, Herr Hoffman. *I* can never forgive you.' Izaac's voice rose momentarily: 'and *what right* ... excuse me ... what right have I to forgive you on behalf of the people you have murdered? Nobody, not even God, can forgive you. You have to *work* for forgiveness; you have to *earn* forgiveness by accepting what you have done in the depth of your heart. Don't ask someone else to do this for you.' A thin, almost apologetic smile crossed his face, and he looked Erich in the eyes for the first time. 'Now, tell me, why have you have come to rescue me alone, out of so many?'

⸙

Deep underground in the salt mines of Altaussee the silence of oblivion wrapped itself like a protective cloak about Louise. The slender threads of consciousness that had given her life had been burned up in the horror of what the Nazis had done. All that remained for her was a lingering awareness of self and, just occasionally, a sound that might have been the whisper of a pen moving on paper.

She knew nothing of the conversation that took place between Erich and Izaac on the train; a conversation that ended, not so much in reconciliation, but in understanding. She was unaware when the SS manoeuvred a five-hundred-pound bomb into the mine directly above her, with the intention of blowing the entire collection sky-high should Germany lose the war.

Spring came slowly in the mountains above where Izaac lay hidden in the loft of Sabine Hoffman's house. He heard a sudden commotion below, and sat up. It was Erich, who had been waiting to engage in a peaceful handover of the priceless contents of the mine to the victors. What had happened? Izaac heard the ladder being put in place, followed by the agreed tap on the trap door. He slid the bolt. Erich stood shoulder high in the light from below.

'Herr Abrahams, you must come. The Americans are about to enter the valley, but I have just heard that the SS have planted a huge bomb in the salt mine, and that they will explode it before the Americans arrive. I must take action now. I have been in touch with the salt miners, who are horrified, partly because of the art, but chiefly because this is their place of work. They know of ways into the mine that the SS don't know about. As I know where the pictures are stored, and have been trained in defusing mines from my SS days, I am going with them. I may not succeed and I certainly can't do it carrying Louise's portrait under my arm. I want you to come, take Louise's portrait and escape with her picture from the mine. I promised her she would be safe; I need you to help me fulfill that promise.'

'I will come,' Izaac said.

They entered the mine through an old drainage tunnel and waded in until they came to an iron ladder. At the top was a grill with a padlock. Long handled cutters soon disposed of this and they were into the modern workings. While the miners searched for the bomb, Erich led Izaac down to the underground chapel. The package containing Louise's portrait was still there, the seals intact. This was the moment for Erich to hand it over. A sudden urge came over him to open it and see Louise for a last time.

A shout from above indicated that the miners had found the bomb. He would have to go. But down in the chapel a bizarre tug of war was taking place. Erich, having initially offered the package to Izaac, found that his hands just would not let go. Suddenly old resentments and old hates resurged and boiled between them. Then, as quickly as they had come, the resentments passed. Erich managed to give the package to Izaac; they embraced briefly, then one of the young partisans showed Izaac the way out of the mine. It was May 1945; in a few days the war in Europe would be over.

⤠〰⧈〰

Izaac returned to Vienna later in the summer. He half expected to find that his apartment had been requisitioned by some Nazi family, but when he rang the bell, it was Lotte, her hair nearly white now, who opened the door and welcomed him with tears of joy and sadness. She told him how his mother and father had been taken away, not long after he was transported. She was sure that he would have met them there? 'No,' he told her, tearfully. No, he had not met Father or Mother, nor, indeed, Uncle Rudi or Nathan and his family. Lotte supposed that the east must be a very big place, then, and Izaac agreed.

For weeks he occupied himself in searching for their names on lists; but it was too soon. All he could do for now was put their names down as 'missing' and hope for a miracle. He sat in the music room, but every corner held memories, and he decided that he must get away. Gretchen and her husband implored him to come and live with them, but he couldn't bring his countless ghosts into that happy family. So he sold the apartment and in doing so released Lotte to take up Gretchen's offer of a place in her home where, if she wished, she could help look after Konrad, the little boy who had waved to 'Uncle Izaac' the day he was taken off to Terezín. He made over half the proceeds of the sale of the apartment to Lotte by way of thanks for looking after it throughout the war. A pension would follow, but that would have to wait until he had persuaded their Swiss bank to open an account for him. It was time for Izaac to leave. When Konrad asked him where he was going, Izaac told him he was going to visit Herr Schnurrbart.

'Mummy, Mummy, Uncle Izaac is going to visit Mr Moustache! Isn't he funny?'

Gretchen was the only person he told where he was going. 'Gretchen, people keep telling me that I have to learn to forget, to blot it all out and start again.' Izaac could feel his voice tightening, rising. 'But, Gretchen, I don't *want* to forget.' He got himself under control. 'I've told you about the children in the little opera we put on! Am I to blot them out of my mind just for my own survival? Or the people I played with, or the weary Hungarians on their way to nowhere? No, there is something I can do for them still. I feel it in my bones, but I can't do it here. Every evening as the dark creeps out of the east, the black dogs come padding with it. Years ago, after I was nearly lynched by a Nazi gang in Berlin, I found myself in Ireland. There, between the mountains and the sea I found a place where I felt I was safe.'

'And Louise, can't she help you? I notice you haven't unwrapped her picture.'

'Oh, Gretchen, how can I explain? I played Louise into the gas chambers with them. She is just a memory too.'

'Look, Izaac, we created music together, and I know its healing properties. I want to see you happy. I don't know what you can do, but don't try to do it alone. Think of us and we'll think of you. Perhaps one day all three of us, Willie, Konrad and I, will come and find you in your place between the mountains and the sea.'

Gretchen and Konrad came to see Izaac off the following day. He had with him just one suitcase, Madame Helena's violin, complete with clown sticker, and a square package securely wrapped and sealed. Konrad was fascinated by the clown sticker.

Izaac stood on the deck of the mailboat from Wales, his back protected by the ship's funnel, watching their approach to Dublin. Early morning sun sparkled on the waves and lit the creamy underside of the seagull that hung close above him, riding the updraft from the moving ship. The two arms of Dublin Bay seemed to be held wide in welcome. Colour-washed houses lined the shore, and grey spires pierced a thin veil of mist. The humpy hills beyond the city were just beginning to glow.

Going through customs on arrival was disturbingly like arriving at a concentration camp. He chose his customs officer with care; a sleepy one.

'Just an old violin, you say?' the man said when Izaac opened its case. 'Well, it's not wrapped in silk stockings anyway.' He yawned and prodded Louise's portrait. 'A portrait, you say?'

'Of a friend.'

'Will you look at the wrapping, we'd never get that back together again.' A quick rummage in Izaac's case, and he was through. He was still blinking in the doorway when he got a hearty thump on the back and turned to see Paddy McCormack – he of the mighty moustaches – beaming down on him.

'Well, how are you, Mr Izaac? You don't look a day older!' Paddy lied happily. 'Give me that case. I got your telegram and I have the perfect little house for you. Near to where you played your violin to the seals all those years ago. Thirteen is it, well, time flies.' He heaved Izaac's bag into the train that stood waiting on the pier. 'We'll take the train to Galway, sir; petrol is terrible scarce these days. It'll be an ass and cart from then on.' He roared with laughter at his own joke and Izaac, who had no idea what an 'assncart' was, leaned back in the stuffy carriage. Apart from his expanding waistline, Paddy had hardly changed from his last visit. When he said, 'Which way, Mr Izaac?' Izaac remembered the response: 'West, Paddy bitte. To the sea!' and they laughed together.

∽⊶

It wasn't an ass and cart, but a rickety old car, hired from a garage in Galway, that Izaac eventually watched drive away, leaving him to survey his new property and his new world. The property was a thatched cottage. It had been empty for a year and looked it. There was grass growing from the thatch and the walls needed a coat of whitewash, but it was its sur-roundings that held Izaac spellbound. The cottage was tucked into the arm of a small semi-circular bay. The tide had been in when they arrived, so full that it seemed that one deep sigh from the Atlantic beyond and the cup would overflow. While they had unloaded the vast pile of things that Paddy had insisted on Izaac buying for his bachelor existence, the tide had secretly slipped away. So now, when Izaac turned from waving goodbye, he found himself gazing at a golden half-moon of sand with, in the far distance, a line of white breakers marking the sea. It drew Izaac like a magnet, crispy little pink flowers led down to the shore. Here he stepped cautiously on to the sand; it was firm.

∽⊶

Michael Joyce had stopped on the ridge looking down into the bay when he saw the car leaving. The cottage stood on his way

272

to the place, on the opposite side of the bay, where he kept his boat in a sheltered creek from which he could launch it at any tide. He had heard that someone had taken the cottage. He could see him now, walking out on the sand, picking up sea-shells like any child. The man's driver had told Kevin, the man at the petrol pump, that the new owner was foreign; a bache-lor who – God help him – had had a bad time in the war. As the figure was virtually out of sight, Michael diverted down past the cottage to look at the state of the place. He made a mental note of the hole in the thatch on the back of the roof and the meagre pile of the turf in the lean-to as he passed.

～✳✳✳～

Izaac had taken off his shoes and rolled up his trousers. Even on a calm day, the Atlantic rollers sent wavelets thick with foaming bubbles up the sand. They massaged his feet. The sun, sinking towards the horizon, glowed on the mountains; a warm and friendly barrier against things sinister and things past. He could hardly see his new little house. He must find out how to paint it. His supper had to be cold, as he couldn't get the strange fuel to light. He managed to light a candle but the oil lamp defeated him. When he opened the door in the morning, to his surprise he found a fresh fish on the windowsill.

～✳✳✳～

A year passed. Twice a week Izaac would get the bus into Galway where he gave violin lessons to half a dozen worthy but uninspired pupils. His humble ambition now was for them to pass their next grade in their violin exams. In an unfulfilled sort of way, he was happy. He was known to the locals as 'The Professor', and they watched over him as a sort of mascot. Things would happen to his little house without any prompting from him. The thatch would be raked down and a hole in it repaired, and one day just before Easter, he came home to find the walls newly whitewashed. He got to know his neighbours by trying to find out which one to pay. A cheque would arrive monthly from his Swiss bank and he would think, gratefully, if sadly, of Uncle Rudi and his little bags of gold. There was still no word of him, nor of the rest of Izaac's family. Michael Joyce, the fisherman, would often call with a fish and stay for a chat and a bottle of stout. Izaac developed both a taste for Guinness and a Galway lilt to add to his Austrian 'brogue'. He was urged to come down and play in the pub when the traditional musicians were there. He played Viennese airs for them, but when he tried to join in their traditional sessions it was a disaster. He could play the notes, but there were rhythms and subtleties he knew he could never master.

'A powerful violinist, but he's no fiddle player,' was the verdict in the pub.

Spring came, and Izaac became restless again. He practised his violin, and played for his pupils, rather as he did in the pub, to amuse. He realised more and more how much he had relied on Louise, until the idea that he couldn't play without her crept into his mind like a maggot. Her picture, still wrapped, lay propped against the wall. Time and again he was on the verge of opening it when he lost his nerve. What if her picture was no longer as he remembered it? Would she be reproachful for what he had done, or worse, would her eyes now be glazed with the violet bloom of death? On these occasions he would go out and climb the rocks above his house and let the Atlantic storms batter at him until these images faded. So the picture had remained unopened.

The post came by bicycle, ploughing through the blown sand where it invaded the road. There was the monthly envelope with a Swiss stamp and less frequent letters from 'Wien' with an Austrian one. This always brought out a smile in the Professor. When an official-looking letter with a Galway post-mark arrived, the postman lingered in case the foreigner needed help with it.

When Izaac asked, 'What does this "*Feis Ceoil*" mean?' the postman was already fishing in his pocket for his glasses.

'Well, now sir, it means Music Festival, sir. Would you like me to read it for you?' Izaac, not at all affronted, agreed. 'Dear Mr Abrahams, Knowing your reputation as a distinguished violinist, the Music Festival Board would like to invite you to participate in our annual Feis. We would be greatly honoured if you would conduct a master class for the winners in our strings sections. The fee ... ' The postman, pink to his hair, hastily thrust the letter back at Izaac. 'We're honoured to have you here, sir. Will I call for a reply tomorrow?'

'No, no need.' He began to close the door and then changed his mind. Would he? Could he? He wouldn't really have to play. Let them do the playing ... Just a bar or two. *Yes!* If he refused this, he might as well give up music completely. He opened the door; the postman and his bicycle had foundered in the sand. 'Herr Post!' he called. 'Can you spare me five minutes? I will reply!' As he could find neither ink nor paper it took longer than five minutes. 'Herr Post' didn't seem to be in a hurry and a bottle of stout eased the time.

To be honest, the master class was a disappointment. While there might be splendid fiddle players in the west of Ireland, classical players were few and far between. Izaac found him-self with time on his hands so he began to play what the great Fritz Kreisler used to call 'lollipops'; short pieces to bring a smile to the face of an audience. Izaac was beginning to enjoy himself when he noticed, perched alone on one of the empty seats at the back of his circle, a boy of perhaps six or seven who wasn't smiling. Izaac looked away ... then he looked back. The intensity of the child's gaze began to bother him. It was a challenge, but Izaac didn't feel ready for a challenge, he was out of practice. He'd finish with the Schubert 'Rosam ...' But he didn't because, without any warning, he found himself remembering the music room at home in Vienna. There were people in the room. They had their backs to him and looked strangely large, but facing him, in a positive drift of scarves, was the Cloud Lady. Her eyes were fixed on him and she was playing for him ... for him alone.

It felt as if the Stradivarius was rising on its own. There was only one piece of music that he could play in the circumstances. He tightened his bow, flexed his arm, and played. The Galway audience stirred uneasily. Here was something new, and a little frightening, but Izaac wasn't playing for them. He was playing for the child at the back just as intensely and just as irresponsibly as Helena had played for him. He played Helena's 'Humoresque', the piece that she had played for him first when he was a three-year-old. The Strad responded. Technically, Helena would have been ashamed of him, but musically her piece had probably only once been performed so well. While Izaac played he watched the boy's face as challenge changed to awe, and then to rapture. As Izaac lowered his violin he saw the boy turn to the girl sitting beside him with a radiant smile just to share his delight. The girl was Louise.

�⁓

Izaac waited until morning before he attempted to open the parcel. When he had arrived back from Galway last night it had been dark and he didn't want his first sight of the picture to be by candlelight. He cut the string. Erich had done a thorough job with layers of tissue, waxed paper, and then corrugated card. Izaac had moved his kitchen table so that the light from the half-door would fall across the picture as he unwrapped it. Now he took a deep breath and lifted the last sheet of wrapping.

Izaac staggered back. He thought he was going to have a heart attack. What appalling trick was this? Adolf Hitler! He dashed to the door, gasping for breath. Rabbits scuttled for their burrows. How could that swine Hoffman have done this to him? He turned to get a kitchen knife to slash the hateful image into strips. Then he hesitated. That frame was not the one he knew; it was a funny shape. He walked back and carefully turned it over. There it was, the so familiar Dutch interior. He carried it to the door. And there she was too, as the Master had painted her all those years ago, as fresh and as demanding as ever.

⸻✳⸻

It was just as he expected; she gave out severely to him over his playing. He was contrite; she was unforgiving. How could he have let himself slip like this? It was like old times. There was, however, one difference, and it affected them both. In mid-sentence Louise would pause, and Izaac would look up and see her lip tremble. She would turn away then and come back full of unnecessary bustle. The same would happen to him; some two-note phrase would remind him of the Brundibár lullaby perhaps, and he would have to stop and blow his nose.

One stormy evening when they had both hovered like this on the edge of the abyss, Louise said, 'Izaac, this has got to stop, we've got to stop playing for ourselves; just this once let's play for them.'

⸻✳⸻

Michael Joyce hesitated above the Professor's house and looked out over the bay. A luminous half-light lit the sand. The storm had just about blown itself out; he had been checking his boat to see that it was safe, and had thought to call in at the cottage on his way home. When he looked out over the sand, however, he saw that the Professor was out there, but this was a surprise; he had company!

There were two of them walking away from him, the Professor and a girl in a dress of almost luminous green. As Michael watched, the girl broke away from the older man, and ran barefoot on the sand, spinning to let the wind whip at her dress and at her hair. Michael blinked; a whole flock of children had appeared, laughing and swirling about her as if playing tag. They must have come down by bus, Michael thought, and turned towards the road to see. When he looked back, however, all he could see was the Professor. Of the girl and the children there was no sign.

A flock of shore birds flew past Michael in an excited twitter and settled further down the sand. A curlew called. The Professor bent to pick up a seashell, put it to his ear, and then he walked on out towards the sea. Curious, Michael crossed the sand to where the children had been playing; the only footprints he could find were the Professor's. But he could see where the Professor had turned to watch them play.

For as long as the Professor lived in the cottage, Michael would often see the girl in green, and sometimes see the children playing on the sand. He never told anybody else. It seemed to him to be a purely natural phenomenon.

ABOUT *IN THE CLAWS OF THE EAGLE ...*

In April 2003, while on a visit to Czechoslovakia, my wife and I visited the Terezín (Theresienstadt) concentration camp, a former Hapsburg fortress, about an hour's drive from Prague. Our older than usual guide was a cultured, soft-spoken lady, who nevertheless managed to convey to us the horror of the conditions in the camp. One hundred and forty thousand people passed through the camp, most of them on their way to the Nazi gas chambers. Three thousand five hundred died from the appalling conditions in the camp. Our guide concluded our tour with the following words:

'We mustn't forget the victims of the Nazis, and this terrible history mustn't be forgot. Ladies and gentlemen, that is all. Thank you for your attention and your pleasant company, allow me to wish you a beautiful stay in the Czech Republic.'

It was only after we had left Terezín to return to Prague that we learned that our guide had, almost certainly, as a child, been a prisoner in Terezín. It was with her exhortation in mind that I began to look at the Terezín story. It is a story of horror, but it is also a story of human and artistic triumph. It is the story of Jewish musicians, dramatists, comedians and teachers who not only entertained their fellow prisoners, but composed and performed to the highest level. Not least among these were the children who sang in choirs and played in the seventy-odd performances of Hans Krása's opera 'Brundibár'. Sadly, most of these children died in the gas chambers of Auschwitz in the period of the war, as did most of the adult musicians and performers in the camp. Many of the situations and incidents that I have described in this book are based on fact, and my characters have been inspired by real people. However, the book is a work of fiction; the scenes and characters are simply as I have imagined them. My main source of information on the musical life in Terezín has been the book: *Music in Terezín 1941-1945* by Joža Káras.

Ever since I first visited, and fell in love with Austria and its people in the 1950s, I have been haunted by the question: would I have been able to resist the lure of, for example, the Hitler Youth. My interest in outdoor activities could easily have drawn me towards them and thence into Nazism. As a teenager I was easily impressed by people more confident than I. One of my great heroes of this time was Heinrich Harrer, a climber famous for his ascent of the North Face of the Eiger, and subsequently for his wonderfully humane account of his seven years in Tibet. How, I wondered, would he have reacted to the emergent Nazism of that time? Then, when halfway through writing this book, I learned to my surprise and dismay that Harrer had indeed served in the SS. More recently still the great German pacifist writer, Günter Grass, has confessed to having been a member of the SS. In Erich I have attempted to show how easy it can be to be drawn into a position of prejudice, and how difficult it is to break out of it.

Izaac Abrahams could be any one of the many Jewish child prodigies that sprang from the nursery of culture that was Vienna at the turn of the last century. There is an excellent description of Vienna at that time in Amy Biancolli's biography of the great violinist Kreisler: *Fritz Kreisler. Love's Sorrow, Love's Joy.* Though I learned the violin for a year or two as a youngster, my eyes were opened wide by sitting in on a master class conducted by violinist Mary O'Brien in the Royal Irish Academy of Music in Dublin. Madame Helena Stronski is not modelled on anyone, but she is wholly inspired by the way in which Ms O'Brien worked to bring out the musicianship in her already competent players. I hope she will not wholly disown my Izaac.

Izaac's home is based on my parents' apartment as it was in Vienna in the 1950s, close to the Volksgarten where the lawns were then still being mown with scythes.

In 1938 Hitler had the idea of creating what he intended to be the largest collection of art in Europe. As an aspiring art student he had applied to the Academy of Fine Arts in Vienna and had been rejected. He never forgave Vienna for this rejection and so chose Linz, his home town, to be the site for his future gallery. The great Jewish art collections were to be his principal source of art, but as his armies swept west and east across Europe this soon turned into wholescale looting of galleries and collections in the conquered states. The Jeu de Paume in Paris was one of his collecting points. Situated in the Tuileries Gardens near the Louvre, it is now a museum of modern art, but during the war, lorries drove in at night from the Place de la Concorde stuffed with looted art. Old masters and the realistic art of the nineteenth century were what appealed to the Nazis. Picassos, Van Goghs, and other 'degenerate' works were separated out to be sold. Göring was a regular visitor, travelling in his private train to Platform 1 in the *Gare de l'Est*. He seldom paid for what he carried away.

It had been known for some time that the atmosphere in the salt mines in the Austrian Lake District was perfect for storing pictures. Altaussee is every bit as beautiful as Eric and Louise found it. The salt mine where the art was stored can be visited. Because of the atmosphere, the timber of the Nazi shelves looks as new today as the day it was put in. So does the box marked 'Marble, do not drop,' that once contained a bomb designed to destroy the whole collection. A level or two lower in the mine, reached by a wooden slide, is the chapel where I imagined Louise's picture being stored. This fascinating story is told by Peter Harclerode and Brendan Pittaway in *The Lost Masters. The Looting of Europe's Treasurehouses*.

As always, Norman Davies' *Europe, A History*, provides the backbone of my research. There have been numerous television documentaries and videos on the Holocaust in recent times. The Internet is a valuable source of information but I find it is necessary to verify everything I use, checking where possible against a reliable source such as the *Encyclopaedia Britannica* or Norman Davies.

This is the final book in the *Louise* Trilogy. In *Wings Over Delft* we met Louise as she was in life, three and a half centuries ago. In *The Rainbow Bridge* and *In the Claws of the Eagle* I have used the tools of fantasy to bring Louise to life, while in reality the only way that Louise could come to life would be through the eyes of those who looked at her portrait, or perhaps those who read her story.

Aubrey Flegg

Other Books by Aubrey Flegg

WINGS OVER DELFT
Book 1: the *Louise* trilogy

Delft, Holland, 1654. Louise Eeden reluctantly agrees to have her portrait painted. Things are moving too fast in her life. Everyone believes she is engaged to Reynier DeVries; she is chaperoned and protected – a commodity to be exchanged in a marriage that will merge two pottery businesses. In the studio with Master Haitink and his apprentice, Pieter, Louise unexpectedly finds the freedom to be herself. Friendship grows into love, but unknown to Louise, her every move is being reported, and behind the scenes a web of treachery is gradually unravelling. Then fate, in the form of a careless watchman at the gunpowder store, steps in ...

Winner of the Bisto Book of the Year Award and the Reading Association of Ireland Award.

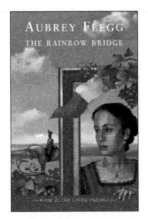

THE RAINBOW BRIDGE

Book 2: the *Louise* trilogy

France, 1792. As revolution sweeps through his country, Gaston
Morteau, a lieutenant in the Hussars, rescues the painting of Louise
from a canal in Holland. Louise becomes a very real presence in his
life, sharing his experiences: the trauma of war, and his meeting
with Napoleon. When Gaston is forced to give up the portrait to
the devious Count du Bois, Louise becomes embroiled in a tale of
political intrigue and Gothic horror.

THE CINNAMON TREE

When she steps on a landmine, Yola Abonda's leg is shattered, and with it her dreams for the future. Who will want her now? Yola travels to Ireland for treatment and makes a special friend – Fintan. She returns home with a mission: to do all she can to end the menace of landmines.

KATIE'S WAR

When Katie's father returns from the Great War he is suffering from shell-shock. Four years later, he has almost recovered, but now Ireland is on the brink of civil war. There are divided loyalties in Katie's family – how can Katie make a choice? Who is right?
Winner of the Peter Pan Award (IBbY Sweden)